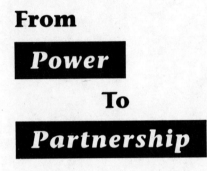

From
Power
To
Partnership

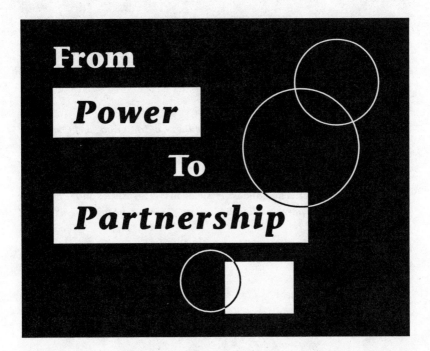

From
Power
To
Partnership

Creating the Future of Love, Work, and Community

Alfonso Montouri, Ph.D.,
and Isabella Conti, Ph.D.

HarperSanFrancisco
A Division of HarperCollins*Publishers*

FIRST EDITION

Text design by Irene Imfeld

Library of Congress Cataloging-in-Publication Data
Montuori, Alfonso.
    From power to partnership: creating the future of love, work, and
community / Alfonso Montuori and Isabella Conti.
      p.   cm.
    Includes bibliographical references and index.
    ISBN 0-06-250548-3 (alk. paper)
    1. Social history. 2. Social evolution. 3. Dominance
(Psychology) 4. Sex role. I. Conti, Isabella. II. Title.
HN18.M658   1993
303.4—dc20   91-58921
                                            CIP

93 94 95 96 97 ❖ HCMG 10 9 8 7 6 5 4 3 2 1

This edition is printed on acid-free paper that meets the American
National Standards Institute Z39.48 Standard.

—

To our mothers

—

FROM POWER TO PARTNERSHIP

Books, like babies, are often conceived out of passion. As readers of *The Chalice and the Blade* and *The Partnership Way* know, the idea that animates this book, that partnership is a viable alternative to domination, is one for which I have a great passion. Not only that, but in significant ways my husband and partner David Loye and I have acted as midwives for *From Power to Partnership*. These are some of the reasons that it is such a pleasure for me to write this Foreword. But the main reason is simply this: *From Power to Partnership* is a book that is a pleasure to read. It is brisk yet thoughtful, imaginative, and at the same time factual, sensitive, and also sensible. Best of all, it is fun to read, humorous without trivializing, persuasive without being preachy, full of intriguing information and lively quotes.

When Alfonso Montuori and Isabella Conti began to talk of a book based on interviews with many diverse people (from artists and poets to astronauts and economists) using the partnership and dominator framework introduced in *The Chalice and the Blade,* David and I had already known Montuori (or Monty, as he is known to his friends) a number of years. Through many stimulating conversations, we had become convinced that with his keen intelligence, unusual creativity, and unique multicultural background (by the age of thirty he had already lived in Lebanon, England, Holland, Greece, China, and the U.S.), Monty was just the right person to write such a book. We had also more recently become acquainted with Isabella Conti and were impressed both by her abilities and accomplishments and by her sensitivity and warmth. Moreover, we could see that her life experiences, from sailing around the world in a small boat to cofounding a leading management consulting firm, would give the book even more breadth and scope. So without hesitation we urged them to proceed.

The result is precisely what we had hoped. *From Power to Partnership* probes almost every aspect of human relations—from the relations between women and men to our relations with our planet and even with ourselves, with our bodies, hearts, and minds—in terms of their underlying framework. And while it is not a how-to book in the conventional sense of the word, it is very much a down-to-earth book. This is why I believe that everybody with such interests, who wants to tune their lives better to the future, will find this book useful as well as entertaining.

From Power to Partnership should additionally be of very special interest and use to what is in effect the partnership movement, which in recent years has begun literally to spread over the planet. This has been happening in the wake of the publication of *The Chalice and the Blade* in Japanese, German, French, Finnish, Spanish, Portuguese, and Greek, with editions in Russian and Chinese forthcoming. (A British edition distributed throughout the United Kingdom also reaches Australia, South Africa, and India.) As of this writing, in the mainland United States there are Centers for Partnership Education in Arizona, California, Colorado, the District of Columbia, Illinois, New Jersey, New Mexico, New York, North Carolina, Ohio, Texas, and Virginia, as well as our fiftieth state, the island of Hawaii, and the Seychelles Islands off the coast of East Africa. People from many of these countries and centers recently gathered on the Greek island of Crete (the home of one of the most fascinating ancient partnership cultures described in *The Chalice and the Blade*) for the first International Celebration of Partnership. In ways such as this an informal network of individuals and groups is today working for personal and social transformation all over the world.

We of course hear a lot these days about transformation, about paradigm shifts, about the search for more satisfying and more sustainable ways of living on our increasingly endangered planet. We hear a lot particularly about our environmental and international problems, and how the old conquest-of-nature mentality—along with the notion that there must in human relations always be winners and losers, dominators and dominated—is not adaptive to the crises, and opportunities, of our age. But much of what we read focuses primarily on the problems, or at best on short-term solutions.

By contrast, *From Power to Partnership* takes a holistic, or systems, view. It focuses on both short-term and long-range processes. Most important, it shows how many seemingly disparate aspects of contemporary life—the ecology, women's, men's, new spirituality, peace, holistic healing, personal growth, civil rights, humanistic psychology, and human rights movements—are all part of a larger movement to replace a dominator with a partnership paradigm. It shows how women and men from all walks of life, from so-called ordinary people to leading-edge thinkers, are fashioning in bits and pieces the various elements we need for a fundamental shift in how we think and live. Illustrating, time and time again, how these pieces fit together into a coherent whole helps accelerate that shift.

I could say much more about *From Power to Partnership*. But I want to make this foreword brief, as the book speaks for itself. So I will end as I started, on a personal note, to say how exciting it has been for me to see this book come to life. Since the publication of *The Chalice and the Blade*, a number of other excellent books have used the partnership and dominator framework, books as diverse as Suzi Gablick's *The Re-enchantment of Art*, Barry and Janae Weinhold's *Breaking Free of the Co-dependency Trap*, and Samuel Noah Kramer and John Maier's *Myths of Enki*. But this book is particularly special for me, not only because of David's and my personal involvement in its conception and birth, but because it vividly shows that we can re-connect with our partnership roots and thus make more conscious, and effective, choices for our future. I know it will also be a very special book for its many readers.

Riane Eisler
June 1992

We owe an immense debt of gratitude to Riane Eisler, whose work inspired us to write this book. Her theory of cultural transformation and its template of partnership and domination outlined in her book, *The Chalice and the Blade* lie at the root of our work, and form the basis of the conceptual framework we are proposing.

David Loye's friendship and his unwavering support of this project from the beginning to its completion has been invaluable. His insightful editorial suggestions helped us in the writing of this book, while his concepts and ideas inform a large part of it.

The understated genius of our teacher, Frank Barron, guided us both through our dissertations—though in different decades—and eventually arranged for our meeting somewhere in the hills of Umbria. His thinking has profoundly influenced both of us, and we are grateful for his guidance and friendship.

We thank all the women and men of action and wisdom who have agreed to be interviewed for this book. Their words and their examples are forces shaping our future today: Ralph Abraham, Isabel Allende, Royal Alsup, Art and Elaine Aron, Bela Banathy, Frank Barron, Debi Coleman, Scott Coltrane, Dominique Di Prima, Riane Eisler, Joel Federman, Judy Flanagan, Roddy Frame, Todd Gitlin, Susan Hales, Willis Harman, Bob Haywood, Hazel Henderson, Mara Keller, Stanley Krippner, Joan Levinson, David Loye, Joanna Macy, Sheldon Margen, Edgar Mitchell, Ashley Montagu, Dean Ornish, Ishmael Reed, Paul Saffo, Stuart Schlegel, Philip Slater, Tom Stone, William Irwin Thompson, John Todd, Vivienne Verdon-Roe, Paul Watzlawick, Robert Anton Wilson, and the others who preferred to remain nameless.

From
Power
To
Partnership

Introduction

Welcome to the End of the World

In the year 999 some very peculiar things were happening all over Europe. Shopkeepers began distributing their goods to the poor. The pope was consumed by his studies of astrology and necromancy in a desperate attempt to divine the future. Masses of people swarmed to Jerusalem. And, miracle of miracles, husbands and wives forgave their adulterous spouses.

The millennium madness got to everybody, and fears of eternal damnation were running high. A general feeling of moral decay was prevalent, and this translated into royal charters about "the wanton fortune of this deceiving world, not lovely with the milk-white radiance of unfading lilies, but odious with the gall-steeped bitterness of lamentable corruption, raging with venomous wide-stretched jaws." The end of the world was nigh, and sinners were repenting. At the stroke of midnight, the year 1000 was ushered in, and, in somewhat of an anticlimax, not much changed, apart from the date.

We are now approaching the third millennium, and although we like to think of ourselves as less superstitious than our ancestors, we will likely succumb to some form of millennium madness. A United States president has already referred to a "moral malaise"

1

sweeping the country, and another has consulted an astrologer. Thousands of people, inspired by an interpretation of the Mayan calendar, converged harmonically at sacred sites to usher in a new age.

At the end of the first millennium, the Europeans saw omens in the sky and on the earth, mystical signs of change and apocalypse. We are also seeing signs, but they are of an altogether different nature. They are not angelic or demonic messengers but rather situations we have created ourselves, in the form of war, poverty, deforestation, homelessness, pollution, rapid and confusing social changes, and a general feeling that the world is on the brink of something we don't quite understand. The difference this time is that we are dealing not with acts of God but of humans, and we are ultimately accountable for them. For us, repenting is perhaps somewhat more difficult: prayers are not enough, because unlike our ancestors, we're beginning to understand the source of our own predicament.

If the threat of nuclear war seems to have receded at the time of this writing, no one can predict what the geopolitical landscape will be like even one month from now. The former Soviet Union has witnessed coups and secessions, commonwealths and confusion. When Deng Xiaoping and his antediluvian colleagues in Beijing kick the proverbial bucket, we may be in for more surprises.

Humanity has not been able to eliminate war as a method for conflict resolution, and we have employed it with gruesome regularity since the beginning of our recorded history. Nor is the world any closer to solving the problems of hunger, crime, and widespread violation of basic human rights. To these long-standing issues, our century has added a few of its own: overpopulation, environmental disruption, and enough nuclear weapons to obliterate life on earth. All these factors seem to be converging to form a crisis of exceptional proportions.

Astronaut Edgar Mitchell, the sixth man to walk on the moon, brings a perspective born of a look from space at the beauty and "oneness" of Earth. Back on Earth, he founded the Institute for Noetic Sciences, with the intention of studying those occurrences on the edge of our paradigm that point the way to tomorrow. He is one of the many forward thinkers we have interviewed for this book.

"Our problems are only going to be solved with the participation of all people, all societies, and all cultures, because we're dealing with a systemic global problem. Anything short of perceiving its global scope is putting on Band-Aids," he told us. "The notion of a more cooperative, collaborative universe is absolutely essential. Historically humans have resolved conflicts by armed assault on each other. This must be either reduced to a minimum or eliminated completely, if for no other reason than the weapons we use today are too darn awesome. We risk destroying the whole planetary system if we use them. The elimination of armed conflicts is not as utopian as it sounds; I think it will fall into place fairly naturally once we really understand and internalize the notion that we are in a wholly connected universe as opposed to a universe with discreet particles.

"I don't think there is a specific course of action that everyone can follow, except to examine your beliefs and your life and ask yourself if you find it satisfactory. Of course crisis creates dissatisfaction. That's the only thing that's going to move civilization in a different direction: crisis. As life becomes less satisfactory and pain becomes more prominent, you do something to alleviate the pain. We are still a reactive, not a proactive, civilization."

Indeed, the world is facing a monumental crisis. Some prefer to minimize it: What else is new? Every generation claims this challenge for itself and proclaims its own crisis as the most difficult one ever experienced. The crisis that our generation faces, however, does have certain distinctive characteristics.

Its scope is global. We are all affected by it, more or less directly, more or less immediately. Only six centuries ago, around 1330, the Aztecs were establishing Mexico City, a civil war broke out in Japan due to a succession dispute, and Yusef I became caliph of Granada, marking the peak of Arab civilization in Spain. Each event had no bearing whatsoever on any of the others. Today this is almost unthinkable; our actions have inescapable global consequences. The way humanity satisfies its energy needs, for example, and the environmental implications of each method are no longer the business of separate sovereign nations or sociopolitical groups. They have become a global issue. The radioactive clumps of debris spewed by the Soviet nuclear-power disaster in Chernobyl rained as far away as Poland; Iraqi and Kuwaiti alike choked under the burning oil fields in Kuwait in 1991; the destruction of the Brazilian rain forest collapses the lungs of all humanity.

When we are not directly affected by something that takes place halfway around the globe, we're nevertheless subjected to its psychological impact. Television has brought the world into our living rooms, courtesy of CNN, whether that living room is in New Delhi, Paris, New York, or Isla Tortugas somewhere in the Atlantic Ocean. Within twenty-four hours of the 1989 earthquake that shook the San Francisco Bay area, phone lines were jammed with 250 million callers from all over the world worried about loved ones. Our sheer

3

number has multiplied our ties to one another, and the very density of the population creates a contiguity through which ripple effects pass very rapidly.

The crisis is multidimensional and complex. We are dealing not with one problem but with a seemingly endless array of them, somehow connected with one another in an inextricable Gordian knot. Our parents had to deal with the Great Depression and World War II. These were major disruptions that challenged some fundamental assumptions, but at least they came in sequence. We have to deal with the threat of nuclear war, dwindling resources, overpopulation, pollution, the drug war, the death of God, the erosion of the family, the crisis of beliefs (the list goes on), all at the same time.

Baby-boom journalists are annoyed because they don't see their own reflection in today's youth, but the much-maligned "twentysomething" generation resents being called uncommitted. Today's youths did not experience the Vietnam War; they have dozens of wars but no photo opportunities. Their problems are quite complex and pernicious. Many give up. Others, the more optimistic ones, say that this is not about stopping a war. It's about transforming the world, changing the mentality that creates wars. No wonder they get depressed and wear black a lot. But, as we shall see, they're determined to do something about this mess, and they're looking for answers and working at it, without much fanfare.

As we pick one thread and try to unravel one problem, we seem to run only into more knots. We make tougher laws to curb the "crime problem" and fill our prisons to capacity, so we create a "prison problem." We're dealing with a system-wide problem, a system pathology that does not fare well with piecemeal solutions.

In China, for example, an ingenious campaign to get rid of sparrows—one of the "four pests," along with rats, mosquitoes, and fleas—was launched in 1958. The idea was to get everybody to make an enormous racket at certain times to scare the sparrows and force them to stay in the air. Since sparrows can only stay airborne for three hours or so, they figured the terrified birds, unable to land because of the gong-bashing, screeching, flag-waving, shooting masses, would eventually drop dead, which is exactly what they did. With the sparrows almost gone, the crops were invaded by pests who devoured them undisturbed. The Chinese were forced to revert to using DDT and other chemicals, which eventually ended up in rivers and canals, poisoning the fish.

The world is made not of so many isolated bits but of complex systems of interrelationships and networks of interaction. If you mess with one part, it's going to affect something or someone somewhere else. The traditional approach to problems does not help us deal with these complex situations. The relatively new discipline of *systems science,* however, emerged specifically in response to complexity. It helps us deal with apparently overwhelming complexity and distills from it a manageable simplicity, without making it simplistic. Once you take the "systems approach," you realize how many of our problems are connected and how many of the alternative solutions are connected as well.

Many of us feel that our individual actions mean little on the global stage. We feel that we can only do so much, and only in a limited arena. But precisely because of the complex interconnections that tie the world together, a single act can reverberate very far. "I call it the pebble effect," author Isabel Allende told us, and she smiled remembering all the pebbles whose ripples changed the face of Chile.

The rate of change has increased exponentially. So many things are happening so fast that we are losing any illusion of control. Even our most cherished accomplishments contribute to our feeling of disorientation and confusion. The twentieth century has seen some of the most dramatic changes in history. Television, radio, computers, and nuclear energy, cars and skyscrapers and airplanes, new medical technologies, satellites, and moon landings would have been scoffed at as science fiction only 150 years before. The changes brought about by this massive outburst of human creativity are so enormous that futurist Alvin Toffler has coined the term "future shock" to express what is often our dismay at trying to grasp the implications of it all. The volume of information we have to process is so overwhelming and the pace of change is so fast that we feel unable to predict and control the outcome of our actions.

The 1980s and early 1990s witnessed high drama in the Eastern bloc, with the reunification of Germany, the remarkable shifts in Poland, Hungary, and the Soviet Union. Yet in other respects not much has changed, because many people in those countries—and in the capitalist countries that claim to have won the confrontation—are still hungry, miserable, poor, out of work, and homeless.

But beyond the technological and political realms, change is occurring in areas that until recently were considered impenetrable fortresses. Wholesale racism was still rampant fifty years ago. Segregation was standard in many places—buses and toilets, not to mention jobs and schools. Black performers often played in clubs that barred them as patrons. Before World War II Americans thought of the Japanese as squinty-eyed, buck-toothed incompetents, while the

5

Japanese were out to prove the superiority of their race and the inherent weakness of the clumsy and degenerate Americans. Both countries actually knew very little about each other. Although racism is still widespread, now at least it is legally forbidden and considered less socially acceptable.

Wars used to be a legitimate and unquestioned extension of politics, a perfectly sensible way of getting what you wanted. In battlefields boys would become men. If there was no war, the army performed that rite of passage nevertheless, albeit less dramatically. The army, and war in particular, was the perfect place for a man to express everything that was manly, a place where he could be tested and reach his full potential, to be all that he could be. Wars were glorious until World War I, when Flanders' fields brought home the muddy slaughter of innocents. Since then the viability and legitimacy of war has been questioned more and more vociferously. Subtle yet quite revolutionary changes are taking place. Cultural historian William Irwin Thompson, for example, points out that during the Gulf War in 1991, U.S. spokespersons emphasized repeatedly that it was not the Iraqi *people* America was at war with. This may not sound like much, but compare it with the propaganda of other wars, showing the enemy's men, women, and children as bloodcurdling monsters, and you get a measure of the distance we have covered in less than half a century.

Fundamental Transformation

The alignment of these three conditions—global scope, multiplicity and complexity of factors, rapid rate of change—seems to portend a fundamental shift, the end of an era and the beginning of a new one. We feel the very fabric of our lives unraveling, readying itself to be recombined in yet unknown and unforeseeable patterns.

Futurists of all persuasions have spoken about the radical changes awaiting us just around the corner. Many authors and politicians, along with a large number of people in general, suspect that something of considerable importance is happening—the old ways are fast becoming obsolete. We are not just changing mores from one generation to the next, as when Victorian society's grandchildren invented the sexual revolution. We are actually in the process of changing our collective mind about some fundamental things that have been in place for hundreds, even thousands, of years. No wonder we are feeling unsettled.

Have you ever watched the turning of the tide? If we could see the patterns made by our collective ideas, the ones we hold in common with large numbers of people and do not even think about most of the time, they would look pretty much like the clashing waves of a changing tide. From a mountaintop you can spot the two currents, one coming and one going, a well-defined pattern. But if you are a cork bouncing on the waves, all you feel are the whirlpools; you have no idea where the next push will come from. This analogy sums up *chaos theory,* which holds that there are predictable patterns that contain within well-defined boundaries completely unpredictable variations of events. If you live in the state of New York, for example, you can pretty much bet your life that there will be a winter followed by a spring and two more seasons. But you will never be able to predict the weather for, let's say, Tuesday after next. If you are planning an early summer wedding in the garden, nothing can help you schedule a sunny day; but if you are planting a crop, you can rely on the knowledge of what season is coming up next. If you are a cork caught in the changing tide, having a bird's eye view of the situation will not help you avoid the splash of the next wave. But if you had such a view, if you could see the shape of the underlying currents, you could set a meaningful course of action. Instead of a pawn you would become a player. If you knew the pattern, even the relative chaos of the surface would begin to make sense. You could catch a wave and ride its crest all the way to the shore.

If we dig deep, what's underneath the dust kicked up by the change? What forces are pushing it? Deep down, what is the shape of the movement?

This global change of mind is still in the process of defining itself. We know we are headed somewhere, but it is uncharted territory. We can feel in our bones that our present view of the world—our underlying system of beliefs, our fundamental paradigm—is running out of steam. We are collectively getting ready for a jump, a major paradigm shift.

Brother, Can You Paradigm?

The term *paradigm* has been used a great deal recently. It has been used so much that its original and revolutionary meaning has been considerably diluted. The intent of philosopher of science Thomas Kuhn, who first used the term in the now popular sense, was essentially to describe a set of assumptions about reality. These assumptions are so pervasive we don't even know that they're just hypotheses. They form an invisible web of beliefs about the world, beliefs that we take to be reality, and they function as a compass that guides our lives at an unconscious level.

Before the Copernican revolution in the sixteenth century, for example, when people still believed that Earth was the center of the universe, they automatically assumed that man was the focus and purpose of creation. Eventually we learned that we occupy for an infinitesimally short time a peripheral planet in a minor solar system among the billions of stars of one among countless galaxies. Since then our sense of self-importance has shrunk a size or two. If nothing else, the word *man* no longer represents adequately the totality of our species.

Paradigms are like the rules of a game. They allow a group of people to play bridge together and have fun for an afternoon. When a population shares a paradigm, all its people view the world essentially the same way. They may still argue with each other, and spend days debating whether women have souls or how many angels fit on the head of a pin, but no one questions the sanity or the relevance of the discussion. Everyone has bought into the same model of the world unquestioningly and often unknowingly.

The peculiar nature of paradigms makes them invisible for the most part. While the rules of the bridge game are clearly spelled out and can be taught and learned relatively easily, the paradigms that shape major historical eras (e.g., Imperial Rome versus medieval Europe) are recognized only partially by the people of the time. It is only later, when a paradigm begins to lose its power to shape a period's worldview, that its components, underlying structure, and limitations are revealed.

Paradigms don't last forever. Once every corner of a given worldview has been explored, and new data accumulate that do not fit the existing model, the predominant paradigm starts to chip at the edges. A paradigm shift occurs when the way we see reality stops making sense and an alternative emerges that we think makes more sense. It may take a hundred years, but before you know it, one paradigm stops working and a new one grabs its place.

A paradigm shift occurred in the way the economy was run during the Industrial Revolution. Artisans and craftsmen and farmers were replaced by factories and machinery. People had to learn different skills and slowly began to think differently. A new, industrial age was dawning.

The emergence of the industrial age didn't affect only the economy. It ended up changing just about everything, from the family to housing to the way people think about themselves. With the industrial age we stopped defining ourselves in organic terms, with crops and seasons as our frame of reference. We became little machines in a big machine. Even the body became a machine, designed to function according to specs. But more about this later.

Now a new, global paradigm shift seems to be happening, comparable in scale to the one that occurred with the Industrial Revolution. The difference is that it's happening faster. Like travelers to a distant land, we don't understand the language, we cannot read the unspoken social messages, and we do not know how to behave. If we're culture shocked abroad, we at least know that there is a home we might be able to get back to. But when a fundamental paradigm shift happens in our very home, it changes the quality of our life down to its most intimate details. As a paradigm starts losing its hold, events and situations become unpredictable. These anomalies can be distressing, because a relatively stable and predictable world feels reassuring. On the other hand, nothing beats the fascination of a new world where anything can be invented afresh and the future is being shaped as we speak.

Well-established, still partially unexplored paradigms have enormous solidity and inertia. Only when a paradigm has ceased to be functional can a new one emerge. According to sociologist Kurt Lewin, a new belief can be entertained only when the previous one has been demolished or seriously cracked. We happen to live in interesting times, as the ancient Chinese curse goes. We have been denied the comfort of a stable, solid, unchanging worldview; and we have been blessed with the gift of unformed clay. We are living at the turning of the tide, when ebbing and flowing waves crash with each other, and for a time all we can see is chaos.

This book offers a set of binoculars to look at the world we are leaving behind and begins to sketch the outline of the new world's emerging shape. Once we become aware of the fundamental characteristics of our present age, we acquire the power to engage in purposeful action and to participate consciously in the creation of the future. Without this clarity of vision, actions remain isolated anomalies lacking the focus and the momentum necessary to guide the changes now occurring.

Our search is for the underlying patterns and fundamental meaning in thousands of messages sent daily through the ether. If

9

we listen closely enough, can we hear the compelling rhythm of humanity's tom-tom? Beneath the din that five billion of us produce on a daily basis, can we grasp the message that we are trying to send to one another?

We'd like to tell you what we hear and ask you to compare notes, to see for yourself if, viewed through the lenses we are proposing, things don't suddenly start making a lot more sense.

Bridging the Mind Shift

Like ants making bridges with their own bodies to cross rivers, we humans manufacture rope bridges with our theories and ideas and launch them across the chasm of chaos to reach the other shore. We, the authors, invite you to travel across one such bridge, so that having crossed to the other side, you can throw more ropes to help others walk safely across. Like you, we are crafting our bridge with ropes made by hundreds of others, each strand braided tightly with the next until they are strong enough and big enough to do the job.

From this vantage point we perceive that this global change, this major paradigm shift, is occurring on three fundamental levels. We list them here in linear order, but this is due only to the restrictions of writing. In truth they form a circular, self-reinforcing motion, a sort of whirlpool. This could be the movement that defines the boundaries around chaos and holds the seed of tomorrow.

• Our way of knowing—how we think, gather information, and understand the world around us.

• Our way of relating—how we relate to one another, the stance we take when facing another human being or the "other" in general.

• Our way of being—our fundamental capacity as human beings to create our lives, the questions we ask, and the answers we give ourselves about the meaning of our existence.

Pretty fundamental issues, encompassing every aspect of our personal life and social structures. The first, that is, the way we go about learning and knowing, has been in place for the shortest time, approximately four hundred years in its present form and a little over one thousand in its broadest characteristics.

The second—the way we go about relating to one another—has been in place for about five thousand years in its most basic dimension.

The third is life's fundamental question. Human beings have started to answer this question with countless creation myths, stories about how the world and people came to be, about the way customs and laws and rituals have evolved. For the first time, we may collectively be coming up with quite a different vision of what it means to be human.

Way of Knowing

As people educated mainly in the scientific method, we go about the business of knowing and learning invisibly guided by the prevailing paradigm. We perform a series of almost automatic mental operations that strongly influences the structure, and therefore the outcome, of our thoughts. First and foremost we focus on one aspect and then try to determine cause and effect.

When we deal with complex issues, for example, we have been trained to take things one step at a time. We begin with something we are sure we can handle. Although hardly the scientific method in all its glory, this principle is nevertheless one of its foundations. This approach is effective because it allows us to reduce otherwise complicated phenomena into manageable chunks that we can examine. In school, when we're taught how the body functions, we study digestion, for example, but not its relation to our mental and emotional state. The technical term for this cornerstone of scientific analysis is *reductionism,* which basically means holding the working assumption that the world is made up of many separate parts, whether atoms or individuals. In order to study and understand the world, it is thought that one has to be able to find the single most manageable bit to which it can be reduced, and start there.

This kind of thinking goes back quite a way, to the emergence of the scientific method and the rise of individualism and capitalism, a process that began somewhere around the Renaissance. The industrial age was made possible by the use of the scientific method to study the world. Taking a part of something, isolating it, and tampering with it to see how it would react was a practical method that allowed people to begin to question the supposedly unquestionable wisdom of the church, which at the time dictated every aspect of life. It became possible for people to check things for themselves, to run little experiments to see whether the combined wisdom of Aristotle and the Bible via Thomas Aquinas could stand the test of observation and experiment. The enormous success of the scientific approach led

11

to its widespread acceptance in the West and to a vastly improved standard of living for a greater number of people.

This way of thinking has obvious powerful advantages, but it also has inherent limitations, which we are beginning to discover. For one, it subtly introduces a fundamental schism in our way of thinking. From childhood we are trained to think that something is either one way or the other, and if you and I are stating two opposing views, unless we are both wrong, only one of us can be right. For centuries, if not longer, we have been encouraged to think in terms of opposites: mind versus body, reason versus emotion. From the very beginning we are programmed for opposition and conflict even within ourselves.

A second aspect of this inherently dichotomous way of thinking is the deadlocked controversy between the part and the whole. In the process of focusing on certain aspects of a phenomenon and shedding light on the way it works, reductionism obscures other aspects. Historically some groups have emphasized the part over the whole, and some the whole over the part, with far-reaching political and social implications.

This seemingly abstract speculation translates into such real-life questions as, What's more important, the life of one individual or society? Should society, the government, the community, interfere in any way in a person's life? Should a person's life be sacrificed for the sake of future generations? Should a whole generation be sacrificed, as communist regimes were wont to do, for the sake of a revolution that would supposedly bring untold happiness to millions? What right has anyone to dictate what anybody else should do? How much should the individual give up for society? This debate takes the form of the polarity between rights and responsibilities, freedom and equality, for instance. Usually people who focus on the part—the individual—stress rights and freedom, whereas people who focus on the whole—society—emphasize responsibilities, equality, and duties.

As you may have guessed, we don't like this either/or split. The paradigm that generated it seems to have exhausted its usefulness. A different approach is beginning to emerge. Over the past fifty years or so, General Systems Theory, or simply the systems approach, has become the preferred method for studying the world. In a holistic way, it allows us to see both part and whole and to focus on the relationship between the two. It has given us a refreshingly new perspective on the world, one that reminds us of the basic connection between the parts that make up the whole.

All these parts, which the traditional scientific method isolated in a laboratory, muttering the incantation "all other things being equal," have become increasingly linked. Stock markets collapse together in a neat row like dominoes and then together get back up again. Automatic teller machines allow people to access bank accounts in different continents. This global interdependence creates situations too complex to be understood simply by taking things apart. The systems approach, focusing on relationships rather than essences, provides the way of knowing we need at this point in history. Also known as the science of complexity, systems theory is designed to deal with issues that are complex, unstable, and even chaotic and that must be viewed simultaneously as part and as whole in order to be understood.

Just as reductionism constituted one of the pillars that supported the predominant view of reality for centuries, systems theory is laying the foundation for our new perceptions. The more people become exposed to it, outside the mathematical circles to which it was confined in the first part of this century, the more deeply it will influence our way of conceiving the world. Systems theory is beginning to shape a new paradigm, and because we are at the beginning of it, we inhale the perfume of undiscovered possibilities without experiencing the limitations. (We are happy to leave the task of dismantling systems theory to a future generation, when this paradigm has run its course too.)

Bela Banathy, former president of the International Society for Systems Sciences, told us what got him into systems thinking in the late 1950s. He was designing curricula for foreign language education at the time. "The most fascinating aspects of systems is revealed to us when we understand what language is all about. We seldom think about it, at least consciously, but one of the major gifts given to us by God, the ability to express ourselves in language, is the most remarkable example of the way systems work.

"The basic characteristics of systems are *connectiveness* and *emergence*," he continued. "Just think about the basic linguistic building blocks of language—sounds like *p, e,* or *g*. From them a sound system emerges. From this sound system words emerge, and words are then arranged into meaningful patterns and emerge as sentences. But sentences become meaningful only if you organize them or understand them in the context of the referential system of language, which is always culturally conditioned and determined. So that was for me the most remarkable example of what systems are about."

13

We asked Paul Watzlawick, author of one of the most important books to date on human communication and an early proponent of systems theory applied to social sciences, to describe how the systems perspective is drastically changing our view of the world. One significant change, he said, is in our notions of causality. It used to be thought that there was a one-way, linear cause-and-effect relationship: A caused B—I push you, you react. But the systems approach shows us a circular causality: I shove you, you react, but your reaction affects me in turn, and so on. A "mutually causal" process occurs, Watzlawick explained.

This new view of causality focuses our attention not on *why* something happens but *how*. The more complex the system, the more crucial the *how*. Historically we've tended to want simple solutions to complex problems. There's nothing inherently wrong with that, unless we end up scapegoating a person or a group of people. When economies fail, for instance, it's easier to blame ethnic minorities than to examine the complex social, political, and economic forces at work. The shift to *how* offers a more pragmatic approach, which Watzlawick finds effective in problem resolution. In psychotherapy, for instance, instead of digging into the past to see who cast the first stone, we can focus on the relationship's problem. No scapegoating, no "You started it!" The question for the therapist or mediator then becomes not why but how do we keep this relationship going, and how do we make it better?

We all have mental models of the world. We don't truly know reality. We simply have an interpretation of it. On the basis of my mental construct of "you," I behave in a certain way toward you. How I interpret the way you react to me in turn affects my next behavior toward you, and so on. The systems approach reminds us that there is a system doing the watching, and that system has a certain way of seeing the world. To demonstrate, Watzlawick got out a booklet of transparencies from his desk. "This usually gets the idea across to my colleagues who have trouble with it initially," he said. He pulled out two transparencies. One had a series of red concentric circles ("representing a well-rounded person") and the other a series of parallel straight green lines ("a very straight person"). Then he superimposed them and a completely different pattern, a so-called moiré pattern, emerged from the two. "This is an *emergent quality*," he said, "more than the sum of its parts, arising out of the relationship between the two."

With linear cause-and-effect thinking went the assumption that to get a big effect you needed a big cause. Wrong, said Watzlawick.

Minimal causes are highly effective. Who would have thought, he said, that the Hungarian government's decision to take down 150 miles of barbed wire on the Austrian border would cause the exodus of East Germans that precipitated the end of the Berlin Wall?

Chaos theory also strongly supports this idea of minimal causes, giving it the catchy term "butterfly effect." Studying the chaotic and unpredictable nature of weather systems, researcher Edward Lorenz suggested the weather in Africa could be changed by a butterfly flapping its wings in China. The importance of this finding, which is counterintuitive and goes against the commonsense view of causality as proportional cause and effect, cannot be overestimated. Isabel Allende told us that she has "always thought that there is a link between human beings and the world. Everything is intertwined, like a braid. Everything I do has consequences for myself and very often for others, so I try to be careful with myself, because by being careful with myself I am also careful with others. I believe that what I do now will make someone else's life easier in the future."

She has something of Scheherazade about her as she recounts anecdotes of her native Chile and of her life in exile after her uncle, Salvador Allende, the democratically elected leader, was deposed by a U.S.-backed military coup. Her experiences have made her acutely aware of the power small events can have and the responsibility one has for them. "I am careful, and I plant these little seeds in my writing about the necessity of having a world that is more gentle, where equality would be a possibility, where everybody would have equal chances that we don't have now. I believe that if I plant this in my writing, someone might take it and it may become a tree in somebody's heart one day. I do this consciously: it's the pebble effect."

The systems perspective is a different knowledge system, one that is more suited for an era of increasing complexity and rapid change. Throughout this book we will be coming back to it to illustrate how it is changing our way of knowing.

The Dutch novelist Janwillem van de Wetering spent several years in a Zen monastery in Japan. He tells the story of how the head monk explained that all beings are connected and that anyone who realizes this will be careful and aware of what he is doing. Van de Wetering was not aware, the monk said. "I saw you turn a corner the other day and you didn't hold out your hand. Because of your carelessness, a truck driver, who happened to be driving behind you, got into trouble and had to drive his truck on the sidewalk where a lady pushing her pram hit a director of a large trading company. The man, who was in a bad mood already, fired an employee

15

that day who might have stayed on. That employee got drunk and killed a young man who could have become a Zen master."

Buddhists believe that the intellectual aspect of the Buddha's enlightenment consisted of seeing the interdependence, the "dependent co-arising" of all things. Once we fully understand and appreciate the incredible web of interrelationships that holds our world together, they assert, we will behave in radically different—and more enlightened—ways.

Way of Relating

Great quantities of ink have been spilled in an effort to discover and describe the different ways human beings interact. Systems scientist Riane Eisler has presented a new template that expresses the complexity of human interactions very simply.

In a revolutionary theory of social structure and organization, this remarkable woman has opened our eyes to the existence of two fundamentally different ways of relating. In her book *The Chalice and the Blade,* drawing from a variety of fields and bringing together ten years of her own research, Eisler goes far beyond any existing construct of human interaction to create an overarching theory of "cultural transformation." With extraordinary insight, she identifies the unifying paradigm that has run through our entire recorded history as "the dominator model." This model has shaped the relationships of individuals, groups, and nations over the past five millennia. She juxtaposes this with a very different organizing principle, which she calls "the partnership model."

Since we will be using Eisler's partnership and dominator paradigms throughout this book, we will introduce it here briefly. We will then explore its multifaceted implications in the chapters that follow. Described in a few words, a dominator system is based on social ranking: men (and nations) dominate women, children, nature, and other men (and nations), enforcing rank through violence, either physical or psychological or both, and fear. The civilizations that flourished at the beginning of our recorded history are long gone or transformed beyond recognition. Yet their social organizing principle continues to operate today, unchanged, mostly below our conscious awareness.

"Societies that are conventionally viewed as very different," says Eisler, "like Khomeini's Iran, Hitler's Germany, Stalin's Soviet Union, and the Masai of nineteenth- and early twentieth-century Africa, all have striking similarities. They are characterized by rigid male dominance, a generally hierarchic and authoritarian social structure, and a high degree of institutionalized violence. They are also societies where so-called 'masculine' values such as toughness, strength, conquest, and domination are given high social and economic priority (as in the emphasis on weaponry) and so-called 'feminine' values such as caring, compassion, empathy, and nonviolence are, along with women, generally held in contempt by men and relegated to a secondary, subservient sphere that is cut off from the 'real world' of politics and economics. Finally, this is a model where difference (be it on the basis of sex, race, tribal or ethnic origin, religion or belief system) is equated with inferiority or superiority, and where in-group versus out-group thinking and behavior are the norm."

We do not need to look very far for examples of dominator systems. Even in our Western democracies, where freedom and equality form the basis of the political system, we witness daily examples of the dominator mentality: racial prejudice and discrimination, second-class citizenship for women and other "minorities," corporate hierarchies with rigid levels of employee ranks, and TV violence, just to name a few. The dominator system has so thoroughly informed our vision of the world that we (citizens of Western democracies) firmly believe it is an integral part of life, a "law of nature," and therefore inescapable. According to the most widespread interpretation of Darwinian evolution, for example, life is a competition to stay on top, it is survival of the fittest, an adapt-or-die categorical imperative. The dominator model assumes that there is one fundamental way of doing things, and one has to learn a specific set of survival rules in order to be the fittest (or at least fit enough to survive and reproduce), and everyone must race and fight for a place at the top of the heap—devil take the hindmost! The fittest would be, naturally, at the top of the pyramid, the hierarchy of domination. Too bad for the individuals and species that become extinguished—that's just the way it is. Or is it?

Recent studies have led to a new and different understanding of evolution. Rather than thinking of evolution as a process whereby nature or the environment exerts some kind of force that causes us to behave in a certain way (again, a dominator view), we can speak of *viability*, of a mutual "fit" between us and our environment. In other words, "nature" sets certain constraints within which we can adapt in myriad ways: creative diversity is a better evolutionary tool than brute force. It's not a question of survival of the fittest but of reciprocal compatibility, of mutual survival.

Recent archaeological findings and reinterpretations of Neolithic art and artifacts have led some historians and archaeologists

17

to cast some doubt on the belief that violent aggression is an inevitable aspect of our genetic heritage. Popular images still depict early men clubbing wild beasts and each other and dragging women by the hair to a cave. But evidence gathered by new research paints quite a different picture. Capitalizing on these recent discoveries, Riane Eisler has constructed her partnership theory of cultural transformation.

Envision an early agricultural society where the organizing principle was based on a profound reverence for life, for each other, and for nature in all its diverse manifestations. According to Riane Eisler, "In these societies, the characteristic social and ideological configuration or pattern appears to have been basically nonhierarchic or egalitarian; although there were differences in status and wealth, these were not extreme. There are also specific indications that these were not male-dominated societies: Women were priestesses, women were craftspeople, and to us most surprising if not shocking, the supreme deity was female rather than male, a Goddess rather than a God. Finally, these were societies that do not appear to have had wars. Throughout the digs there is a general absence of fortifications, as well as an absence in their very extensive art of the glorification of warriors and war." So much for the theory that violence is built into our genes! It may turn out to be yet another dominator artifact.

Eisler's concept of partnership not only reinterprets our prehistoric past but holds the key to our future. As a society we have reached a paradigm dead end: The dominator system has revealed its own destructive paradox. The awesome potential of nuclear weapons is showing us the folly of trying to dominate the world. Our attempts to dominate nature are backfiring in a most visible way. Dominator practices from the workplace to the home are being questioned. Basic human rights are being extended to those who until remarkably recently were denied them, including laborers, women, children, and so-called minorities.

A new (or revisited, as the case may be) paradigm is emerging, and it is the paradigm of partnership. In this paradigm, Eisler explains, women, men, and nature are linked rather than ranked, and the driving force is not an attempt to dominate and have power over others but to create a better world for oneself and others. Partnership is about that overused but underapplied word *synergy*—about the whole that is not just more than the sum of its parts but that is also qualitatively different.

The dominator/partnership template takes the complexity of human relations and simplifies it for us, but it is not simplistic. Like the baffling equations of chaos theory that produce those beautiful fractals, it's possible to start with a very simple equation and watch, as it is repeated over and over, the most remarkable complexity appear. The dominator system has evolved in often bizarre and terrifying ways. From Nero watching Rome burn to Hitler and Stalin, from McCarthyism to Mai Lai, from serial killers to history's torturers, our imagination has turned to new ways of dominating—and submitting. The paradigm of partnership is equally simple and straightforward, and that's the beauty of it, but it offers a wealth of applications. It is a vast territory waiting to be explored.

The dominator system is a self-perpetuating, self-organizing system, which can keep on going of its own accord unless an alternative supplants it. Dominator dynamics are fed by the desire to escape fear and pain. But in the double bind created by this system, whether we dominate or submit, we cannot escape fear. We may think that once we're on top we'll be safe, but this is simply not true. The higher up we go in any dominator system, the greater the paranoia we encounter. This paranoia leads one to perpetuate a fear-based system in order to dominate others: dominator husbands who are completely obsessed with the "faithfulness" of their wives; dominator leaders who spy on their own people.

This is the paradoxical nature of the dominator system: Our quest for domination is really an attempt to eliminate domination from our lives, but the way we go about it actually increases the dynamic of domination in both self and others. We want to be free, safe, and happy and are convinced that in order to do this we must restrict the freedom, safety, and happiness of others. The solution has become the problem. To escape this vicious circle we need a new paradigm with an equally self-organizing power. Without it, all the hard-won advances remain isolated attempts, struggling with the prevalent worldview, while abuse, violence, prejudice, exploitation, and discrimination become more subtle.

An entirely different outlook emerges as we begin to explore the complexities of partnership, as we begin to articulate it and apply it in various aspects of our lives. Many obstacles stand in the way, but partnership, as a self-organizing system, develops its own momentum once we know the basic concepts and begin to apply them and share them with others. As Paul Simon wrote, "the thought that life can be better is woven indelibly into our hearts and our bones." The concept of partnership gives us a framework to begin bringing that thought into reality.

In order to create partnership, we need to revise drastically our entire understanding of the world, and this is by no means an easy task. People often assume, for example, that partnership stands for cooperation and domination for competition, but it's not quite as simple as that. Riane Eisler clearly states that partnership does not mean the elimination of competition, since competition can be extremely beneficial. And dominator systems have thrived on cooperation—after all, she argues, the Nazis cooperated very well to achieve their hideous goals. In a dominator system, people cooperate for the purpose of eliminating their adversaries, their competitors. The whole system is based on competition to reach the top, and cooperation is a subset of competition. In a partnership system, people compete not to eliminate others but to bring out the best in themselves and others, much like runners do. The competition acts as a stimulus, but it is ultimately a subset of an effort to cooperate. The basic difference is between fearful and playful competition. Creativity and learning are possible only without fear.

Two radically different interpretations of power emerge from the two systems: Dominator power is power over others, motivated by the fear that if we don't control others, they will control us. Partnership power is power from within, power to enable ourselves and others to achieve the ends we desire. This power is motivated not by fear but by the desire to realize the possibilities inherent in us and in others. This power rests on the security of one's own abilities, one's personal mastery, and it is therefore a power that empowers others too.

In order to understand these two different principles of social organization, we have needed Riane Eisler's revolutionary theory. What we are going to do about it, however, will depend on what each of us believes to be human beings' basic responsibility.

Way of Being

Ancient Greek tragedy made it very plain: Human beings were born to obey the wishes of the gods. Virtue was the courage to obey, unquestioningly fulfilling the actions that were each person's destiny. If the outcome was unpleasant, tragic in fact, or made little sense by human standards, it didn't matter. It wasn't human beings' prerogative to question their fate.

Philosophers and theologians have been debating for centuries exactly how much of human life is predetermined, how much obedience (to the gods or the genes or the environment) and free will (if any) define the human condition. The silver lining in a view of the world based on obedience is that we do not have to take much responsibility for anything, except for following the divine or natural or scientific or the latest cult's "law." Life becomes very simple. One is spared the agony of having to decide. Just follow directions and everything will be OK; you will be safe or saved or right or chosen, as the case may be.

People are beginning to have some problems with this concept of following orders, however, as famous trials from Nuremberg to Oliver North's Iran-Contra case testify. On a larger scale, we are beginning to admit that we have no one else to blame or to thank for the current state of the world. It is our responsibility, whether we like it or not.

We are also becoming aware that our imagination shapes not just us and our relationships, but also the structure of our political and social institutions. Physiological and genetic parameters do, of course, define the range of our experience. But beyond these, we have the complete freedom, and therefore the awesome responsibility, to create our life. This means we become morally and esthetically responsible for creating our model of the world, our particular angle on it. Systems science also reminds us that we exist in relationship, not as isolated globules bobbing along waiting to bump into each other. So we have responsibility not just to create but to co-create. We create with others, and what we create affects others. We all live in a consensus reality, a world shaped through stories we tell ourselves and each other about who we are and what we do, where we have come from and where we are going. Our judgment is constantly influenced by this consensus.

If we decide that our highest responsibility as human beings is to construct our world as consciously as possible, to create our reality knowingly, then it becomes necessary for us to question our basic assumptions.

This book offers examples of people who are questioning consensus reality, who are taking seriously their responsibility for creating and co-creating the world. Before exploring their solutions and contributions, we will explore the meaning of *creation* and *creativity*, because these concepts too have been profoundly influenced by the prevailing paradigm based on reductionism and domination.

The popular imagination, shaped by reductionism and pseudo-individualism, sees the creative genius as a fundamentally isolated man, driven by sudden inspirations either divine or genetic. In typical old-paradigm fashion (the part against the whole), our hero

21

struggles against the prejudice, disbelief, and plain stubbornness of more conventional types, who resent his brilliance and more often than not label him a crank. The genius of Mozart, as portrayed in the movie *Amadeus,* is eccentric, childish, unrecognized by the masses. They prefer the empty bombast of the envious Salieri, who fiendishly plots against the brilliant, feverish "Wolfie," whose abilities seem supernaturally inspired.

This is a profoundly reductionistic conception of genius: It reduces creativity to a lone, isolated figure devoid of social and historical context. It focuses on the moment of illumination, the Aha! experience, the light bulb turning on, the divine inspiration. Science writer Dennis Overbye writes that Einstein "the absentminded, frizzed-out dreamer has become the archetype of male genius. ('Don't bother Daddy. He's working on the space-time continuum.' Substitute 'novel,' 'fast ball,' or 'takeover plan,' for the end of that statement, and you have the image of the lone genius.)"

Creative people are often depicted as unbalanced individuals who have to suffer a thousand physical, mental, and spiritual woes all through their lives. The songwriter Paul Simon recently said that "one of the worst aspects of this culture is that we romanticize that early-burnout, self-destructive, die-young attitude. For some people, that's their destiny, but then they become cultural icons, and you got a whole people out there dying for no reason."

The movie *Bird,* about jazz alto saxophonist Charlie Parker, is replete with images of Parker's excessive drinking and drug abuse (not surprising perhaps, given the social abuse he and other African Americans had to endure), with no substantive reference to Parker's evolution as a player, his intensive, sixteen-hour-a-day study of his predecessors, such as tenor-player Lester Young, and his collaborations with Dizzy Gillespie and other innovators at Minton's Playhouse. Movies like this one perpetuate the myth that creative people are simply divinely inspired and do not need to work hard. Despite the attempt to glorify the individual, this viewpoint is rather demeaning. Individuals feel powerless when they believe that their abilities are determined by forces beyond their control and that no amount of work is going to make any difference.

We can see a perfect example of a dominator self-validating and self-fulfilling prophecy at work in the individualist view of creativity. If genius surfaces regardless of social conditions, then there is no need to create a supportive, nurturing environment for young talent. If women or blacks or Latinos and Latinas don't rise to the top, it's obviously because they haven't enough talent, so why bother with special programs or even decent education for them? The ones with talent will make it, after all, and we can chalk up one more rags-to-riches success story. This is a classic dominator strategy to keep people in their place—in the kitchen or the ghetto.

The predominant paradigm sets up an antagonistic relationship between creativity, creative people, and society. A split results between creative and conforming types, with the latter seen as the convention-bound herd oscillating between a dominant and a submissive—but decidedly adversarial—relationship to the creative types.

The characteristic dominator-system either/or polarization thus occurs: a person is either creative or conforming. This kind of thinking does violence to our nature as complex creatures who can at times be brilliantly creative and then suddenly remarkably slow and dense—all within the space of a few minutes!

Although we value creativity highly, we isolate creative people and secretly resent them. We idolize cultural stars for periods of time, for instance, but eagerly welcome any dirt on them or allow them to sink into oblivion the moment another star eclipses them.

In a dominator system, creative people can't be trusted: they might disturb the status quo and become too powerful. In the dominator system, the power to control others is highly valued, and creativity is all too often channeled into the development of instruments of domination. More than half of the world's scientists are working in weapons-related fields.

In summary, the prevailing view of creativity is not only profoundly elitist but also ultimately destructive. It separates creative individuals from their social matrix. It holds no hope for those who do not belong to the elite and fosters suspicion and resentment.

A partnership perspective on creativity is holistic and seeks to develop an environment in which everybody is allowed and encouraged to develop their creativity. Partnership creativity, like partnership power, fosters the expression of both the individual and the community. It enables others to create in ways that may be radically different from ours, it opens up a space for further creativity, as it were, rather than confining creativity to what is acceptable. Frank Barron, a leading authority on creativity, urges us to consider the *ecology* of creativity.

Creativity must become an ongoing process of participation and co-creation with the world, rather than something which occasionally strikes us on the head and spends the rest of its time hiding behind some mental clouds. We must learn to befriend creativity

23

rather than treating it as an unexpected guest that comes when we least expect it, bringing mixed blessings and urges we sometimes cannot quite manage.

Outro

The partnership system offers the matrix for an alternative that makes us aware of the connections among such seemingly disparate issues as women's rights, the environment, economic and political change, war, and the search for happiness and fulfillment.

A partnership approach does not ask us to look at utopian visions. It gently draws our attention to what goes on around us all the time that we have thus far trivialized and neglected—those people and those actions that we have taken for granted for so long. It invites us to be creative and learn from them.

The kind of change we are suggesting is not about using a few buzzwords or following a recipe. It asks that we begin to figure out for ourselves how we can contribute to the creation of a new world. We are presenting food for thought. We asked experts and laypersons, the famous and not-so-famous, how they are overcoming the old ways, what partnership means to them, what they are endeavoring to create. Their examples can assist us in our own journey and help us make a difference in the process of change.

Preview of Coming Attractions

In this chapter we have gathered the thoughts of three persons who are quite different in age, interests, and concerns. Yet a common thread unites them, a thread we will find time and again in the chapters that follow.

This selection is a bit like a wine tasting. There is a look into the future from a global perspective; a reflection in the present driven by a personal quest; and a discovery of the past through the eyes of people who live in today's world but whose customs and values echo those of our distant ancestors.

Futurist Paul Saffo and the Power of Zero
When you have questions about the future, where do you go these days? Why, to a futurist of course. Paul Saffo has practiced law in Silicon Valley, New York, and Tokyo and is now a research fellow at the Institute for the Future in Menlo Park, California, conveniently located near Silicon Valley, Stanford University, SRI International, and other trend-setting, information-gobbling institutions. A walking, talking encyclopedia, he was casually dressed when we met him and exuded an air of relaxed confidence and not a little mischief.

"We really are headed toward the mother of all New Year's Eve parties," he told us, "and it has to do with our love of zeros. We always get nervous around New Year's anyway. The greater the number of zeros in the year, the sooner we get nervous, the more nervous we get, and the longer it lasts. So you see, the end of a decade, one zero, usually lasts two to two and a half years. Each decade has had something like this. At the end of the eighties we saw things like the harmonic convergence and new age movements really taking hold. At the end of the sixties it was the Age of Aquarius. Take two zeros, the end of a century, and you have end-of-the-century thinking like the so-called fin de siècle in France, which was this world-weary sophistication and artistic despair that everybody really got quite sick of, and it lasted about ten to fifteen years.

"With two zeros you have a real impact for a ten- to fifteen-year period. We've only been through one millennium, three zeros, in recent memory, and that opened a period of change and upheaval that disrupted the better part of a century of European social history. This did not happen so much among the intelligentsia, the Christian establishment at the time, who said, 'Don't be silly, this is not the end of the world.' But among normal folks, among the Joe Six-packs of the year 1000, many people really expected the end of the world.

"What's interesting about millennial movements in that society is that part of the effect happened after the year 1000. It is no coincidence that the Crusades followed close on the heels of the first millennium, because it turns out that when millennial predictions do not come to pass, the majority of people say, 'Oh, that was silly,' but a minority believe more fervently than ever that we just got the date wrong. So the people had assumed that even though the year 1000 had passed, they had entered into the end of time and that, of course, after Armaggedon, the second coming of Christ would happen in the Middle East. How inconvenient for it to be controlled by Muslim infidels and not by Christians!

"We have the same sorts of millennial traditions today. Part of it is fueled by plain old calendric chauvinism. Every generation that's ever lived on Earth thinks that it lived in the most interesting time and the most important time in history. Calendric chauvinism and religious fundamentalism seem to go hand in hand. We have a long tradition of millennial fatalism in our society. The single best-selling book of the 1970s was *The Late Great Planet Earth* by Hal Lindsey, a book of predictions loosely based on the Book of Revelation and biblical prophecy.

"There are fundamentalist Christian groups who were opposed to arms control on the theory that the Russian premier was the 'Beast' and that Armaggedon would arrive in the form of a nuclear exchange between the United States and Russia. If you had arms control, there would be no Armaggedon; and no Armaggedon, no second coming. They thought they would be raptured into heaven when the bombs exploded. Drive down the freeway and you'll notice people who have bumper stickers on their cars that say, Warning—In the Event of Rapture, This Car Will Be Unmanned. You scratch the surface and there is a real lunatic fringe.

"I suspect that the twentieth century is the century that started a decade late and ended a decade early. In essence, it was a seventy-six year century that opened with the assassination of Archduke Ferdinand in Sarajevo, which precipitated WWI, and ended the moment that Saddam's tanks crossed the border in Kuwait.

"Until 1457, when the first books came out of movable-type machines, the dominant skill of scholars was not literacy, the ability to read, but memory, the ability to recall, which by then had become a very formal science. Thomas Aquinas achieved sainthood in the 1200s on the strength of inventing a memory-palace mnemonics. And in fact it was so formal a technology that around 1520 a Jesuit priest by the name of Matteo Ricci went to China armed with the 'memory palace,' a mnemonic system of visualization to remember information, and presented it to them convinced the Chinese would be so blown away by Western 'technology' that they would all become Christian.

"By 1480 with the advent of print there was a shift from the brain as a storage medium to the brain as processor of printed information. It's no coincidence that the brittle palaces of memory collapsed under literacy, and it was a shift from a static, medieval worldview to the dynamic worldview of the Renaissance. I think we're going through a fundamental shift like that today. And it's a shift from worrying about understanding information to trying to see some links between different kinds of information. From saying, What's the price of this stock? to saying, What's the trend of this stock? We are looking for patterns in huge amounts of information. We are looking for indicators.

"The whole scientific visualization revolution is really about nothing more than how to cope with information overload. The solution is graphics. Abstraction is the solution. During the time of the Renaissance, they managed information overload in their financial environment with an invention created by a Benedictine monk: double-entry bookkeeping. Today the equivalent of double-entry bookkeeping on Wall Street is probably chaos theory. Apply chaos theory to commodity prices and they map out as what is called a strange attractor. It's a specific pattern. The invasion of so-called rocket scientists, mathematicians, and theoreticians on Wall Street is also an indicator. In the long run, what I argue is, we're shifting to something new. Information is a wave about to engulf us, and the solution is to surf. We're creating a whole new generation of information surfers who have a new set of skills that they'll bring to bear on how to cope with information overload."

The Christmas Spirit Is Not What You Drink

Tom Stone is a college student in his junior year, coming to terms with the different heritages in his background. Tom shared with us a way in which he's going about it.

"I first heard about Kwanzaa last December, when I was twenty years old. My aunt called to wish me a merry Christmas one night. We talked for a while, and before she hung up she said, 'Oh, and happy Kwanzaa too.' 'Happy what?' I said.

"She explained to me what Kwanzaa was, and said she had been celebrating it for the past several years. The fact that my aunt, who is white, was celebrating an African American holiday did not surprise me—she's always been considered the most liberal and daring relative on my mom's side of the family.

"After hearing my aunt's description of Kwanzaa, I decided that it sounded interesting and set out to learn more about it. I went to the bookstore the next day and found a Kwanzaa cookbook, which also contained a brief history of the holiday and an explanation of the traditions and necessary materials for those, like myself, who were new to Kwanzaa.

"I read the first chapter in the book and knew I had started a new tradition in my life. Kwanzaa was exactly what I had been looking for; it appealed to me for several reasons. The first is that Kwanzaa is not a religious holiday. Since I am not a religious person, I could celebrate Kwanzaa to the fullest extent without going against any of my beliefs. Instead of focusing on a god, and how he or she may influence your life, you are encouraged to look to yourself and consider how you control your own life, and how you may affect the lives of others. Another reason it appealed to me is because it offered an alternative to Christmas. It disturbs me that Christmas has become so commercialized. During the holiday season, it seems that everywhere you turn someone's trying to sell you Christmas at fifty percent off. Too many people have forgotten the reasons, whatever they may be, why they celebrate Christmas. It was refreshing to find a holiday celebrated by people who know why they're celebrating it. Finally, the main reason I decided to celebrate Kwanzaa is because it made me think about what it really means to be an African American, like my father. Much pressure is put on people of color in America to assimilate, to try to melt into the crowd and copy white American culture. But after celebrating Kwanzaa, I realized how important it is to hang on to our heritage and proudly acknowledge every bit of our background. Kwanzaa showed me ways to tie together aspects of African culture and American culture to form one unique way of life."

Here are the seven principles of Kwanzaa—an African-American holiday celebrated from December 26 through January 1 as described by author Eric Copage:

1. *Umoja* (unity): To strive for and maintain unity in the family, community, nation, and race.

2. *Kujichagulia* (self-determination): To define ourselves, name ourselves, create for ourselves, and speak for ourselves, instead of being defined, named, created for, and spoken for by others.

3. *Ujima* (collective work and responsibility): To build and maintain our community together, and to make our sisters' and brothers' problems our problems and to solve them together.

4. *Ujamma* (cooperative economics): To build and maintain our own stores, shops, and other businesses and to profit from them together.

5. *Nia* (purpose): To make our collective vocation the building and developing of our community in order to restore our people to their traditional greatness.

6. *Kuumba* (creativity): To do always as much as we can, in whatever way we can, in order to leave our community more beautiful and beneficial than we inherited it.

7. *Imani* (faith): To believe with all our heart in our people, our parents, our teachers, our leaders, and in the righteousness and victory of our struggle.

Finding Partnership All Over the World, or
How Stuart Schlegel Lived in the Rain Forest
of the Philippines with the Tiruray

"Ever since high school I had wanted to be a priest," Stuart Schlegel, professor emeritus of anthropology at the University of California, Santa Cruz, remembers. "Prior to seminary, I decided to go back to the Philippines, which I loved very much from visiting while I was in the navy. I went there for about eight months and worked up in the Mountain Province with Igorots, people who until very recently were headhunters.

"I loved it, and thought when I was ordained an Episcopal priest I would go back to that area as a missionary. In fact I was sent to the south to Mindanao, to an area where the church was working among people called the Tiruray. I spent three years there as a missionary and enjoyed my life there very much. I would have stayed on permanently except that we were turning all the church work over to Filipino priests and bishops and nuns. So there was no real future for an Anglo priest in that area.

I knew that the forest went a long way back into the mountains, and I knew that deep in the forest were people who lived the old, traditional life. And so I determined to do a study among those people as my anthropology predoctoral field work. "I went back into the forest, and I was guided by a priest friend who was a Tiruray man himself, a Tiruray Episcopal priest who kept contacts with the old, traditional folks. And he took me way in, it was many hours' hike from the nearest road to where they lived. He took me into the interior, way into the interior, to this community called Figel.

"I stayed there for the better part of two years. He introduced me to the Tiruray and told them I was harmless and didn't want to convert them to anything and didn't want to change anything. Didn't want to cut the trees down for logging. Didn't want to become a rancher, just simply to live among them and learn their ways. I think the Tiruray found that rather bizarre. But they accepted me at face value and were always very lovely to me.

"After a while of being a little defensive about whether I was trying to convert them to something, they settled down with me and we became good friends. Over the next two years, I learned lots about their way of life, how they hunted, fished, gathered, farmed the forest, how they drew livelihood from the deep forest.

"What I came to realize, as I worked with the Tiruray material and thought about it and as I was myself influenced by feminist thinking, was that these Tiruray were something quite unusual, at least to my knowledge. Maybe they were not unique in the world by any means, but at least unusual to what you typically see in so much anthropological literature, in that they were what I called radical egalitarians. In all of their doings—in their terminology, their daily activities, their marriage system, their legal system, and so on—they do not institutionalize power and they don't ever rank people.

"They see very clearly the difference between a man and a woman, the difference between childbearing and cutting down big trees. But they don't rank them. In their cultivation system, for example, women will normally do the weeding and men will normally cut down the big trees. It's not that a man wouldn't weed or that a woman couldn't cut down a big tree, it's just that they don't usually do that. They have role-specific behaviors. The difference between that and what you have so often in the West is that it would never occur to a Tiruray that cutting down trees was a superior or a more high-tone thing to do than weeding.

"When I read Riane Eisler's *The Chalice and the Blade,* it made me realize how many other aspects of Tiruray culture embody the partnership system. Tiruray cooperate with the spirits, for example. They're not afraid of the spirits, even though the spirits can make you ill if you offend them, just as they believe a human will get back at you if you offend a human. But they don't rank the spirits; they interact with the spirits. They have social relations with the environment. They respect the environment; they don't try to dominate it. They try to work with it. Their whole way of life can be understood as a sort of cooperative venture with the spirits to make use of the forest for the good of the community."

What We Can Learn from the Tiruray

The Tiruray can teach us about many things, according to Schlegel, about "oneness with nature, the possibility of peaceful human coexistence, the possibility of a society based on cooperation and equality rather than power and domination. And they can teach us that it is possible to have authority without power, violence, dominance, and oppression. The whole of life for the Tiruray is saturated with trust and goodwill for others, and with the benevolence of nature.

"Tiruray love peace and harmony and social cooperation. They have a deep dislike and distrust of individual domination and control. Fighting is not idealized as warfare; it is seen as self-protective at best and immoral at worst. Fighting and killing among Tiruray do exist;

they are seen as part of human nature, but wrong. Tiruray traditional society was a kind of island of partnership in a sea of dominator-oriented societies in the world.

"Tiruray don't glorify battle or even hunting. Battle is seen as the result of wrong behavior. It happens, but it's never right. Hunting and swidden cultivation are purely for subsistence needs, for social sharing. They are accompanied by a most humble appeal to the caretaker spirits for understanding our dependence upon each other for life. So, for instance, before the Tiruray will cut down the first rice of a harvest, they will always honor the spirits of the rice and say to them, 'We are cutting down this rice not to do it harm but because we depend on it for our life and we thank you for your help in our living.'

"All ways of assaulting the common good and social harmony are considered foolish wrongdoing. The Tiruray who know English will often translate the word *dufang* as "foolishness," but what it really means is that you have done something against the harmony of nature or against the harmony of human beings, which will bring retaliation either from the spirits or from other human beings. That's why it's foolish to behave violently. People will lose their temper; that's a natural thing to do. But it's not the ethical, not the moral, thing to do. What you should do (in their normative system), if you're angry, is to turn it over to the legal leaders to settle the matter nicely.

"These leaders act as justice givers, and 'justice' is a return to harmony in which every person has his or her due, every person has his or her honor restored. You can't do that by mediating compromises, so Tiruray reject the notion of compromise in their legal system. They seek to find out who really was right and who really was wrong, where right and wrong were apportioned in a conflict situation. And they make it right.

"If angered and hurt, people are apt to lash out in disharmonious violence. That's part of 'human nature.' It's not that some people are evil and nasty, it's just that some people are foolish and do foolish things that bring on feuding if they offend another person or bring on sickness if they offend a spirit.

"Their interaction with the spirits is essentially a happy and joyful enterprise, whether in social encounter or in more formal rituals. On top of mountains, in forest clearings around one's settlements, in living areas, interaction with spirits has the quality of play, of recreation. Gongs are played because the spirits can hear the gongs.

Laughter and relaxation are the mode of interaction with spirits, not silence and solemnity or prayerful sobriety. Tiruray ritual, like Tiruray social order, celebrates and dramatizes cooperation. It's meant to invoke the powers of the cosmos and to bring well-being to the society and to the world.

"So often in dominator societies, cooperation is based on fear and aggression toward an out group," Stuart Schlegel told us. "Nothing like that exists among the Tiruray. Cooperation for them is based on trust and reciprocity with each other. Their attitude is 'I'll do this for you because I need you to do things for me.' It's not a kind of moral calculus like 'I'll scratch your back if you scratch mine.' It's just a sense that we're all in this world together, and the world is good if we cooperate. The world is good if we share, if we help each other."

The Self

One

This is the place where everything starts. In our current worldview, this is the point of reference, where "I" begin, my sense of self, me, the one that is my self. Somehow we assume that this experience is both universal and primordial, in the sense that it has been with us since the beginning of our lives. But it is not.

The sense of self develops over several years. Our consciousness emerges slowly. By nine months of age some children recognize themselves in the mirror, and by age two most can scream "Mine!" This does not mean, however, that they have the same sense of identity and awareness of self that an adult has. It takes about six to ten years of life before one can reflect upon the idea of one's identity. Do you remember that moment when you said to yourself, "This is *me:* This face, these eyes, my left hand touching my right arm, the smell of my skin, this inner presence so known, so . . . me, like no other"?

From that moment on, we spend years patiently gathering layers that add consistency and strength to our identity and sense of self. In the polarized system of knowing and learning that is still prevalent, one culture might emphasize the part, or individual, while another culture might emphasize the whole. In the Western world, particularly in the United States, we make a big deal of our individuality, individualism, and the accompanying virtue of self-reliance. Americans are the most individualistic society in recorded history; in every facet of our culture we emphasize finding, expressing, understanding ourselves. The emphasis is on the concept of individuals as isolated atoms, as fully autonomous entities.

In many other societies people get their identity from the group they belong to—from their family and village. Boys follow in their fathers' footsteps and take over the family business or employment, girls marry into a family where their husbands will provide for them a new identity as wives. Historically most people rarely lived more than forty miles from the place they were born, which meant kith and kin accompanied them from the cradle to the grave.

The famous Russian psychologist Alexander Luria did some interesting research in an isolated area of the Soviet Union called Uzbekistan. When he asked the farmers there to describe themselves, he did not get the usual self-congratulatory characteristics like "kind," "considerate," or "intelligent." What Luria got was quite different. "I came here from Uch-Kagan," one of them replied. "I was very poor and now I'm married and have children." Luria asked another one if he was satisfied with himself: "It would be good if I had a little bit more land and could sow some wheat," he replied. "Well," Luria continued, "some people are hot tempered, others calm, what do you think about yourself?" "We behave well," another farmer replied. "If we were bad people nobody would respect us." As he asked more questions, Luria slowly realized that these people never actually referred to their own inner self. Everything was explained in terms of the collective, or in terms of external indicators, like the weather, crops, or social relations.

According to Luria, it is likely that our preindustrial, agricultural ancestors did not really think of themselves as independent, autonomous human beings capable of self-definition. This sense of separateness and uniqueness only really emerged in the West after the Renaissance and the Industrial Revolution, some scholars argue.

In Asia the far-reaching influence of Confucianism has important implications for the creation of a sense of self. In the Confucian world, there are no individuals, only family members. People are at no time seen as separate from the family and the larger social unit. Maturity involves an ever-greater understanding of one's place in the social fabric, of the roles, duties, and responsibilities one has to take. The idea of self-actualization and the abandonment of group responsibilities in favor of some half-baked "inner search" would be considered rude, selfish, and even foolish.

The Western, individualistic mentality recoils at the idea of submerging the self in a group. It gets just as turned off as Chinese do when they see Westerners insisting on drawing attention to themselves. But some profound differences exist even among Westerners. "I come from a society where life is so hectic and the individual counts so little," Isabel Allende of Chile told us, "that you can think of yourself only in terms of the group, as part of a group, part of the family, the tribe, the society."

The predominant polarizing viewpoint would set the two approaches, individualism versus community, in opposition. But what would happen if we switched worldviews, put on different glasses, and started reasoning with a systems mentality? What might we see? An agile movement from part to whole and back again? Designated times in the course of the year when the part or the whole would be celebrated? A simultaneous awareness of self as separate and as part of the whole?

Royal Alsup, a psychotherapist and social activist who has worked extensively with African and Native Americans, believes that "the reason African Americans and Native Americans lasted through all this genocide is because of their community orientation, the partnership that they have in community. This is the dream of Martin Luther King and Gandhi, Indian people, and the black church—they're all community artists sculpting a beloved community and a partnership with each other. This is totally opposite to individualism, where the individual is self-elevating at the expense of everybody else.

"I'm not talking about the negation of individualism. In fact in this community orientation of Native Americans and African Americans, you have the uplifting of the individual through the community. In any community, for instance, you have a boat maker, a dancer, a spiritual singer, medicine people; so each individual creates in community their own individual way, but in conjunction, in partnership with the rest of the community." As we have seen, the Tiruray have a similar kind of orientation toward roles in society.

This thinning of the boundaries between the one and the whole is a recurring theme in spiritual traditions the world over. In our Western world, influenced by reductionistic thinking, we have made it increasingly difficult to relinquish our separateness for an occasional dive into wholeness. We are afraid of giving up our individuality and

37

getting lost. In a world where either/or thinking is emphasized, and where the predominant form of interaction is based on dominator dynamics, these fears are perfectly understandable. Yet we long to recreate from time to time that experience of belonging that we knew before we became one.

According to religion historian Mircea Eliade, a most important celebration for ancient and "primitive" societies is the beginning of the year. Interestingly enough, beginnings are times when both the part and the whole are present: the matrix and the emerging one.

Beginnings

Before we became a separate psychological being, there was the time when we became a separate physical being: the moment of birth. Most of us do not remember what birth was like and thus can never know that experience directly. But we can experience a birth from the other side, so to speak, by either becoming a mother or assisting a woman who is giving birth. It is not the same as being born, of course, but it comes close.

Yet it is only in the last twenty years that males (other than those in a medical role) have been attending births. Generation upon generation of men have gone through life without knowing what the source, the spring, the beginning of life is all about. The closest they got was to waiting rooms and antechambers. This is not just a historical curiosity. According to Riane Eisler, dominator societies tend to isolate birthing from the mainstream of life, to separate as much as possible sex and birth (as in the notion of the virgin birth), and to represent the woman's role as "baby container." This systematically downplays the notion that birthing completes the cycle of a woman's sexual experience and symbolizes her creative sexual power.

In sociological terms, birth has not been a partnership experience. Things are changing, but even now for every man who feels expanded by the experience of attending the birth of his baby there is one who has to fight fainting and nausea at the "messy" sight. The poor guy has fallen prey to the predominant paradigm that focuses on one aspect at the time: the breathing according to Lamaze, the centimeters of dilation, the place of birth, the medical progression of it. Nobody has told him that the best way to attend a birth is to focus on the woman, to center completely on her and her experience. Nobody has taught him to look into her eyes and be brought along, close, very close, to where he could never venture alone; to be with her, not with a "delivery." If this was common knowledge and a widespread experience, would the world be different?

In the dominator world, birth and pregnancy have been made into something not a little repulsive. One can see people get shot on TV, but a birth is hardly ever shown. When actress Demi Moore appeared pregnant and discreetly bare on a *Vanity Fair* cover in 1991, some circles protested, and certain convenience stores refused to carry the issue. Common sense prevailed as most people found the photo not just inoffensive but beautiful. Yet the incident reveals lingering traces of the dominator revulsion toward life, creation, and the "filthy mysteries" of women.

Judy Flanagan is the director of Nurse Midwifery Programs at the University of California, San Francisco, General Hospital. She has assisted over a thousand births and has trained hundreds of nurse midwives. When she was interviewed on a radio talk show, it was apparent that Judy and her host, a well-known local politician, were coming from two different paradigms, two worldviews separated by an immense gulf.

From the host's perspective, the presence of a physician during delivery was unquestionably preferable. He agreed that given the great need, it was a good idea to train nurses to be midwives so that less affluent women, or women living off the beaten track, could have the comfort of competent assistance. Judy, by contrast, talked about giving birth as not merely a physiological event. She held the whole experience of the woman in the process of becoming a mother, and explained that the word *midwife* comes from the German *mit* (with) and means "to be with the woman." He was talking "part," she was talking "system"; he was talking mechanics and economics; she was talking life experience.

Isabella had just witnessed a birth facilitated by a midwife who had been Judy's student. This is how she describes that experience:

"My friend Mona had asked me to be with her and her husband at the birth of their first child. I remember the first part of the day as a dance, a ritual dance that moved us slowly through every corner of the house. Walking seemed to be the easiest way for Mona to handle the pain that within a few hours would open the way for her baby to be born. Through the day the three of us grew closer together; we lost the sense of separate parts and we became a system. We had only one focus: her well-being. We were being nourished by her strength,

39

she by our caring attentions. Toward the end, when exhaustion was beginning to set in, we had created a tight knot of solidarity. The boundaries were thinning out, like the placenta that was about to relinquish her fruit.

"The midwife and her assistant joined us during the last few hours. They were amazed at how gently and thoughtfully Mona's husband, Edward, was ministering to her. When the true pain came, the one that stretches and tears, descending on the whole body like a hurricane and rushing through the brain like water falling three thousand feet down a rock wall, like lava exploding from the mouth of a volcano, he did not pull back. The other women in the room remembered their own labor, the opening of the water, the tide rushing out. Gathered around the bed, our breathings followed Mona's rhythm, we were all shouting, not loud, in a whisper, but we were all shouting to encourage her because we knew her hour had come and she would be ripped apart and *life* would be present. Through her pain and her bearing the pain with such bravery and honesty, Mona had invoked a sacred presence. For a short second I slipped out of my complete concentration and looked around. I saw we had created a circle of light around her bed that glowed and pulsated like a roaring bonfire on a beach . . . and then her son was born."

Not all births sound the trumpets of angels, only one in several hundred. But so what? The idea is to allow different views to exist. The midwife is there to be *with* the woman, whatever her trip turns out to be. We asked Judy Flanagan what the best way is for friends and relatives to be with a woman who is giving birth, what one should do to be useful. "Love her," said Judy. "Love is all that's necessary. You are there for her, your attention is wholly concentrated on her. Whatever she does is fine. Never stop telling her that she is doing great, whatever she does, however she wants to do it, however she chooses to live this time of her life." Compare this with the common experience of women who are constantly told what they are supposed to do and how they are supposed to feel during delivery.

We cannot help but wonder what would change if the paradigm were different. If women did not think of delivery as merely a medical event but were prepared during gestation to look upon it as their moment of truth, as a most powerful chance to become one with life? If husbands and loved ones were made an integral part of birthing the world over and taught to become part of that miracle of creation, would the world be different? Would the children be different? Perhaps it's worth a try.

No Sense, No Feeling

By young adulthood most of us reared in the West have developed a powerful set of tools to differentiate ourselves from the surrounding whole in order to maintain, above all—the supreme good—our individual identity. We erect walls around our hearts so we may not be vulnerable to the attack of others. With time, the self becomes stiff like our joints, more unshakable, heavier, less porous, closed to new ideas and to change. Armoring of all sorts, both physical and psychological, accumulates over the years until we become like clunky medieval knights in rusty suits of armor.

Yet in spite of all this work, the "one" turns out to be more elusive than we were led to believe. The very worldview that motivated us to pursue this goal makes it impossible for us to achieve it. The predominant paradigm affects not only the relationships between the one and the whole, it pervades not only the process of birth, it actually works within the self in insidious ways. It splits us into parts and sets them up against each other: emotions versus reason, body versus spirit.

Most of us were taught early to separate reason from emotions and to conceive of these two parts of the self in opposition. In typical dominator fashion, we were taught to rank them rather than link them. Reason is thus considered superior to feelings.

Despite the valiant attempts of romantics throughout the ages to sing the praises of emotion, at least since the seventeenth century we have considered reason to be superior in every way to emotion. A decision arrived at on the basis of reason was indeed considered "reasonable." An emotionally tinged decision was inevitably suspect, and the term *emotionality* implied instability, untrustworthiness, and "femininity." Men were supposed to be cool, silent types who never showed emotion, whereas women could get away with swooning and other displays of loss of self-control.

A quick look at the movies of the 1940s and the 1950s can show how much we are already beginning to change our minds on this point. Remember the cool Manhattan home of some intrepid anthropologist, who amid the Naugahyde furniture and dry martinis and views of Central Park had a couple of "primitive" masks hanging in his living room, to be studied while furiously puffing on his pipe? He represented the pinnacle of rational and scientific Western society; those masks, icons of savage emotions, inevitably caused him no end of grief, supposedly because they were elaborately cursed, conjuring up "those drums . . . oh, the drums . . ." It seems this emotional hex came in with the masks, like a pest U.S. Customs officials make you swear you haven't come near. All of this means that the West considered itself rational and scientific, and therefore inherently peaceful and good, in contrast to the primitive heathens. And if something occasionally unleashed some mysterious, hidden genie, it was our duty to find the cork and close the bottle. Shedding the light of reason on wild superstitions was a matter of progress. And if the light of reason came from the firing of cannons, then all the worse for those at the receiving end.

Along with this image of the savage brute came his counterpart, the Noble Savage, the "natural man" with none of society's dreadful inhibitions. Starting with Rousseau and then in a number of ever more simplistic ways, the "heathens" were cast as role models for our alienated society. Today some circles still romanticize everything that's exotic and non-Western, just as others trumpet the supremacy of Western logic.

It's important to perceive the ways a dominator system can polarize us into different, mutually exclusive camps. This creation of illusory or imaginary oppositions, presented in either/or fashion, is integral to the dominator dynamic that in the guise of giving us a choice, really creates a damned-if-you-do, damned-if-you-don't situation.

Remember those science fiction yarns where squeaky-clean people dressed in white would interact with robots and computers and never show any emotion? The aliens encountered by our intrepid heroes were usually paragons of unbridled, destructive emotion, large hairy creatures from outer space and black lagoons, mindless monsters from the planet Id. Dr. Zachary Smith in *Lost in Space* and Dr. "Bones" McCoy in *Star Trek* were typical examples of how the emotional person was out of place in the technological future.

That the conquering West didn't quite live up to its noble self-image is no mystery by now, and in fact it seems to have used its reason and science to fuel some rather base desires for territory and power. The reason-emotion split was particularly interesting because scientists wanted to eliminate emotions and values from their investigations, and this made the very study of values and emotions out of bounds. They consequently became even more mysterious and powerful forces. They may have been taboo for scientists but not for greedy politicians and pirates.

Reason was so highly valued in the West that the eighteenth century hailed itself as the Age of Reason. The hope emerged that through scientific, rational, and reasonable thinking, human beings might improve their lives dramatically, eliminating disease, poverty, and war. The Enlightenment proclaimed the gospel of reason, education, and linear progress (every day in every way we're getting better and better).

Now, however, our collective images are changing. The modern, or machine, age is turning into the postmodern age. We are beginning to doubt optimistic linear projections, and we are beginning to understand the role of feelings in the wholeness of life. Our science-fiction screen heroes, like Han Solo and Chewbacca of *Star Wars*, are much more conversant with their own emotions. The aspiring Jedi knight Luke Skywalker knows that the greatest danger is not in feelings but in letting one destructive feeling dominate his whole self. Even Darth Vader, the worst of villains, turns out to have a good side. Aliens are also becoming warm, funny, inquisitive, and friendly creatures like E.T.

We are becoming aware of the inner damage the dominator model can do within the "one." We are beginning to view reason and emotion as mutually dependent. We are beginning to understand that when emotion and reason are split, with one dominating the other, the results are not pretty. Reason alone is an outwardly sterile affair motivated by sinister, hidden, and most likely "sinful" feelings. Emotion is a roller coaster of joy and rage and depression, but with a nasty, calculating edge. This split creates enmity within the self.

David Loye, a former faculty member at Princeton and the UCLA School of Medicine, is a social scientist committed to human betterment and social change. He is the author of the prize-winning *Healing of a Nation,* as well as a highly acclaimed work on the psychology of ideology, two important books on brain and futures research, and a pioneer in the application of chaos theory to social theory. He has also worked for over a decade with his wife and partner, Riane Eisler, in developing and applying her dominator/partnership model analysis in many areas. Loye notes that typical dominators in a dominator system show the same symptoms as people suffering from alexithymia, which means "no words for feelings." Clinical alexithymia comes from brain damage or stunted development. Loye hypothesizes that the dominator system could be said to have the same effect as this type of brain damage. Dominators are typically insensitive and don't have words to translate their feelings. Some feelings can be expressed, but the range is very limited. It is an interesting hypothesis in light of our typical childhood experience of being systematically discouraged from laughing at the

43

table or in class. Our natural excitement, inquisitiveness, and ebullience were considered a nuisance. We were rewarded for being quiet, docile, and emotionless.

Mara Keller, a professor of philosophy at San Francisco State University and head of the Peace Studies program, believes that "in our culture, most of us, but especially boys, are taught not to feel their own pain. 'It doesn't hurt!' 'Don't cry!' 'Be a man!' 'It's just the way it is!' 'No pain, no gain!' All these admonitions are designed to dismiss the significance of pain. But Nature's way not only in humans but in all creatures is to seek pleasure and to avoid pain as much as possible.

"If women want to rise up the ladder of success in this culture, we are told that we must play by the same rules as the men—who have been taught to suppress their feelings to such extremes, especially the feeling of pain. But as soon as we discount the value of pain, then we've lost a great teacher. Pain is Nature's way of telling us something is wrong and we shouldn't do it, whether it's pushing our muscles beyond their limits, or pushing our emotions or our social relations beyond the limit of what's healthy. If we can feel sympathy or compassion for our own pain, our own humanity remains. To the extent that we shut down around our own pain, we are unable to feel or care about anybody else's. Out of that indifference comes the disregard, and all the other social problems that bring us to such a desperate crisis in the world today.

"The first time I was able to feel compassion for myself was only a handful of years ago, during a Buddhist meditation retreat with Ruth Denison, an important teacher to me. I was so very fatigued, so tired, but I was trying to be the good student, which is one of my roles, and to sit right and to meditate right and to get more enlightened.

"She told me, 'Feel your fatigue, feel your weariness, be aware of yourself.' I was touched by that because I really had not allowed myself to feel the *negative* feelings. My mother always taught me to be cheerful and positive. Having positive emotions is fine, but not if you always dismiss or deny or ignore the negative feelings. So that was my problem, and it created a lot more pain than I expected. Finally I allowed myself to feel my own pain and be aware and care about my own pain. It was quite an experience, it was good for me. I felt my heart open because of that. I do shut down. I can't always be that open. Sometimes, in order to make a living, I feel a need to put up my walls, my defenses. But I know it's possible to be open and if I was in that place more often, I'd be happier, and my work would be more effective."

Mara Keller illustrates beautifully a point that will keep coming up in these pages: To the extent that we shut down around our true feelings we are unable to consider or care about or feel anybody else's. We must develop greater sensitivity, what David Loye calls *moral sensitivity.* In a dominator system, morality emphasizes control and punishment, Loye points out. The term *morality* has become associated with moralizing, judging, and imposing one's rules of conduct on others. In a partnership system, by contrast, morality emphasizes bonding and linking. Loye believes it is vital for us to recast the definition of morality and begin a serious and open dialogue on issues concerning progressive rather than regressive right conduct.

The Mixed Blessings of the Flesh

The split between mind and body, flesh and soul, matter and spirit has been even more painful than the split between reason and emotion. In the Middle Ages the flesh had to be denied and humiliated so that the spirit could triumph. The flesh was notoriously weak and had to be kept in check so it wouldn't become easy prey for the devil. The body seemed to have an uncanny ability to make us lose *control,* the crucial word that still sums up our attitude about the body. Bodies have to be controlled, not in the least because they represent the "animal" in us, the part that is susceptible to brutish lusts and sexual passions.

Woman, as temptress, was believed to have almost supernatural power to bring out devilish lusts in men, particularly chaste, religious men. In the twelfth century, a guide for women recluses warned that if a man "commits mortal sin through you in any way, even with desire for you, be quite sure of the judgment: you must pay for the animal because you laid open the pit." In the sixteenth century Saint Bernard avoided any contact with women, including his sister, since according to him, "to be always with a woman and not to have sexual relations with her is more difficult than to raise the dead." Only a hundred years ago the sight of elbows, ankles, and, God forbid, knees could still make people swoon and whoop and holler.

After the paradigm of the dominator system swept over the ancient world, "women were seen as chaotic and dangerous," according to Ralph Abraham, a mathematician and noted chaos theorist, who has written a book entitled *Chaos, Eros, and Gaia.* Chaos theory seems to have found a perfect embodiment in Ralph Abraham, a maverick mathematician who clearly is uncomfortable within the

45

confines of a single discipline. Abraham told us that "the serpent, who was Eve's teacher, is well known as a symbol from prehistoric times. Eve is a relic of the *hyerosgamos,* the priestesses of the temple of the Goddess. We have the temples of Inanna in Sumer, the temples of Ishtar in Babylon, the temples of Isis in Egypt and continuing in classical Greek time up to A.D. 632, when the Moslems destroyed Alexandria.

"A positive aspect of Eve continued for a pretty long time, in spite of the Old Testament, right up to early Christian times and the beginning of Islam. Today there is an emerging consensus on the association of chaos and the Goddess, particularly within the feminist revision of history." Whereas, at the dawn of history, chaos was seen as a source of creativity and change, the patriarchal dominator system viewed it as threatening to the status quo and to the existing power structure. Eve's role in humanity's fall from grace replaced her role as the mother of all.

When not the source of devilish, uncontrollable lust, bodies evoke uneasiness for other reasons. Bodies are the source of urine, feces, blood, and a variety of noxious gases and fumes. Not all of us can easily reconcile within a unified image of the self our highest aspirations and our "base" bodily functions.

The most positive metaphor for the body in the last several centuries has been the body as a work implement, a tool for bringing food to the table. Muscles were desirable because they gave one the strength to perform the tasks that today are done by machines. In the last few decades, the shift in the way we see our bodies has been considerable. From being a work machine the body is becoming an instrument of pleasure and esthetics. Now muscles and a tan are there for our pleasure and enjoyment—and that of others, yet we are still, in many ways, prisoners of the old worldview.

If Looks Could Kill

In the traditional dominator system, women's identity depends very much on their looks. The revolution in Iran that led to the fall of the shah and the rise of Khomeini in 1979 was fueled in part by the fundamentalists' disgust with Iranian women who had cast aside the traditional veils. In a dominator system, how women look is not defined by the women. Men, by contrast, are judged on their achievements and the tokens of that achievement, the car, the job, the house.

Women know what they should look like, what they really look like, and how they should feel about not looking the way they should look. Women have a far greater investment than men in their bodies, because in a dominator system, women *are* their bodies to a far greater extent than men are.

They are destined to be companions to men and therefore have to be attractive. Women are enormously concerned with the way they look—not unreasonably, given the system's demands—and tend to get depressed about their looks no matter whether they're "objectively" beautiful or not. When they get older and lose their slimness and firmness, they are discarded like overripe peaches, to be replaced by younger, more attractive companions. Never mind that the old geezer can't keep up with his new bride on the sidewalk, let alone in the bedroom, because she is there to make a statement about him, about the property he owns.

Yet men don't always get a free ride in the body department either. No matter how powerful a man is, the body can still be a source of pride or shame, depending on whether he's the kind that gets sand kicked in his face or the kind that does the kicking. Being physically weak or short or fat or somehow different from the physical norm is no laughing matter for a boy, and the memories of beatings and taunts from the schoolyard and the neighborhood are not easily erased. The ensuing feelings of powerlessness and inferiority last a lifetime and create a scar that will not heal unless carefully tended to.

The dominator system has no room for losers and yet ensures that everyone becomes one ultimately. Even muscle-bound high school heroes get old, and their bodies begin to change and lose their power. Inevitably someone will be faster and stronger and better, and the prowess of their youth will be no consolation.

It is no mystery either that girls do not tend to seek out the nerds and the wimps. This double rejection from both boys *and* girls can lead to feelings of isolation and anger. This anger then comes back to haunt a person in adulthood. It is the kind of anger at women that can express itself in rape and domestic violence—anger taken out on somebody who's lower on the totem pole.

Riane Eisler points out that "we live in a society where violence against women has traditionally not only been visible but eroticized." The dominator system objectifies women and men, and both fall victim to the "parts-is-parts" game. *Metonymy* is the word used when a part is taken to represent the whole. It's inoffensive when the waitress refers to you as "the chicken cacciatore," but it becomes absolutely demeaning when a woman becomes "a pair of tits" or a man is judged by his "buns." Only when the body is viewed as part of a larger system that is the self does it stop being some kind of alien

47

creature we inhabit or a perennial source of dissatisfaction because we don't measure up to the latest airbrushed, five-hours-in-the-makeup-room screen god or goddess.

Not long ago, education about the body was minimal. The body served simply as a kind of locomotion vehicle for the I that was located between the ears. Philosophers would get worked up about the mind-body problem, amazed at this kinky cohabitation of flesh and soul.

When something went wrong with the old workhorse, we'd take it to a doctor, who'd suggest some remedy or other. If things got really bad, he'd poke around inside us and usually take something out. Preventive medicine consisted of removing the tonsils or the appendix, parts we couldn't figure out and therefore considered useless. We were not educated about diet, for instance, or the effects of smoking, saturated fat, and a thousand other potential killers. Today when they're offered a high-cholesterol, high-fat meal, some people assume that the host is some kind of culinary terrorist out to dispatch them prematurely. Because of the new concern about skin cancer, many people are forgoing tans, putting concern for the body above esthetic or faddish preoccupations. Despite a certain initial overkill, the health movement seems to be helping us to establish a partnership with our bodies and to understand the systems nature of our well-being.

Sheldon Margen Defines Health and Pokes Some Sacred Cows in the Ribs

Sheldon Margen used to be a researcher in biochemistry, working on the synthesis of proteins. "Eventually I found myself in an area where only about four or five others in the world were interested in the research I was doing. It's nice to be lecturing to people who are impressed with you but have no idea what you're talking about. But what effect did this have on society or on knowledge? It was contributing to knowledge, but whose knowledge, and for what purpose? I think that sort caught me—'Hey, what am I doing out here?'

"I then got involved and interested in food and nutrition, and then peace and wellness," he continued. Now he is professor emeritus of public health and director of the Peace and Conflict Program at the University of California, Berkeley. His own drive to learn and change motivates him to advise people to take stock of their lives every ten years or so and probably change their routes, just as he did his.

We asked him to define health. "Health, very briefly, is the optimal state of an individual in terms of functional capacity—at the physical, psychological, and social levels. Obviously this involves value judgments and ethical concepts. Value judgments are extremely important, even at the physical level. If you examine the children of the developing world, you observe that they develop at a slower rate. They do not grow as fast, they do not grow as tall, and they do not get as large. And the people end up smaller, in stature, body build, and so on.

"Is this because these people are genetically determined to be small? No, it is not genetic. It's the result of a deprivation of some sort. Ultimately it would have to come down to some biological deprivation, like food. If their newborns migrate out of a village or the slums and into the middle class, they will grow at a rate approximately equal to the rate of growth of those of us from the West. Their stature will be similar to ours. Therefore genes do not come into it.

"Now, what does stature indicate? This is where value judgments come in. Some experiments done a number of years ago suggested that these deprived children would not have the mental or intellectual capacity of the children who were bigger. Was that because their brains were not developed as well? The theory was *yes*. According to the theory, their brains' development was impaired, which meant they did not and would not have the mental capacity of children who had an opportunity to get taller and bigger. Therefore these people of the third world, these small people, were lost. There wasn't anything you could do. The critical time of their brain development had passed, and they were doomed to be inferior people from here on in, a lost generation, and essentially labeled as such.

"Is this correct, or is it not correct? Well, a beautiful theoretical model was built. This theoretical model said that in order to satisfy our 'genetic potential,' the genetic potential of the human race, we had to become relatively bigger people. Even in our country, it's rather interesting that children of smaller stature, again on an average, score lower on IQ tests than taller children. The theory was that what is important is to satisfy the genetic potential, and therefore getting large satisfies the genetic potential, so maximum is optimum. The theory states that anyone who doesn't get to that 'optimum' has been handicapped in some way and is (to use my term) unhealthy.

"Well, we have to ask, unhealthy in what respect? Maybe unhealthy in terms of mental health. Try to demonstrate that, and you can't, because you cannot separate the developmental influence of the biological effects from the social deprivation that these children are suffering. The orphans in Romania illustrate this. If you take a child born of perfectly normal parents who should otherwise develop normally, and you put this kid into an orphanage or a hospital, and you leave this child without human interaction, you can feed this kid whatever you want, but you'll get a child who will be permanently impaired. To blame this on a biological phenomenon makes no sense. In fact this whole idea of 'satisfying the genetic potential' also makes no sense because we don't know what the genetic potential is.

"So what we do in our society? Our children get fed, overfed. We now know that if you exceed a certain maximum, then you are really at greater risk, and almost all of your functions will start deteriorating. This is what we may be doing in our society right now. With all this pushing to achieve the genetic potential and continuing this manner of overfeeding, we've extended the so-called life expectancy. But this increase in the average life expectancy was produced mainly by decreasing child mortality through better physical environments. Has this increased life expectancy really increased the quality of life, especially for older individuals? We've now started producing a new spectrum of diseases at the other end of life, which seems to be due in large measure to forcing our functional capacities beyond the organism's ability to process them. The result of pushing our genetic potential has been to produce a whole spectrum of chronic illnesses."

Sheldon Margen is saying that the idea of "more is better" and "bigger is better" (a typical dominator belief) influenced our supposedly scientific conception of genetic potential, which in turn influences policy-making on issues such as nutrition, third world development, and life-style. Now we're beginning to admit we really don't know what this genetic potential is. In fact a better way to look at this is that our genetic potential is the maximum level of adaptation of our genetic map, and to exceed this leads to a deterioration of functional capacity.

Margen pointed out two major implications: "First, we are mistaken to think that we're going to cure or change the lives of children in third world countries by bringing them only food and feeding them, which has been the policy of both our Agency for International Development and of the World Health Organization. In other words, it is nonsensical to try to isolate a single factor and say it alone makes a difference.

"Second, you have to examine the problem within the system. Bringing food in and dumping it on these people for a period of time will probably increase their growth to some extent. Although in fact I did experiments that show this is not entirely effective because it's not possible to reach the target. Not only are these kids hungry, but their parents and everybody else is hungry. The food gets distributed all over and ultimately does not solve the social problem. If anything, it creates even more serious social problems because it creates a dependency on an external source of food and diverts attention from the causes of food scarcity. Instead of looking at why they are not getting food within their social system and how they can get enough within the system to feed everybody properly, through an ongoing process, we offer a piecemeal approach.

"But now, slowly, the major donors and people concerned with development are saying, 'Hey, we've not been doing it right; nutrition is worsening. Let's go back and take another look at our policy.' They have to be a part of the health system, and now they're all beginning to talk about how the health system has to include more than worrying about the immediate physical health of a child or mother."

Don't Worry About Being Happy

Most of the knowledge that science has patiently accumulated about the body and the mind has to do with what can go wrong and how to fix it. Generations of researchers have tried to figure out exactly how people are sick, mentally and physically. Hardly anyone has paid any attention to the day-to-day basic maintenance, let alone the possibility of feeling really good. It's the eat-lard-for-breakfast-and-call-the-doctor-when-we-get-the-chest-pains approach.

One fine day, Elaine and Art Aron, two intrepid researchers on the frontiers of social psychology, foolishly decided to study happiness. They're the kind of people who would do that sort of thing. With a passion for ballet and statistics, meditation and psychology, they've begun to explore areas where most researchers do not even think to look. Studying happiness is a major event in the sense that hardly anyone in academia has looked at happiness seriously.

Elaine points out that most of us think achievements make us happy. Research shows we're quite wrong in thinking this. People interviewed six months after an accident that had paralyzed them from the waist down and people interviewed six months after they'd won a lottery showed the same levels of expected future happiness as measured on tests. The people around them expected the former to be devastated and the latter to be ecstatic, but in fact this was not the case. But this expectation certainly would contribute to making both groups feel isolated.

The work of Art and Elaine Aron is part of a larger movement toward the study of positive states rather than negative ones like aggression and depression. The same is true in medicine. What is the state we're supposed to return to after we've gotten over a bad flu? It's supposed to be some kind of personal baseline, some acceptable "normal" state. We can differentiate between people who are really healthy and people who are not, and we can also make some suggestions to unhealthy people about what they should and should not do to improve their health. But only very recently have we started paying attention to what makes and keeps us healthy.

When we asked Sheldon Margen to define the more generic term *wellness,* he complicated matters by saying that "you can almost interchange the two words *wellness* and *peace.* Conceptually there's not much difference between what we talk about as peace and what we talk about as health. In other words, a society that is at peace is also a society that is healthy. An individual who is at peace is also healthy.

"I've been intrigued by the notion of both of them being positive terms, rather than merely an absence of the negative. Peace is not an absence of war, or health an absence of disease. These two are positive concepts that operate in very similar ways.

"What do we really mean by health, and what are the determinants of health? Health is really a state in which an individual is able to function at his or her best, at the physical, psychological, and social level. It depends therefore upon a number of factors. There are internal factors, like genetics, and how you take care of your body. You're constantly interacting with your environment. So you have to be concerned about that, to try to keep your environment in some sort of state that it is not harming you and to keep interactions with your environment positive for both you and your environment. From this point of view, wellness and peace are extremely similar. They belong to the same general conceptual framework."

In a dominator system, happiness revolves around our place in the dialectic of domination and submission. If we're on top, we're OK, but we have to worry about losing our position. If we're on the bottom, we're anxious and miserable. This dynamic precludes the possibility of fundamental happiness—a basic happiness that seems to be at the core of what we are and do—and allows only ephemeral happiness, the brief happiness following achievement. In a partnership context, happiness is a much more general, whole-system form of peace, as we shall see.

Dean Ornish on Happiness and Low Cholesterol

In his best-seller *Dr. Dean Ornish's Program for Reversing Heart Disease*, physician Dean Ornish proposes a way not only to reduce the risk of heart disease but actually to reverse it. Drawing on a variety of disciplines, including a healthy dose of common sense, Ornish has created a program that is easy to follow but that requires a basic change in life-style. His approach involves a combination of diet, exercise, relaxation, and, generally speaking, a different approach to life. He believes that "mind and body are one and the same."

"The split between mind and body," he told us, "grew out of the Cartesian dualism of the seventeenth century, which allowed people to objectify reality as somehow being different or separate from ourselves. There is some value in looking at the world from that model, but the danger is that it leads to a profound sense of isolation, not only from other people and from the sense of being part of something larger than oneself, but even from our own bodies and from our own feelings. In my opinion, that split is a fundamental cause, not the only cause, but a fundamental cause of why people get sick all the time.

"There is a paradigm shift occurring now, and, if you follow the book that Thomas Kuhn wrote on *The Structure of Scientific Revolutions*, paradigms begin to shift when anomalies become apparent to a number of people. The universe is an infinitely complex and vast place, and our minds have a hard time dealing with concepts like infinity, so we reduce the universe to more manageable proportions by using models or paradigms. Those models have value in that they provide a sense of order and help us understand at least part of the universe more clearly. The problem comes when we mistake the paradigms for the universe as a whole, and we think that all of reality can be explained by one paradigm. And since a paradigm, by definition, is limited, sooner or later anomalies become apparent. Anomalies are simply observations that don't fit within the paradigm or model.

"In the sixteenth century an Italian philosopher named Giordano Bruno came along and said, 'The Earth is not the center of the universe,' and the Catholic church burned him at the stake. When people

53

challenge the prevailing paradigm, they are threatening not only the particular item that they're challenging but also on a deeper level the overall sense of order that the paradigm provides. So when a paradigm is challenged, people often react in intense and irrational ways in order to preserve the order of the universe, literally.

"In the seventeenth century, Galileo came along and he showed people, using a telescope, that they could see with their own eyes that the Earth was not the center of the universe. And although eventually he had to recant under the threat of the Catholic church and the Spanish Inquisition, by then it was too late. He had given people the tool to see for themselves the limitations of the prevailing worldview of that time.

"Now in this latter part of the twentieth century, I think that we are seeing the limitations of the scientific paradigms in a number of ways. In medicine, for example, we are realizing that the approach of trying to fix problems without also addressing their underlying causes is of limited value. The problems tend to come back, either in the same form or in a different one. In my book I use the example of bypass surgery. Half of the bypasses clog up within five to seven years, since we're not changing the underlying cause. It's like mopping up the floor around the sink without turning off the faucet.

"The costs are so high. Last year twelve billion dollars was spent on bypass surgery, even though we know that it's only palliative. And so, in a sense, the medical system now is in a state similar to a patient who has had a heart attack. In other words, it's in a state of crisis, partly because of the disillusionment that many people are experiencing in the active search for alternative approaches and partly because of the exponential rise in health care costs. It's a cost we can no longer afford as a country. It will invariably lead to rationing unless we change the paradigm and address the underlying reasons why people get sick in the first place.

"As with any crisis, there is the opportunity for things to get much better or much worse, whether on the personal level or on the social level. My hope is that through studies like ours and others', people see that they have new alternatives and choices and that those choices can be more empowering. We could use very high-tech, state-of-the-art measures, like quantitative coronary arteriography and cardiac pep scans, to demonstrate how powerful these approaches are even at unclogging arteries or lowering cholesterol. They are comparable to or better than high doses of cholesterol-lowering drugs without the great expense and the side effects that these drugs have.

"Part of the problem is that we tend to believe what we can measure, and it's much easier to measure blood pressure and cholesterol than social isolation, or certainly emotional or spiritual isolation. Yet if you talk with patients and look at the emerging literature on social isolation and social support, you'll see that people who feel socially isolated have three to five times the mortality from not only heart disease but from all causes when compared with people who feel more connected with others. We may not always be able to measure the experience of isolation, but we can measure the effects of it. What's also interesting about these studies is that isolation is a determinant of health at least as powerful and in some ways even more powerful than diet, cholesterol, blood pressure, and even smoking. So I'm hoping that as we begin to see the limitations as well as the benefits of drugs and surgery, we can begin to see that other factors play an important role too. No one paradigm can encompass all different facets of reality. It's not that drugs and surgery are bad. They have their place, especially in a crisis. But they're limited.

"We try to encourage the expression of feelings, for instance. This is part of an overall context that we use to heal isolation. The expression of feelings is a way of transcending our isolation. Feelings connect us more than thoughts do. We pay attention to the way people communicate those feelings so they are not heard by others as an attack or a judgment, otherwise the expression of feelings can increase isolation rather than help heal it. It's not just the expression of feelings but the expression of feelings in a particular way, which can be very healing if done using the kind of communications skills that I write about in my book.

"There is the misidentification of thinking that happiness or peace comes from something external. Having made that misidentification, a person gets into a series of patterns and behaviors and beliefs and expectations that ultimately bring unhappiness and disappointment and often even disease. If I think that external events are going to bring me happiness, I am setting myself up to be unhappy. External factors can't bring happiness in a lasting sense. For a short time they can, but everything that comes, goes eventually.

"Once I quiet down my mind and body, I can experience an inner sense of well-being or happiness. That is really our natural state until we disturb it. Not realizing that, we end up doing things in the name of being happy or getting happiness, disturbing an inner happiness that we could have if we just quieted down enough to experience it. The paradox is that once a person is more grounded

55

in that, he or she can go out in the world and accomplish even more, but for different reasons and without the anxiety and fear that often get in the way. And of course it's a process—it's not all or nothing; I don't claim to be happy all the time. Once we have made that discovery or that identification and at least understand where true happiness and peace really come from, the world itself reminds us when we start looking for happiness outside that we are looking in the wrong place."

How Do We Know What We Know?

According to astronaut Edgar Mitchell, in our present paradigm "we don't account for intuition or creativity because science cannot accept, or does not officially recognize, that consciousness is a valid phenomenon. It's a nonsequitur, because what, after all, are we looking with? What is it that's observing all of this observing? What's doing all this science? What is the mind and consciousness that scientists are using if it's not real?

"So science glosses over a fundamental problem, saying, 'Don't bother me with that, I've got enough mundane problems to keep me interested and happy and prosperous. I don't need to worry about these philosophical questions.' Scientists of that ilk are essentially saying that consciousness studies are about as useful to science as ornithology is to birds. To me, that's living with your head in the sand. It's truly missing the point of science's greater purview, which is discovering the nature of reality, not necessarily solving particular problems.

"I tend to think that science in general has virtually no understanding of how information is transferred in the universe. We are information-processing organisms. Creativity is organization of information that in some sense hasn't been organized before. My approach is to look at what information really means in the universe, how it is organized, how it is transferred, what the mechanisms are. Intuition is clearly the perception of information from the universe beyond our normal senses. Creativity is closely related to intuition. It is gaining information, gaining ideas, in a freshly organized way. I would say creativity is the organization of new gestalts."

Whereas the scientific approach involves a methodical, conscious process, with all the evidence out in the open and every step clearly outlined, intuition occurs in a flash and comes seemingly from nowhere. Einstein said that "the really valuable thing is intuition," and examples abound of scientists who had flashes of intuition and inspiration that came to them like bolts of lightning out of a blue sky.

The dominator system has split the world in two and set us against ourselves. Intuition and empiricism, imagination and observation were meant to function together, and do in our most creative moments. But normally they are woefully unable and untrained to communicate with each other.

By making us see wholes, showing us connections where previously we could not see them, intuition is closely related to creativity. In fact almost all creative people seem to be very intuitive, far above statistical average. Combine creativity and intuition with scientific training and you get a powerful mix. Separate them and you get impractical dreamers on one side and plodding dullards on the other.

Rational, empirical processes function in linear, machine time. The step-by-step methodical process is well suited for a digitalized, bit-by-bit conception of time. But intuitive processes require more time, it seems. Their time is not at our bidding and cannot be forced. Intuitions can be immediate, but they can also result from long periods of hard thinking after which we let go. The process is similar to the functioning of memory: When we forget someone's name, we try hard to remember, hoping for some clues, perhaps in the first letter of the name. Then we give up, and suddenly, at sometimes the strangest moments, the name jumps back into consciousness.

What is intuition? One set of descriptions might be "seeing through," or "seeing into," the idea being that we can see, beyond appearance, a deeper or hidden reality. In this sense we might have an unpleasant intuition or foreboding or a hunch or premonition about someone who on the surface looks pleasant enough.

Based on recent brain research, David Loye has developed a theory of five different kinds of intuition linked to five different experiences of time. In his book *The Sphinx and the Rainbow* he calls the first kind of intuition "left brain serial intuition." In this case we base a judgment about somebody on an intuition that really comes from processing an enormous amount of data about them so quickly that we are not conscious of it. There is nothing mysterious about it, since we are merely reacting to cues, little telltale signs that added together give us a certain feeling. Less easy to understand are kinds of intuition linked to right-brain and holographic-brain processing that seem to access a realm of timeless time. These latter interpretations of intuition are more easily dismissed, since they suggest some mysterious capacity for knowing that remains largely undiscovered and unexplained.

Intuition can also be a sudden click of insight, where previously disjointed elements seem to fall into place. Police investigators on television routinely have this kind of intuition. When all the seemingly random evidence they have collected comes together and points conclusively to the culprit. Great creative insights seem to fall into this category.

In a dominator system, the faculty of intuition is viewed with some suspicion and is considered the province of women. As a way of knowing, it has been shunned by men. Women have been socialized to rely on their intuition; men may occasionally make lucky guesses but usually utilize logic and reason to understand the world around them. Only men in the arts have been permitted to be intuitive. Women, who have traditionally not been educated to be—or allowed to be—outwardly logical and rational, have naturally expressed these abilities as an alternative way of knowing.

What is it about intuition that can be so disturbing? In a system based on control, there is something terribly out of control about this phenomenon. It's not rational, not explainable, and in the dominator system the unknown is a source of profound fear.

People who have strong intuitive capacities are sometimes referred to as "sensitive," which suggests they're picking up things in their environment that the rest of us are not. *Awareness* is a crucial word here. Are we aware of our bodies? Are we aware of what goes on around us, or do we steam ahead mindlessly? Are we sensitive enough to pick up what is going on around us and inside us? The word *sensitive* itself is not particularly favored by the dominator system. It carries overtones of weakness, of crybabies who are affected by everything and need to be toughened up.

Musical improvisation is an example of an art that requires a high degree of intuition. Musicians have to be extremely sensitive to the sound of an entire ensemble. They have to listen closely and be prepared for the unexpected. In improvisation the nature of relationships changes and a partnership network emerges that provides mutual support while at the same time encouraging the greatest amount of individual freedom.

The great psychologist C. G. Jung insisted that the task of life was to fully explore and integrate our disparate processes of thinking, feeling, physical sensation, and intuition. The prevailing paradigm works hard at keeping them separate and keeping us internally disconnected when in fact we yearn to make friends with ourselves.

Creating the Self

As the whole world around us is changing at a feverish pace, and we try to make sense of what is happening out there, in the small hours of the night when we cannot get to sleep and lie in bed wondering, we are still left with the fundamental question of what to do with our own life. The dominator system hands us precise answers quite eagerly. It provides sets of rules that define our proper place in the order of things. If we are not inclined to obey, the system has powerful and often frightening methods to encourage us to stay within our assigned roles. In its most benevolent aspect, the dominator paradigm acts with subtle persuasion to help us choose among the acceptable scripts. Because it is so deeply buried below the level of our awareness, we obey without even knowing that we are delivering the lines someone else has written.

The emerging paradigm, by contrast, encourages us to write our own scenario and to create for ourselves our life story in a spirit of partnership with the world around us. This ongoing process of creation and co-creation of the self becomes a person's basic right and responsibility.

Stanley Krippner's life has taken him around the world exploring the mysteries of the mind. From China to Brazil, from the former Soviet Union, where he spoke at the prestigious Academy of Sciences, to various parts of Africa, Krippner has delved into matters mysterious and unexplained, ranging from shamanic rituals to dreams, telepathy, and creativity. His demeanor is inquisitive, curious, open-minded. He is an amateur magician, alert to sleight of hand and preposterous claims. As diverse as it may seem, all of his work revolves around human possibilities, in particular the ability to effect psychological change. His best-known book, coauthored with David Feinstein, is *Personal Mythology*.

"We all have a part of ourselves that prioritizes, that makes decisions on how we're going to live our lives, and that constructs the inner story," Krippner explains. "Some neuroscientists have called this the 'narrative' brain, yet that is another metaphor. Gazzaniga, for example, believes that the ability to construct a narrative is hardwired in the nervous system. A myth is an imaginal narrative, but it's not always a narrative in words; sometimes the narrative is in pictures, or in images, dance, or movement. Myths always tell a story or make a statement. All of us have personal myths. These myths, whether we know it or not, have behavioral consequences.

59

They probably affect our most important decisions, and in many ways they run our lives. In some societies, especially under dictatorships or under very tight social controls, people do not have much choice, and so the utility of their personal myths is greatly limited. But certainly in Western industrialized nations, again within limits, individuals can make choices, and these choices are governed by the myths that people, wittingly or unwittingly, have constructed."

When we talk of "empowering" people these days we are talking in a very real sense about allowing people to be creative, to create their own world, their own circumstances, rather than to conform to a preexisting pattern.

Willis Harman was a regent of the University of California from 1980 to 1990. An emeritus professor at Stanford University and president of the Institute for Noetic Sciences, Harman has been at the forefront of the exploration of our present social transformation. He told us that "if you firmly believe in some sort of a computerlike model of the brain, you will believe that creativity—because it's done by a machine—has to have some limits. If instead of that, at the other extreme, you have a model that believes the mind can tune in to a universal mind, then there aren't any limits at all. We all participate in creation, all the time. The question is, are we creating what we think we want? My sense is that we're shifting from viewing creativity in terms of its usefulness and as a kind of mysterious behind-the-scenes process to creativity as a code word that describes a whole new outlook: Our existence as part of a unity and involvement in the creation of experience."

Between saying and doing there is a vast, deep ocean, according to an Italian proverb. People may like the idea that they have the freedom to create their own life, and many are taking advantage of this opportunity, which in past centuries was reserved for the privileged few. But freedom can also be frightening. A few years ago, at the beginning of *perestroika,* we were in Europe teaching a course on creativity. A Russian psychologist, an eminent member of the Soviet Academy of Sciences, and his assistant were also invited to lecture. They confessed to us their trepidation and fear about the changes taking place in their country. They were confused by the sudden lack of structure in their lives. They no longer had a blueprint to guide their actions. Closer to home, when we consult in corporations that are trying to implement the principle of employee empowerment, unfailingly many will ask, "I don't understand, what am I supposed to do now that I am empowered?"

The German sociologist and psychoanalyst Erich Fromm wrote an interesting book titled *Escape from Freedom*, in which he argued that human beings have a tendency to run away from freedom and into the arms of totalitarian, or authoritarian, dominator systems. Freedom is a great responsibility, Fromm wrote, one that many of us are not ready to accept. There is an unbreakable connection between creativity and freedom, but there is a fundamental difference between the concept of freedom in a dominator system and in a partnership system. In the dominator model, freedom is purely freedom *from*, in other words, freedom from coercion, arbitrary power, rules, and regulations. In order to implement this freedom from, Byzantine laws and rules and regulations are invented to prevent people from interfering in one another's freedom.

In some societies "freedom" becomes communist or fascist collectivism, where people ostensibly work together to free themselves by following rules and manifestos and ironclad laws of history (which benefit only the dominant elites, who establish the rules). In democratic societies it is often thought of as individualism and freedom of expression. This type of individualism, however, usually implies freedom without responsibility and therefore is called in this book "pseudo-individualism." Its unspoken promise is that once you get to the top, you can do as you wish. Power buys you the right to use it in any way you can get away with. Other people are either obstacles or means to achieve freedom.

Freedom and individualism are highly valued in the United States. But, to paraphrase Henry James, being an American is a complex fate, according to Todd Gitlin, former head of Students for a Democratic Society, now a professor of sociology at the University of California, Berkeley, a novelist and one of the nation's leading media-watchers. "It is to be at home in a certain kind of rootlessness, unsettled in certain ways about who one is, perennially challenged, damaged, and anxious. It is to be pious, since Americans are, after all, the great churchgoers, not the Italians or the Irish. It is to be deeply insecure and brash at the same time, to be convinced destiny is in one's power and to be obligated to make one's life what one can. There is a searching for ground to stand on, and a belief in the American gift of freedom."

Americans also tend to overvalue freedom but don't really know what they want to be free *for*, even as they find more and more things they want to be free *from*, like old age and taxes.

This tendency to want freedom from rather than freedom for is fascinating. Perhaps it reflects the fact that we're still in a "scarcity" mode and want freedom from hunger, fear, and so on. But unless we develop an image of what we want freedom for, we'll have a tendency simply to keep doing what we're doing; and this creates conflict because we don't really know what to do with ourselves. It's a bit like longing for a holiday but being bored when we finally get it because we're so used to the routine of work.

In a pseudo-individualist society, any failure—even the flu or cancer—can be blamed on the individual. Without a strong support network of friends and family, this can place an unnecessarily hard burden on the individual while at the same time exonerating any larger forces.

"Individualism is the last gimmick of authoritarianism," social critic Philip Slater told us cheerily. "It's part and parcel of the old divide-and-conquer ploy," said Slater, author of the classic *The Pursuit of Loneliness* and most recently *A Dream Deferred.* "In this case it says 'You have to fight the system alone.' The lone individual shakes a tiny fist against the all-powerful system, whatever and wherever that may be."

More often than not, however, people fight among themselves. The rise of psycho-killers, according to some psychologists, is a phenomenon of our age of individualism, loneliness, powerlessness, and alienation. It's a way of getting back at society, but not the whole of it, not by trying to create positive change but by killing some of the representatives—*any* representatives—of the system.

Todd Gitlin considers himself a rugged individualist and feels that much of what passes for individualism is in fact merely a cheap substitute, what we're here calling pseudo-individualism. Many people we spoke to point out that we've been duped into believing that we are individualists when in fact we've put on our badges and conformed with the uniform and the behavior of all the other supposed individualists. In the meantime, we're not really sure who the hell we are, which may be why so many of us are going into therapy.

Greedy individualism is indicative of a profound insecurity about the self and society, according to Gitlin. "A true individual," he says, "is one who can cooperate and is not afraid of being submerged by others. People who know who they are have no need to lord it over others or slaughter each other."

The explosion of greed in the 1980s was generally depicted as a period of remarkable shallowness. Movies like *Wall Street* and books like *Bright Lights, Big City* and *Bonfire of the Vanities* (we won't mention the movie) painted a picture of frenzied, coked-out conspicuous consumption, of self-consciously kinky *9 ½ Weeks* yuppie sex, and very little real satisfaction of any kind. What the 1990s will be about no one can predict at this point, but the first indicators appear to show a shift toward caring. Young and old are beginning to find real satisfaction and meaning in working with others and sharing in the creation of a life that is better for all, not in conquering Wall Street. This shift to caring is accompanied by a reevaluation of who and what we are and what the nature of individualism is.

Isabel Allende too sees individualism as a mixed blessing. She stresses how it can in fact become conformism. "We are shaped by others to a far greater extent than we might suppose," she points out. "America is the paradise of self-made people—whatever that means—but I think you are never self-made. You are made by all the people that surround you, by the circumstances, by the place where you were born. So I am not a fan of individualism when it's taken to the limits. Of course a certain amount is necessary and healthy, but when you exaggerate it, as is done in the U.S., you have a very selfish society, very greedy, where people are measured by what they make and not who they are."

Although Allende loves the United States and is happy to be living here, she does see that "certain things that are essential for human beings to be healthy are deteriorating and even lacking in this society. The family, real friendship, a sense of commitment to the group. There is no sense of commitment to the group: You live in a neighborhood for thirty years and then you retire to Florida, where you don't know anybody and have to start all over, making friends in a retirement home! I can't imagine a more horrible way of getting old, and to have to pay for that! They want to live in a neighborhood where there are no children or no blacks. Why would you want to be isolated among people who think like you, look like you, are like you? This is surely a most boring idea."

When we become aware of how others have shaped us, of the influence of our environment on us, we become more aware of who we are. Our unwillingness to accept the impact of social forces on us is an unwillingness to recognize parts of ourselves. This sense of history is evident in Allende's novels.

In a partnership view of the world, freedom is seen as freedom *to*. The freer we become, the more creative we become, the greater our responsibilities become—both to ourselves and to others. Systems thinking shows us we're not alone in our endeavor to create our story; we are a part of many larger systems and networks of connections. It further points the way to recognizing these connections at all levels of life, from the self to the community to the environment.

63

A partnership approach shows us how we can work with others in a cooperative, mutually beneficial way, drawing on all the resources within a system. Creativity research shows us how we can begin to create the kind of world we want by drawing on our human capacities, and it shows us how to do this *with* others, within the larger network of relationships.

Our concept of self, the basic foundation of our life story, is shaped by the interaction between us and the world around us. Susan Hales, a professor of psychology at the Saybrook Institute and a member of the Alameda County Task Force to promote Self-Esteem and Personal and Social Responsibility, describes how the self-concept is formed and its relationship to self-esteem.

"The self-concept is the knowledge you have about yourself, it's everything you know about yourself. You're tall, you're short, you have brown hair, brown eyes, hazel eyes, you're a husband, a son, a daughter, a musician. You know what you like about yourself and what you don't, your affinities, your proclivities, attitudes, values, beliefs.

"Self-esteem is part of the self-concept, but it's different," Professor Hales explained. "Self-esteem is the 'evaluative component' of the self-concept. It has two aspects. Self-esteem is a function of judging who you are. If you know all these things about yourself, then what do you think of yourself? Are you a person of value, a person of worth? In addition to the judgmental component, self-esteem has an affective component. Once you make that evaluation of yourself, it either feels good or it feels bad, and it can be very painful. That's why self-esteem is so important. It is an affective experience that is either pleasurable or painful. People are strongly motivated to protect themselves against the pain of low self-esteem and low self-evaluation. They try to create opportunities to increase positive affect. But sometimes the need to protect one's self-esteem prevents one from taking any of the risks necessary to get positive inputs to self-esteem.

"My parents are migrant farm workers, and I was raised in a particularly harsh, difficult environment," she remembers. "As a 'fruit-tramp' I was discriminated against by people in my hometown, Lindsay, which is between Bakersfield and Fresno in California. When I was a freshman in high school, I had a very interesting experience. We used to travel around in a little trailer picking fruit, and we'd spend most of the year in Lindsay, but we'd start off in the spring around April and go to Lodi and Stockton and further north to Auburn and then to Oregon and Washington and Montana. We would travel further and further north to pick cherries because cherries get riper later the further north you go.

"One year my father stayed in Washington to pick apples. In that town I was treated very differently by the kids in school because all they knew about me was that I was from California. And I guess when you're a Washington high schooler, you think everybody from California is a surfer. They thought I was a surfer from California, and I was a celebrity to them. I had a wonderful suntan, which they thought I got at the beach, but in fact I got it in the fields picking cherries and apples in their town. The quarterback of the football team asked me out, and the cheerleaders wanted to be my friends. I said no to the quarterback. I didn't understand what was going on—I thought it was a joke or something. I didn't understand until later. When I left after a couple of months, these people actually had a surprise going-away party for me. Then I went back to Lindsay, where I was again treated as if I didn't exist. I didn't matter. I wasn't even made fun of or anything. I just wasn't worth the trouble. In both settings I was the same person, yet in neither place was I treated according to who I was, only according to who people thought I was."

At that point, Hales decided she would be in charge of who she was. She subsequently earned a Ph.D. in psychology from the University of California at Berkeley, and it's not surprising perhaps that she became interested in doing research on the social construction of the self, self-esteem, and self-concept.

The Buddha said that all we are is our thoughts, our beliefs. Our very self is kept together through the momentum set into place by beliefs. Suppose a man strongly believes that he is a successful manager. When he retires, and stops being a manager, he'll probably wonder who the hell he is, not know what to do, and die. These paradoxical dangers of retirement are brought about by a literal identity crisis: "My God, what do I do now? Where do I go for strokes, for fun, for excitement, for stress? Where are my routines?" This man's whole self-concept revolves around being a manager. His self-esteem is inextricably tied to it. Take the job away, and self-concept and self-esteem can collapse. He had successfully created a self, but now there seems to be something wrong with it. It doesn't want to let go. In fact it has almost taken over.

In the same way that we may identify with our job and become it—I *am* a plumber, a musician, a secretary—we identify with certain beliefs about how the world should be, what is right and wrong.

65

Going to a foreign country, where untold numbers of people often stubbornly do the exact opposite of what we expect them to do, can give us culture shock. This involves losing our bearings and, to some extent, our grip on social reality. We may become anxious, depressed, and, interestingly enough, may experience a peculiar blurring of our personality and its boundaries.

We don't know what to believe anymore. What is right, and what is wrong? What is beautiful? When everybody else has beliefs that differ from ours, we may start feeling strange. Our identity is largely dependent on outside cues, on a society that is familiar and reassuring. Just like when we shop for clothes, many of us want to look at the designer's label, and make sure it's someone we know.

Our identity is constantly reinforced by outside cues, such as neighborhoods, like-minded people, and television. This is why isolation tanks and solitary confinement, when involuntary, can lead to a quick breakdown of personality. When the cues are gone, we literally forget who we are. Voluntary isolation is, of course, a time-honored method to loosen the grip of society's conditioning, used by yogis, monks, and all sorts of mystics.

Beliefs about who we are and what's going on are clearly useful. But they can also become stifling. In our present system, many labels reflect dominator assumptions that tie us to behaviors, thoughts, and feelings we may not want. Part of our creative challenge, therefore, is to "reimagine" the world and ourselves, as William Irwin Thompson calls it, or "reenchant" them, as others say.

Creating the self, in a partnership way, is not a once-and-for-all project. It is an ongoing, interactive, and organic process. Human beings have the basic equipment needed to create themselves, to define who they are, and to become responsible for their actions. All we need is to be creative.

This Business of Who Is Creative

One of the most common statements we have come across—from all sorts of people in all walks of life—is "I'm not creative." Before we go on, therefore, we should make something clear. When we talk about creative people doing this or that, say, having a tolerance for ambiguity, some have a tendency to think that they're not creative, so they can't have a tolerance for ambiguity. The description of characteristics becomes a depressing catalog of their shortcomings when in fact the whole point of isolating these traits is so we can all learn from them and integrate them into our own lives. We can learn to develop these qualities, whether we think we're creative or not.

Creativity is not something we are born with or something we either have or don't have. Some people are extremely creative painters but never developed their creativity when it comes to finances or romance or music. Creativity is not a *thing* we possess, like some kind of internal organ. It's not even a right or a left brain. It's a process, and it has to be nurtured and encouraged and improved. It's a way of thinking and being, and it can be learned. It can be learned through a gradual process of opening ourselves up to the world. What if we were to learn how to keep an open mind and made ourselves explore and take seriously claims about UFOs or Atlantis, for instance, or the sincerity of some politicians or the claims of postmodern philosophers or the local army recruiter or the proponents of weekly high colonics—without prejudgments? What if we considered these to be thought experiments and entertained and played with these ideas? Perhaps these exercises could help us increase our mental flexibility, our ability to make new connections.

Someone who has made a living out of making seemingly wild connections appear far more plausible than we feel they should be if we are to retain our sanity is novelist and philosopher Robert Anton Wilson. Something about him makes you wonder what's hiding behind his quiet, Buddhalike amusement. If you read his books, you realize part of it is a glorious, unabashed personal utopianism, laced with a strong dose of good old-fashioned no-nonsense libertarian humor that has not been seen since the days of H. L. Mencken. Wilson punctures pretentiousness and dogma with great abandon and likes to replace it with catma—from the predictable Pavlov's dog to the unpredictable Schrödinger's cat, as it were.

Wilson told us he once remarked to a friend—novelist Robert Shea—that he sees at least four or five UFOs a week. Shea thought the cheese had finally fallen off Wilson's cracker, but Wilson pointed out that he simply *did not know* what the flying objects were. For that matter, he also saw a bunch of UNFOs (Unidentified Non-Flying Objects) every week. The psychology of perception is a complicated process, but we know that human beings like to fill in the gaps and reassure themselves that they know what they're seeing. Most of us assume far too much, and Wilson has trained himself not to take too much for granted. "Perception is a gamble," he told

67

us. He has written fascinating and often funny books, like *Quantum Psychology* and *The New Inquisition,* which are all about shedding assumptions and beliefs.

What if we decided to move from a position where we are all knowers, where we value knowing because knowledge is power over, to one where we are all learners? Instead of using knowledge to put one over on someone, we could make an effort to learn together.

In our present system, asking a question is often seen as the result of not knowing, and not knowing requires asking someone else, who, knowing the answer, is by that very fact better and more powerful than you. Asking questions is thus seen as a domination-submission ritual, reminiscent of childhood, when we were "ignorant" and "helpless" and had to ask others what we felt were foolish questions. "You mean you don't know what *that* is?"

Surely there can be a different form of inquiry, one where people engage in dialogue not to come out on top but to go on a journey of discovery together. Even in instances of inequality—say, you know the directions to a place and I don't, or you are my teacher in some skill or other—the feedback you get from me is an indication of how effective your teaching is, and the dialogue we can have if you really allow me to question can lead to shared learning.

Frank Barron, a professor of psychology at the University of California, has spent a lifetime studying creativity and the characteristic behaviors that make a person creative. He found that exceptionally creative individuals exhibit a consistent set of traits that recurs irrespective of the particular area of creativity. One such trait is a *preference for complexity.* This means that they are attracted to people, phenomena, objects, problems, and feelings that are rich and complex in nature, even if theses cannot be explained or are considered weird. But this preference for complexity is balanced by a desire to find some simple and elegant order in the complexity.

If we simply prefer complexity, we may get lost in a world that is becoming messier and messier, with more and more interesting— or frightening—information accumulating and no real sense of what it all might mean. If we prefer simplicity, we may become a little simpleminded. The preference for complexity, as described by Barron, is a constant process of moving toward the complex in an effort to make some sense of it, literally to create meaning for ourselves and in the process to define who we are. Creating our selves involves exploring both the inner and outer world. The challenge of murky, messy, complex, and dark areas stimulates us to look further.

As we step into the unknown, facing experiences we normally would not, trying new ideas or life-styles or work-situations, we may be taking some risks, but risks and learning—and mistakes—go hand in hand with creativity. Only by facing these challenges can we really grow.

Another characteristic of creativity is *tolerance for ambiguity.* The dominator system is based on a logic of either/or. It thrives on a simple black-and-white, good-versus-evil mentality. It allows for no ambiguity, no opportunity for gray areas where good and evil blend confusingly and the bad guys have a human face and the good guys have some failings of their own. John le Carré's spy novels were distressing to some and compelling to others precisely because it seemed as if everything and everyone in his spy world dressed in a drab and mundane gray, with no drooling, torturing evilmongers and no clear, blue-eyed, morally upright heroes. The story goes that Richard Helms, head of the CIA in the mid-1960s, kept copies of James Bond novels on his desk but not surprisingly hated le Carré's work.

A tolerance for ambiguity means one does not judge immediately whether something or someone is good or bad, beautiful or ugly, useful or useless. It means accepting that one does not know and that whatever one is looking at or experiencing can't really be pinned down yet, if ever. It means looking, listening, paying attention. It means, perhaps, "Zen mind, beginner's mind." In a beautiful book of that name, the Zen master Shunryu Suzuki described the nature of Zen mind as the mind that sees everything afresh, without preconceptions and prejudgments. This mind has the same boundless curiosity that children have. It lacks the habits, or the stultifying tendency to take things for granted, that we can fall into as we get older. Creativity research suggests that tolerance for ambiguity, to forego the immediate resolution of our doubt and to embrace the uncomfortable feeling that accompanies uncertainty, is an essential component of creativity.

Independence of judgment and tolerance for ambiguity are closely linked. When faced with uncertainty, the easiest and safest thing to do is to impose some kind of certainty by appealing to authority. As we used to with our parents. Tolerance of ambiguity requires us to suspend judgment for a while, and then make up our own minds. To do this we need to be able to think both critically and creatively.

Most of the time, unfortunately, we make our decisions quickly and unthinkingly. We have a built-in mechanism, it seems, a little

69

robot, programmed to make decisions the way "we" like them. But "we," the "I," as we have seen, is not all of our own making. In fact, according to some schools of thought, the self is shaped largely by society. Who then is making our decisions? Are we responsible? Did we create all this? Or are we largely the product of our social environment, responding with all the preset answers programmed into us by our socialization?

The answer is rather tricky: No, you did not create most of what you call you; and yes, you are responsible for what you do, how you behave, how you feel and think. How's that for a double whammy?

Many of us have consulted astrologers, palm readers, channelers, futurists, trend watchers, and a variety of other crystal-ball gazers in the hope of getting some certainty about where we're headed as individuals and as a society. It's nice to think somebody out there knows, whether through science or through mystical insight. It's more difficult to accept that the future is uncertain and largely up to us. It's the burden and responsibility of freedom: We have to decide what we want, and then we have to make it happen. We can begin by learning a way of knowing that allows us to see wholes, a way of relating that forges partnerships rather than swords, and a way of being that encourages ongoing creativity rather than obedience.

The characteristic Frank Barron calls *ego-strength* is somewhat misleading, because it can give the impression that it refers to an overinflated ego, a big or a tough ego. We imagine some guy with his chest sticking out and his chin in the air, like Mussolini strutting on his balcony. But the term means something far more subtle than that, almost Taoist in some respects. Psychologist Mihalyi Csikszentmihalyi writes that people who survived ordeals "did not doubt their own resources would be sufficient to allow them to determine their fate. In that sense one would call them self-assured, yet at the same time, their egos seem curiously absent: they are not self-centered; their energy is typically not bent on dominating the environment as much as on finding a way to function within it harmoniously."

Ego-strength also involves resilience, the ability to rally from setbacks, and not succumb to discouragement. Resilient people were found to have a more positive self-concept. They were also found to be more nurturant, responsible, and achievement oriented and had a desire to keep growing psychologically. They had a sense of coherence in their lives. They also had the support of friends and relatives.

One of the fundamental concepts to arise out of systems thinking and its close cousin cybernetics is the idea of feedback. In order to get feedback, we need to pay attention to sources that can provide us with it. The popular term *denial*—as in, "he is in denial about his addiction to alcohol"—is used to refer to a state in which one refuses to see something that is patently obvious to others. It is an extreme form of feedback avoidance. We don't want to know. By contrast, the ability to remain open to all input without the fear of being over-whelmed is ego-strength, and it gives us the richness and complexity of experience that fuels creativity.

One of the remarkable characteristics of creative people is their capacity for self-renewal. They periodically make little—or even big—paradigm shifts. This keeps them fresh and young in their out-look; they seem capable of "intrepid aging" as Frank Barron has called it.

Time After Time

In many subtle ways the self is shaped in its relationship to time. Time is not simply that which is measured by a clock, a single phe-nomenon with a single definition. "Time is money, and speed is of the essence." "Next-day delivery ensures your business success." "I can fit you in next Thursday." "This is a waste of my time." "Meet me at eleven sharp." "There's not enough time in a day." These statements reflect a particular view of time. When you contrast this with the *mañana* of most Latin American countries, you realize that not everybody takes time quite the same way.

In Naples there's a story about a guy who spends his days lying on the beach with a bottle of wine. "What in God's name are you doing here on the beach all day?" a businessman from Milan—in the positively Germanic industrial heart of Italy—once asked him. "Well," the Neapolitan replied, "you work all day, running from one place to another, always hurrying, always chasing the next deal, for what? So you can come here to the beach and relax. I just go straight to the beach."

Western industrialized time is machine digital time. It's the time digital watches display down to the last second, a time that is precise and efficient. It's a segmented time, cut up into small fragments, an hour here, a half hour there. This kind of hurry-hurry time is never enough time, there's always more to be done. As non-Americans point out, Americans are always cramming their schedules so full there's no time just to loaf. But then idle hands do the devil's work. God knows what we might think about if we had nothing to do, right?

North Americans like to be on time. They are monochronic, in the words of anthropologist E. T. Hall. Time is rigidly segmented:

Eleven o'clock is exactly that, and 11:05 is five minutes late. Along with this go-go-go time comes the obligation to be *on* time, not to *lose* time, and to *manage* your time so as not to *waste* time.

A huge number of people around the world are polychronic. This means that an appointment at eight means sometime between eight and nine, sometimes ten, and no one gets too frazzled if people are "late." Time expands and contracts along with space, because one can do many different things in the same space of time. North Americans generally segment time so as to do one thing at a time, devoting precisely the required amount of undivided attention to a project to make it on time. Your meeting with a North American will generally be a face-to-face, or other kind of interface, where disruptions will be cause for apologies.

Latin Americans can expand their time to contain many spaces, as it were, and deal with two or three things at the same time. Meetings will be conducted in offices that seem to be more like village squares, making North American "open-door policies" look about as accessible as Greta Garbo.

The Western machinelike time means things are on a schedule, and the schedule has to be followed. But who defines the schedule, and what is a waste of time? Maybe schedules apply to the workplace, but should they spill over into private lives too? Do we internalize this time so much that we don't even have time to think about who decides what it's time for us to do? Do we have "quality" time? Time out!

One of the problems with this extremely linear conception of time is that everything becomes very cramped. With one appointment and commitment after the other, time and space seem to shrink and even collapse in on us, a contraction that makes us feel uptight and stressed out. Our muscles contract. A certain claustrophobia emerges, and we want to take a break and take all the time in the world to look at distant horizons in open spaces far away from home.

This cramped feeling, or hurry sickness, is not just a psychological phenomenon. It turns out that people who are constantly on the run also have a not-surprising tendency to be more anxious and have higher blood pressure and cholesterol levels. They also die sooner. Our organization of time affects us right down to our bodies.

A paradoxical aspect of our relation to time is that as ambitious people we expect to be gratified in the future; we work so that at a later date we may relax and be happy. But while on the one hand we look forward to the future, on the other hand we do everything to put off the ravages of time, the wrinkles and aches and pains that come with the territory. We're very ambivalent about it. This is a typical dominator double bind—you're damned if you do and damned if you don't.

What are we filling our time with? Who is making us be on time all the time?

Most people are familiar with the phenomenon of jet lag, that out-of-kilter feeling we get when we cross many time zones and end up in a place where it's day and we're awake (barely) when we should really be fast asleep. The body has a clock, and it takes longer to reset than a watch. The body's clock works in close partnership with Mother Earth's clock, which doesn't have a reset button.

This kind of natural time is fundamentally cyclical, marked by a rhythm of seasons, moons, and the cycle of night and day. As human beings, we are part of this natural, physical time: the time we all have to live, the time it takes to grow and eventually die, the nine months it takes from conception to birth, and so forth. These kinds of time are in contrast to the linear, machinelike digital time we have become accustomed to.

A single understanding of time is another factor that contributes to the pitting of one part of the self against the other. Rational time is linear, whereas emotional time is cyclical. Emotional time is the time of mood swings and emotional roller coasters, of ups and downs as opposed to the unchanging progression of rational, irreversible time. To be whole, to be truly one, we need all kinds of time.

We need digital, programmed time to build and achieve; we need unstructured, unhurried open time to think, create, and connect. We need to focus on the future to nourish our hope, and we must be conscious of the cycles of nature and emotions to strengthen our courage. We need moments of eternal time to listen to our spiritual side and ease our isolation and connect to the whole. And we need very secular time to fix a leaky faucet.

Yet time is structured in such a way these days that it's quite difficult to experience these different types. The spirit is supposed to awaken on Sunday morning when people attend religious functions, and you do get some unstructured time somewhere between the shopping and the laundry and the yard work on Saturday afternoons.

We (the authors) believe that as the global mind is in the process of changing about a lot of things, it will also begin to reinterpret time in some creative ways. The signs already abound. Corporations are giving employees sabbaticals to pursue other interests. People take unpaid leaves of absence to go on inner or outer pilgrimages. Or they simply quit one job and start a whole new career. The need to structure work and careers to make time for having and being with children, or to tend to aging parents, is becoming more imperative. Time is being restructured according to one's inner needs, and therefore we can expect a blossoming of time diversity based not only on cultural roots but also on personal and family needs.

Checkout Time

Soon comes the end of time, at least of time as we know it. Our bodies will dissolve into their component atoms and melt back into universal matter to be reshaped again through goodness knows how many configurations before we're all gobbled up by a black hole. Before that happens, however, it's going to be a while. Much much sooner we'll come face-to-face with death. We know so very little about the experience of death.

Many older people do not fear death as much as they fear a long, agonizing illness that would rob them of their dignity as human beings and of the experience of dying with their faculties still intact. In modern Western societies, causing the end of life is permitted only under very specific circumstances. It has to be someone else's life, and it has to be specifically sanctioned by judges (capital punishment) or legislators (war). Taking one's own life is always a crime or a sin, considered an act of cowardice or the result of mental illness. The global mind is showing signs of change on this issue too.

First of all we are trying to be less spooked by the whole idea of dying. Interest in death and dying has spurred some important research. This interest is bound to reemerge as the global population gets older. Movements promoting death with dignity are igniting controversies in hospitals and courts. Occasionally a doctor defies the law and helps a patient to die with dignity. It is conceivable that we may see legislative changes to reflect a broader spectrum of options with respect to this "management" of time. Can you imagine a future when people might be allowed to end their own lives after a court hearing (a sort of divorce from life)? Perhaps then people would prepare for death rather than perpetuate massive denial, and the entire society would be made different in the process. Perhaps we will become so attuned with the inner self and the cycle of time, with a firm connection between the one and the whole, that we will simply close our eyes and let go. A rabbi we met told us that one afternoon at the movies, his wife of forty years touched his arm gently. "I love you very much," she said. Then she leaned on his shoulder and died.

How would you choose to die when your time comes?

The Tiruray of the Philippines "have no fear of death or of the dead," Stuart Schlegel told us. "Death, like life, has its place in the great interdependent harmony of existence. Death, like life, is essentially and intrinsically benign. They see the world as benign. Through their work, their thought, their play, and their rituals, Tiruray express joy and sensitivity, love of life and harmony with nature. Tiruray enjoy life and revel in their closeness and harmony with nature. This is the way human beings are experienced, spirits are experienced, and the cosmos in general is experienced. The whole of life is pervaded by this fundamental attitude and faith."

We need rites to celebrate this unity, whether in temples or in meadows, with our friends and with the world. We need, from time to time, to feel the oneness.

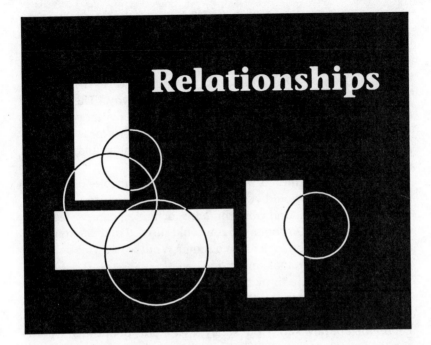

Relationships

WOMEN AND MEN

Dominator Basic Training

Outside the boundaries of one's own self lies this vast territory that carries the label Not Me. Here is where we meet that fabled creature, the Other. From then on, the dance of relationships unfolds. Riane Eisler has shown that the dominator paradigm has been the most popular tune for the past five thousand years. Within this paradigm the tendency has been to polarize the other, make it opposite, view it as different, alien, a potential threat. The "opposite" sex is by definition more "other" than one's own gender. The structure of the relationship between the sexes is the clearest indicator of a society's basic paradigm concerning human interaction. In fact the elemental relationship between man and woman influences every aspect of our lives, as well as humanity's interaction with other species and the entire planet.

According to Eisler, "The way we structure the relations between the two halves of humanity, women and men, profoundly influences everything—values, social structure, institutions. Once we start changing the rules of the relationship between women and men, we really have a hope, a realistic hope, of changing the system, because that's all there is; it's called humanity. But until we do, there isn't much hope. There is simply a change of the dominator guard."

Why are men and women the way they are? And why is there a supposed war between the sexes? One simple answer might be, "Because men and women are taught to be that way." The dominator system has set up certain specific guidelines for what constitutes being a man and what doesn't; and the same applies for women. An entire system of training, or socialization, keeps these guidelines imprinted on our minds.

What do you think it would be like to be someone of the "opposite" sex? What would your body feel like? What kind of worlds would open for you, and what thoughts, activities, careers, feelings, would shut down? Do you think you could succeed in a different gender? What would you look for in a mate? What would you be afraid of? What would you look forward to?

We have only to think back at the toys we received, the activities that were planned for us, the way adults would speak to us and what they spoke to us about, even their body language, to begin to get an idea of how subtly but surely a vital part of our identity was shaped for us by others' beliefs about the significance and role of our gender. When was the last time you saw a little girl with a toy gun or a little boy with a toy kitchen? There is no question that our gender makes a big difference in shaping our lives, and there is little question that, beyond biology, our gender is shaped by others rather than by nature.

These socialization guidelines, which create what we call our gender, are beginning to break down. Although this is causing a considerable amount of chaos and confusion, it has the potential to effect important positive changes. We are at a point in history when the fundamental relationship between woman and man is being questioned, and this gives us an incredible leverage for creating positive social change. Human relationships have been put into question before. Class- and race-based perspectives have been challenged dramatically in the past 150 years. But with the reformulation of the relationship between men and women—the two halves that form humanity, both literally and figuratively—our entire notion of what it means to be a human being is changing.

In a dominator system, our conception of who we are as human beings has been fundamentally male. In other words, politics, business, and economics, as well as psychology, medicine, and just about every other public human endeavor, have been based on perspectives, assumptions, and images drawn from males and by males.

This interpretation of what it means to be male is itself shaped by the dominator paradigm. This is not just men left to their own devices, or the way men *really* are. Let's get very clear before we go on that this is men as they have been mangled and brutalized by a system that in its grimmer moments sets them against each other, brother killing brother, whether literally or symbolically, in the streets or in the office. It's a system that considers this behavior normal, or more, the way to prove manhood.

That Western culture has used the term *man* to describe humanity as a whole is surely not just for the sake of convenience. This extreme one-sidedness has engendered some of the more bizarre outgrowths of the dominator system, as we shall see, not the least of which is a painful distortion of what it means to be a woman and what it means to be a man.

The differences in basic training for women and men give us some important insights into the functioning of the dominator system. This training does not (necessarily) take place in an institution. There is no specific school, no homework to learn and forget. Dominator training occurs everywhere: from the family to the workplace, with friends, on television and in the movies, sometimes just waiting in line at the checkout counter. Dominator training is pervasive inasmuch as it is potentially in every relationship we encounter.

The dominator system's ideal defines four roles for the female and the male, particularly in the West. We are supposed to embody these societal myths or images. If we deviate from them in any way, we feel somehow inadequate. Even if we consciously reject these images, or are unwilling or unable to play the game, they still haunt us, because we are force-fed them every day.

Some will look over these differences and shrug. Things have changed, they'll say, this stuff is outdated. Of course. But even though we're painting a slightly exaggerated picture here, we mustn't forget that one of the great dominator tactics is lulling us into believing that things really have changed. Many young racists in Europe and America, for instance, have grown up with no overtly racist legislation and believe therefore that whites and people of color have always had the same opportunities. For them the fact that many people of color are still poor, what with equal opportunity and all, is a sign they really are inferior. With the same logic, it is said that women and men have achieved equality under the law

79

and any further discussion on the topic is unnecessary. We believe, to the contrary, that further discussion is very necessary.

The four principles for basic training in gender roles are worth pondering not as cultural relics of some historical interest but as active forces in our psyches and our culture today.

1. Men are trained to be independent, women are trained to be dependent.

Basic training for men stresses their independence from their environment. Men should be self-sufficient, capable of taking care of themselves and relying on no one. Women, on the other hand, should be dependent on men for their basic survival. Historically this took the form of the man bringing home the bacon, so that the woman was dependent on her man for food and shelter.

What does it mean to be independent? In essence it means that we do not need anybody, that we are self-sufficient and self-reliant. It means men—"real" men, you understand—don't call electricians or plumbers or even mechanics. They hate to ask for directions even after they've been driving around for hours—they prefer to trust their Davy Crockett-like "homing instinct"—and do it themselves. They don't, or shouldn't, need anyone's help. They are supposed to define their own lives and live at the mercy of no one.

Men are driven to define themselves as autonomous entities. They must become individuals, preferably heroes of some kind, so that they can differentiate themselves from their environment. At some point, some psychologists argue, men have to let go of Mommy's apron strings and go out into the real world. (Mother doesn't live in the real world? In the logic of the dominator system, the private, where Mother is, is not real. Only the public is. That's also why he can beat his wife and still be a good, upstanding citizen.) This process of letting go of Mommy and everything she stands for (unconditional love, support, security, warmth, etc.) is painful but absolutely necessary to become a man. Any hint of Mommy (a "mommy's boy") will be sniffed out and will unleash a thousand taunts.

Women are supposed to be but a reflection of their man, since they are as dependent on him as the moon's light is on the reflection of the sun's rays. If the moon could produce its own light, it surely would. In the same way, women are dependent on men because they cannot generate their own source of light—they cannot do certain things that would allow them to escape from dependence. If women make money and act assertively, then how will we distinguish men from women? No tolerance of ambiguity is permitted here. From the dominator perspective it's not natural for women to do certain things. Lest we think this is all Neanderthal thinking, we should consider that in reliable polls men still find their single greatest source of manliness in being the breadwinner and having the largest income in the family.

The dominator system is set up in such a way that any deviation from it is perceived as a sin against God, or at least against the natural order of things. Women who try—and do—all these unnatural activities get to hear about how different they are, and how sooner or later they will come to regret it. Their lack of femininity will repel every man and they will die spinsters; they will never know the joy of motherhood; they will return to their husbands humbled and repentant, promising never to stray again. All of these have been the plots of countless books and movies until very recently. Worse, all of the above are the "lessons" that countless fathers, brothers, and husbands are still teaching women the world over.

These gender roles may have originated a long time ago when physical characteristics played an important part in the division of labor. Role specialization based on physical characteristics is not wrong in itself. Undoubtedly there are tasks at which nearsighted people excel and tasks that farsighted people do much better. It seems reasonable for people to specialize in those tasks for which they are better suited. What is utterly unreasonable is to make these specializations so rigid as to exclude options. And what is extremely cruel, and ultimately self-destructive, is to assign much greater value to the tasks and activities performed by one gender. Yet this is exactly what the dominator system has done.

If the physically strongest men were to rule the country, then our presidents would be Sylvester Stallone or Arnold Schwarzenegger. For all we know, they may still become U.S. presidents, but it won't be for their physical force, one imagines. In a society where most of the work is done behind a desk and the most powerful men in the world are overweight politicians, these physical criteria hardly apply.

This gender difference seems to make little sense in these supposedly enlightened, postfeminist days. Women work, men are clearly not as self-sufficient as early pioneers, and not all women are helplessly dependent on them.

As ludicrous as they may sound to some, these myths or images are deep inside us. No matter how aware we might be, they still hover around in our consciousness, deposited there through years of training. These myths creep up on us when we feel weak or distressed, when we least suspect it. Both women and men can suddenly find themselves wanting to play their assigned part or wanting the "opposite sex" to play their assigned part. It's still somehow more "natural" in our dominator society that if only one partner works, it should be the man; that a woman should not make more money than her husband; that it is men, not women, who are brave; that women who accuse men of sexual harassment or rape are spurned lovers or a little hysterical; that the president of the U.S. will be a man; that if a woman's career advances rapidly, she should have to put up with accusations about opportunistic sex. But there's nothing natural about any of this.

Our fantasy lives still resonate to these images. Men love the idea of saving a beautiful damsel in distress, who will be eternally grateful. Women occasionally don't mind the idea of a white knight in shining armor coming to the rescue. But perhaps we should invent some images of what this lovely couple will do once they're finally united, after they've spent days gloriously making love and holding hands under the moonlit sky. These independent knights saving dependent damsels are all well and good, but how are they going to fare afterwards?

What happens when men who are told that their fundamental nature requires them to be independent, always moving along, end up marrying women who believe their natural role is to be dependent on their man for every breath they take? These men fear being drowned in domesticity, engulfed by overbearing female mother figures, and these women cling to men who are always attempting to escape the moment they get their prey.

Things have changed rather rapidly over the past hundred years, but most of the change occurred only recently. In Italy, for instance, women did not have the vote until the end of World War II, and in America the entry of significant numbers of women into the paid work force did not start until that same period. Older women are aware that when they were growing up, they had far fewer rights and opportunities than they do now. Real change has only just begun, and although it may appear significant, we should not think that our work is done.

2. Men are taught to control and manipulate their environment, whereas women are taught to be part of that environment.

Many methods exist to train males to gain control of territory and then assert their control over it. Boys are indoctrinated early in organized sports, watching their peers in action, checking out the playground pecking order, through endless displays of domination-submission rituals on television shows ranging from "The Roadrunner" to "Transformer" and "Miami Vice." Boys are bullied into this system. Very few of them have the wherewithal or the good fortune to stay out of the top-dog bottom-dog game that develops in playgrounds and on street corners, and even with brothers. Ask any boy why he got into this whole lark, and if he is truthful, he will mention fear and pain and his desire never to feel them again. In order to avoid them, he has to play the dominator game.

Anger plays a great part in the development of these roles, according to Riane Eisler. "In male socialization, the expression of anger is almost a rite of initiation. In a dominator society, the moment you are permitted to act out your anger, which women and children are not allowed to express, you're initiated into the male fraternity of dominators of various ranks. The degree to which you are socially permitted to express and act out that anger, and the occasions of it, vary according to circumstances. But the expression of anger is a crucial element of a system that is ultimately held together by force or the threat of force."

Social philosopher Myriam Miedzian asserts that the whole process of growing up teaches many boys to be violent, especially through organized sports and its enormous demands—usually for victory at all costs rather than real excellence. Rough and tumble may be a natural part of childhood. But taking out a sports opponent by breaking his leg, with the sanction of a sports coach, is beyond all bounds of good sense, sportsmanship, and even esthetics. Perhaps within the context of the winning frenzy this kind of violent behavior makes sense, particularly if money is at stake; but anyone looking in from outside this world is likely to be appalled. There are not only other sports but other ways to do sports, ways that in older days were more gentlemanly.

Stuart Schlegel gave us a vignette illustrating how the Tiruray of the Philippines play. "When the men come back from hunting or working in the field, they'll gather in the clearing in the midst of their settlement and play a game called *sesifa,* which is like our hackysack. They bounce a rattan ball to each other with the inside of the foot. The idea is to keep it going as long as you can. There's no winner. The longer you can keep the ball going, the happier everybody is. You win by having it go a long time. *Win* probably isn't the right word. The game has a happy outcome if you keep the ball going a long time. It involves a lot of skill, and it's a wonderful metaphor for their life because it's a skill that is used cooperatively and interpersonally in a common enterprise. Every player is dependent on every other player to use his skill to keep the ball going. Which means you kick it to another person not away from another person."

Eighty-nine percent of crimes in the U.S. are committed by males, generally young males. The primary cause of death among black males is murder. If boys have so much fun being violent, they certainly seem to pay the price for it.

Girls, on the other hand, are shown how to become part of the boys' environment. This is one of the main reasons why they typically have to be beautiful, submissive, and good housekeepers: one's environment should, after all, be attractive, controllable, and clean. Television shows from the 1950s featured this image of woman-as-attractive-household-appliance. Like an obedient child who should be seen and not heard, a woman could at the most be the one behind a great man but could not be heard directly.

Most of us were blessed with mothers who cleaned up after us when we were tots. In the dominator system, wives have this same public utility function. The fact that there have been no "wives" in industry and government—or men willing to take the role of the wife/mother—has led to the enormous mess in our environment.

Boys are generally taught to follow the strategy of the lion. They should assert themselves and get what they want by roaring and showing muscle. This is the standard, manly thing to do. If necessary, a knock-out, drag-down fight will sort the men from the boys. The strategy of the fox is looked down upon somewhat, since it is devious and involves more thought than is considered strictly kosher in a dominator system. "You're too clever," we say, "too smart for your own good, you sneak." The fox strategy is for nerds. It's also for women, who normally can't get what they want John Wayne style. Women are devious, as we all know, and their "little minds" plot away to cause the downfall of the poor men.

Yet it's fairly obvious that not everyone can be a lion all the time. The game of domination and submission that lies at the root of the dominator system requires far more followers than leaders, far more submissive, dominated people than dominators. But here the dominator hierarchy comes to the rescue in a most democratic way. If we're dominated at work by an overbearing boss, he's the lion and we're without real power. We have to play the fox, sneaking in an extra few minutes of break time here or there, arriving a few minutes late and working out some outrageous excuse, being nice and friendly to the big man—we all know the fox routine. Moreover, the beautiful thing about the dominator system is that unless you're just a complete "wimp," almost inevitably someone will be below you somewhere in the hierarchy. If not at work, then perhaps a busboy in the restaurant, perhaps a recent immigrant, or the wife and kids. After all, if we are real men, we have to flex our muscles every so often.

3. Men are taught to think abstractly; women are taught to communicate.

It is not unusual in many parts of the world to find men heatedly debating politics on street corners and in cafés, discussing the fine points of political theories and the merits or demerits of the local candidates or of world leaders. Women, on the other hand, will be found "gossiping" about this and that (but mostly about "little things").

Here dominator basic training presents us with a lesson in dominator psychology: Men are supposedly better at abstract, visuospatial processes; women are better at the use of language. This seems to make sense, since men are required to build theories and explanations on a high level of abstraction so as to govern home and country with some kind of homespun rationalization. Women, who are generally the governed, talk about the web of relationship they are enmeshed in. Although these differences used to be apparent in test scores, mounting evidence shows that the gap is closing, and that these differences have to do with education and socialization, not with biology.

We have already mentioned the peculiar illness called alexithymia, which involves the inability to express emotions. David Loye suggests that many people in Western society suffer from a chronic low-grade form of this problem. When men do talk, they discuss sports, cars, politics, and other issues of a technical nature. But, as we all know by now, they supposedly have trouble expressing emotions. Not all men have this impediment; some, after all, are poets. Others are very good at showing anger but would never get a role in a movie playing anything else.

"Alexithymia," explained David Loye, "is a pathological condition that makes the verbalization of emotions extremely difficult. The theory is that people with alexithymia begin to feel emotions in the right brain, but then something goes wrong in the crossover into the left brain across the corpus callosum. It is as if a gate were there that didn't allow the feelings to come through. The consequence is

85

that the affect is blunted. I find this an extremely suggestive explanation of moral sensitivity in dominator systems, where you repeatedly find the brutalization of people. The whole thrust in the training of the stereotypical dominator male is not to show weakness, to be tough, and at the extreme to be brutal. It's a blocking of empathy, a blocking of tenderness, a blocking of caring in dominators and, stereotypically, in males. An enormous body of literature corroborates this blunting of affect in the male. Men's lack of emotion is also a common complaint of women. Now men's sensitivity groups are trying to open men to their emotions and get them to express their feelings. What I see very vividly is the degree to which all of us are brutalized by this training, males and females.

"The most fascinating analysis I've seen is by the late Silvan Tomkins, who developed a theory of nine primary affects, or emotions, upon which all others are built. In other words, there are nine primary building blocks for the whole structure of emotions. In his view, all nine were operating in the earlier Neolithic partnership culture and were shared by both men and women. This is equivalent to my view that in earlier times there was a single morality that prevailed, shared equally by men and women. Then with the Kurgan invasions, which ended the partnership cultures, the emotions were split. To the males were assigned the emotions of disgust, excitement, contempt, surprise, and anger—all of which fit that brutalizing, tough power requirement for being a warrior. To the females were assigned the tender emotions, distress, shame, relaxed enjoyment, and fear. Since then, for the past five thousand years, you've had these stereotypes prevailing in many cultures of the tough-minded, macho male (and the tough-minded women who identify with a male ideal) counterposed with tender-minded, sweet, potentially servile, obsequious, distressed females."

The difficulty in the expression of emotions is not simply a lack of poetry and song or a deficit in romantic wooing skills or other seemingly nonessential characteristics. The dominator dynamic has crippled the free expression of human beings' full emotional range. Our First Amendment rights are being violated deep inside our souls, and we don't even know it. It's not true that women are emotional and men are not. Men can be extremely emotional, and women can be cold as ice. When a woman is emotionless—a trait valued in a man, who is then typecast as the strong, silent type, Clint Eastwood being a great example—she is called a frigid bitch. In fact many people express only a small part of their human emotional range, and in some cases people actually experience only a tiny portion of it.

Riane Eisler is passionate about the need to develop new arche-types or role models for women and men. We are constantly bom-barded with images that reinforce the dominator society, she argues. "We have suffering heroines, sacrificing heroines, masochistic hero-ines, helpless heroines, dying heroines, and deranged heroines, but how about some adventurous heroines or wise heroines or healing heroines?" The same applies for men, where new characters are sorely needed. Writers may have to stretch themselves to develop this new pantheon of heroines and heroes, for which Eisler and Loye pro-vide models in their joint book *The Partnership Way,* but the potential rewards are immense.

For Eisler, the media represents one of the most powerful forces in society. It can contribute to reinforcing the dominator system or move us toward partnership. The challenge now lies in creating new im-ages, new characters, and new visions to populate our imaginations.

Philip Slater has fun figuring out the rationalizations movie critics give for panning movies with women as the heroes. He sus-pects the critics themselves don't even know that they're doing it be-cause they're disturbed by not finding a male hero. But movies like *Thelma and Louise* and even *Terminator 2,* with powerful roles for women, are beginning to point another way.

"I remember years ago before I understood much about any-thing," Riane Eisler told us, "I was in the park near my house and there was some wailing and crying nearby. I was sitting under a tree and there was a man hitting a little boy. The little boy kept crying and the man was saying to him, 'I'm going to keep hitting you until you stop crying because boys don't cry.' It's very sad. It's such a com-pletely messed up system from A to Z that the wonder, frankly, is not that people have so many problems and difficulties in relating; the wonder is that we do as well as we do.

"In my new work I argue that our fundamental desire is plea-sure, what I call the human yearning for connection. And yet we've constructed a system that systematically rewards the giving and tak-ing of pain rather than the giving and taking of pleasure. Isn't that amazing? I'm not just talking about the repression of sexuality by Christianity, I'm talking about the dominator system."

It is not surprising that, according to research, a major cause of domestic violence can be traced to mistaken perceptions of emotions as dark and basically forbidden, coupled with a profound inability to express them. If a man cannot express what is happening to him in his most intimate moments, with the person who is closest to him, if expressing these feelings in itself casts doubt on his manhood, and if any kind of conflict is always viewed as a zero-sum game with a loser and a winner, as a war, what chances do we stand of establishing a decent relationship? Stay tuned.

4. Men are taught to emphasize the importance of justice and absolute rules, whereas women are taught to be more concerned with caring and contingency.

We are all familiar with the good cop/bad cop routine that goes on in police stations during interrogations (at least in the movies), and in families when kids misbehave. There's the warm-hearted cop that softens you up, and then there's the tough guy who knocks you out with a quick one-two to the chin. They're a team. At home, Dad is usually the tough one, the one whose final rules can't be broken, the one with whom no excuses matter anymore. Mom is the one who cares about you; yes, she loves you unconditionally—until you go too far or she just gets fed up and defers to Dad. This duality reflects to some extent the way the dominator system splits off the role of men and women in matters of law and ethics.

Research has shown that men get upset when rules are broken or principles or individuals are interfered with; women are more concerned with caring than with rules, and they get more upset if one doesn't help someone who asks. Men are interested in the fact that a moral or legal principle was broken (the importance of law and order). Women, it seems, want to know the circumstances under which the breach occurred and the intention of the accused.

During Isabella's last year of law school, after she had supposedly learned all the theories and rules of the Italian legal system, which traces its origins back to ancient Rome, she was finally taken to see the administration of justice in action. It struck her that despite the pomp and the elaborate procedures, nobody was interested in establishing the truth. They cared only that the legal system, this intricately constructed house of cards, be kept intact, procedures followed, and principles respected. No one seemed interested in finding out what had actually happened, what truly motivated the players in that drama. It was such a shock that she silently vowed never to become a part of this charade. She completed her law degree and a couple of years later enrolled in a psychology program.

Men's concerns with rules, abstractions, and ideas have led to a certain willingness to sacrifice people for the sake of ideas, faith, "progress," the revolution, or even science. Women have different priorities.

Psychologist Susan Hales gave an example of how a parent might instill an internalized motivation to live a moral or caring life. She explained what is meant by teaching kids "the moral point of view." "If a child is taking some other child's toy, the mother would say, 'How would you like it if he took your toy? Do you remember when Jimmy did that to you two weeks ago? When he took your train? Do you remember how you felt? That's what you're making Timmy feel like. That's bad, I won't let you do that. It's wrong.' You teach the moral point of view by focusing on the child's feelings in relation to his actions. You focus on the consequences of their actions, but you do that using their own feelings. You ask, 'Remember how it felt when he did that to you?' or 'How would you like it if he did that to you?'"

The importance of seeing the connection between justice and caring, reason and emotion is crucial to developing this whole-system, partnership perspective. By becoming aware of how we would feel if others behaved toward us the way we behave toward them, we gain more insight into ourselves and develop greater sensitivity. David Loye's term *moral sensitivity* originates precisely in this empathic dimension of morality. According to Loye, this sensitivity tends to be blunted in males because of dominator-system pressures. But there is little evidence that this blunting is innate. Instead we see in prehistory—and all around us today—the evidence that moral sensitivity is a powerful drive within men as well as women.

Since men are taught to strive for independence, they view as oppressive any outside force that interferes with that independence. Women, who are usually taught to see themselves as part of a larger web of relationships, feel the need to help others because of this common connection.

The Tiruray have a way of dealing with moral issues that draws more on feelings and sensitivity toward others than laws and regulations, according to Stuart Schlegel. "The fundamental rule of Tiruray life is not to give anybody a bad gallbladder," he said. "They believe that the gallbladder is the center of emotion and feelings, much as we say the heart is. It's a symbolic place in the body. So you don't give anyone a bad gallbladder, meaning you don't hurt them, you don't make them feel bad, you don't frustrate them. You try to do things that will be helpful to one another. I call it the *fedew* rule, because the gallbladder is the *fedew*. You never give anybody a bad fedew. That means you always try to help people achieve what they want to achieve, and you try not to interfere with them.

89

"Now, Tiruray, like all human beings, don't always live up to their moral codes. They do things like steal each other's wives or husbands, and end up getting in trouble with each other, and end up feuding. That's why you have a law system, to bring harmony back. But on the whole, the basic rule of their morality, and the basic rule that informs the legal system, is that it really disturbs harmony if you give somebody a bad gallbladder, by offending them or hurting them or not helping them out in life. So that's a very clear case, I think, of treating people as ends and not as means."

Differences That Make a Difference, Part 2

We find that danger is among the things men and women perceive differently. Men see danger in close, intimate relationships that may somehow drag them down and lead to entrapment. This is the archetypal fear of commitment. But notice that it is the fear of commitment to an intimate relationship; men can become absolutely committed to causes, parties, theories, and sports teams—no problem there.

Women fear achievement since it can set them apart, displacing them from the web of relationships they are in. Achievement means potential isolation (it's lonely at the top), and making decisions which may hurt or displease others. It also means entering an entirely different world, assuming roles that women are simply not educated for. An entire shift of identity is called for when joining a game whose rules have already been set—by men. This is why figures such as Margaret Thatcher appear even tougher and even more masculine in their orientation than the men they work with.

Another interesting difference is that women view aggression as a fracture of human connection. They see activities such as caring and nurturing as a way of preventing isolation by maintaining connections and thus avoiding possible aggression. According to Harvard psychologist Carol Gilligan, in this view aggression is not something to be kept under control through rules but a sign that there is a failure in relationships.

If a Gentleman Doesn't Hit a Lady, How Come So Many Women Get Beaten Up?

One inescapable fact of the relationship between men and women is the inordinate amount of violence.

"Violence against women is still not taken seriously," Eisler notes with profound regret. "It's very interesting: You get people writing passionately about violence where men are involved, about anti-Semitism, racism, and gangs. Not that it shouldn't be so, but look at the statistics on women and violence in this country.

"The mind says 'Domestic violence, an interesting issue, but it's just a family affair.' In the old days, you see, when a man's home was his castle, you should not under any circumstance get between a man and his woman. So if a stranger beats you, it's a crime, but if somebody who says he loves you beats you, that's domestic violence. For women it's the largest cause of injury, larger than practically all other causes combined.

"The Surgeon General reports that battering is the largest single cause of injury to women in the United States, and every fifteen seconds a woman is beaten by her husband or boyfriend," Riane Eisler quotes from a U.S. Senate report. "According to the FBI, a woman is raped every six minutes in this country. More than one third of women slain in this country die at the hands of husbands or boyfriends. Over ninety percent of all murders of women are committed by men. And this one really does it: 'Three out of every four women in the U.S. will be the target of at least one violent crime during their lives.' People feel it's OK. There's always an excuse: he was drunk. Well, yeah, he was drunk, but he didn't go out and beat the guy on the corner, he beat the woman he says he loves. Or, he was out of a job, so he killed his wife. Wonderful. It had nothing to do with it actually. He killed her because he lived in a society where male violence against women is encouraged and where male violence against women and the eroticization and glamorization of rape has become a part of male identity."

How can men's relationships be good if their entire sense of identity comes from a constant struggle to differentiate themselves from other people, a game where one person will be top dog and the other under dog?

"Why does it take the tears of a woman to see how men are?" asks Roddy Frame, the leader of the rock group Aztec Camera, paraphrasing the powerful song he wrote called "How Men Are." "It came up because of situations in my life. We were sitting there with a couple of guys, and just saying, 'Man, we're just shit, why did we behave so badly?' I don't really want to be an apologist for my gender, but it seems to crop up again and again, so I wrote that song. Men grow up to embrace these macho values and are taught to stress ambition and power. I think that's really sad, and sexism is really sad. Long live Anita Hill for bringing the issue up like that!"

Increasingly men are getting together in groups to discuss the new meaning of manhood. What does it mean these days to be a man? How does masculinity define itself once it sheds the simple requirement of not being femininity? As we move away from a polarizing dominator system with a black-and-white, either/or logic toward a more complex partnership world, we cannot define ourselves negatively anymore. Both men and women are complex persons transcending what were formerly stereotypical gender traits.

Riane Eisler warns that "to the extent that men's groups today buy into the old macho scripts, they are reinforcing precisely the kind of society and family where men and women (and this obviously includes mothers and sons) both consciously and unconsciously continue to hurt one another in all the old ways. Myths such as Freud's Oedipus complex—which sets up the angry sons to take over from the equally angry fathers and in the process 'possess' as many women as possible (including in fantasy even their own mothers)—and Jungian archetypes that still idealize 'heroic' male violence reflect not the human psyche but the dominator psyche."

Feminism Through Teenage Eyes

The daughter of noted poets Amiri Baraka (LeRoi Jones) and Diane DiPrima, Dominique DiPrima is an African-Italian American who seems to have gotten the best of three worlds. Watching this young woman, whose occasional baby-sitter was poet Allen Ginsberg, in action on her television talk show "Home Turf" is quite revealing. Surrounded by a studio audience of teenagers and young adults, she is at home and clearly enjoying herself. But the show is not just a party; often it deals with extremely touchy issues, like sexism, gay youth, and racism. It's a testament to Dominique's professionalism that, unlike the prima-donna talk-show hosts, she manages to stay out of the way long enough for the kids to speak their minds, which they do with surprising candor and eloquence. The show restores our faith in young people and in the power of dialogue. Interestingly enough, for a show by and about a supposedly uncommitted and apathetic generation, it deals with tough issues a lot more honestly, incisively, and with less hype than the big-ticket, checkout-counter-tabloid afternoon shows. And the music is much better.

According to Dominique, "A lot of young women recognize sexism, and a lot of women are just willing to ignore it because they don't want to put themselves on the line and deal with it. I try to set an example. The teenage girls know I'll go toe-to-toe with a guy about something that I consider sexist. I tell him, 'You're wrong. That's sexist. You can't behave that way.' Yet that same guy calls me up two weeks later and wants to go out with me. What is that telling you? He can handle it, he can deal with it. Some of the biggest admirers I've had are men that I feel I've had to put in check. I've found they tend to respect you ten times more because they know that you're strong, and they know that you're not going to take any shit."

Dominique DiPrima also has some clear ideas about teenage women and feminism. "What's unpopular is that stupid image of the woman with Birkenstocks and hairy armpits, the idea that if you believe in women's rights you can't wear lipstick. That's not an image that works for this decade. It doesn't fit. The young girls coming up now don't want to give up beauty and glamour. Everyone wants to be glamorous and have fun. It's the whole question of style. If the activists of the sixties or seventies are unable to cross the gulf of style, then they're never ever going to reach the young people today. Because they can't listen to a rap record, because they don't like the style of the music, they can never see where the political consciousness of this whole generation is. Since they can't look past the lipstick, they cannot see the political consciousness of a generation of young women. Today you've got women calling themselves womanists, Queen Latifah calls herself a common sensist, whatever, anything other than feminist because they don't want to be associated with that.

"I think that most of the young women I talk to are aware of the principles of equality, and they want to strive for those things. I did a song last year called 'Equality' which dealt with this issue. I think it got a lot of kids in this area at least talking about it. But it's still so hard to overcome the television commercials and the fashion magazines that show us a way of behaving that's very passive. We still have a lot of the same problems—expectations of how a guy wants you to act in order to be considered feminine or sexy. I think we're getting more role models, rappers like Salt-n-Pepa and Queen Latifah are creating more models for a stronger woman, a stronger female image. Madonna is controversial, but I guess to an extent and in her own way, she is a role model because she runs her own show and it's very obvious that she does. What I like about her is that she can come out with the lipstick and the platinum hair and the spike heels and whatever she wants to, but she's obviously running the show.

93

"I think this is an area where there's a big need for more role models, not just for people of color either, but across the board in pop culture. A lot of the young women out there in a feminist role model teach by example more than by what they say. People don't want to be preached to. Latifah's songs are not that political, for example. But she projects an attitude and carries herself, dresses, and handles her business in a way that sets an example. I think that's probably more effective at this point.

"I'm a political activist, so it's important to me to fight for what I believe in and to maintain my integrity. But it's important to have fun in life, to enjoy life, because otherwise what's the point, what are we fighting for? People need to see that it's not either/or; the dumb one is not the pretty blonde, and the smart one is not the ugly one. Things are changing. Young men's attitudes are changing now too. The pretty-and-dumb image is not as appealing as it once was; I'm getting that feedback from young men that I interview out in the field.

"I've been doing the show for seven years, and a lot of kids have grown up with me. I think that I try to teach by example. The girls see that Dominique is out there, and she's going to give her opinion anytime she feels like it. That's just the way I am. They also see that their guy friends like me. They're attracted to me even though I'm that way. When I go to their schools, the guys try to get me to go on dates with them. It tells the girls that you can have it both ways."

People Are Talking

Things are changing between men and women, and they're changing fast. In a 1990 Yankelovich Clancy Shulman poll conducted for *New Woman* magazine, only 31 percent of women said that they needed a man to be truly happy. But 67 percent of men felt they needed a woman to be happy. In 1970, 66 percent of women felt they needed a man to attain true happiness.

Only 6 percent of women told the pollsters that if they could be born again, they would come back as a man. In 1940 the figure was 25 percent. Women feel work is a much more integral part of life, and "essential to a vision of a satisfying life."

The pollsters concluded that "the traditional concepts of masculinity and femininity are nearly extinct." Particularly interesting is this conclusion: "Personality traits that were once considered strictly feminine—being caring and nurturing, open with thoughts and feelings, gentle—have become the new standard to which almost all

American *men,* as well as women, aspire. And most of us think formerly masculine traits, such as being ambitious and being assertive, are desirable in *women* as well as in men."

These fascinating results point to a profound shift in our conception of what it means to be a human being and what it means to be a woman or a man. "The ideal human being," the pollsters continued, "is both female and male: gentle and ambitious, open and assertive." They pointed out that many Americans felt comfortable with this "paradoxical combination," yet others were "still struggling to accept such ambiguity." As we have seen, tolerance for ambiguity is a critical characteristic of creative persons. Where America is going, according to this poll, a considerable amount of it will be required.

The article concluded that now "women feel comfortably feminine when they feel physically strong *and* when they feel vulnerable; men have a firm sense of masculinity when they are assertive *and* when they are open with their feelings." This mélange of feminine and masculine characteristics in the same person has been referred to in psychological literature as androgyny.

Androgyny
Cultural stereotypes have defined for centuries what men and women should be like. Research in creativity conducted about thirty years ago showed that creative individuals did not usually fit in the mold provided by society. Creative individuals tended to be an interesting blend of feminine and masculine characteristics. In retrospect, this is not surprising. Creativity involves breaking out of stereotypes, and what could be more stultifying than the stereotypes of our gender roles? Breaking out of those roles can in fact be an extremely therapeutic way of nurturing one's own creativity. The work of James Melaart, Marija Gimbutas, and others on Neolithic Crete has pointed out that the partnership relationship between the sexes was probably a major reason for Crete's highly advanced and sophisticated art.

Men who become actors must explore greater emotional depths. Women in the arts must learn to be assertive and businesslike, and artists like Madonna, k. d. lang, and Michelle Shocked have shown some of the many ways this is possible. Both men and women artists must have the ego-strength to overcome occasional accusations about becoming "soft" (in the case of a man) or a "bitch" (in the case of a woman).

95

It seems that creative individuals can freely inhabit the spaces of the self and do not close off parts of it quite as firmly as most of us do. If creativity involves going beyond the preestablished grooves we're in, then being able to explore roles, attitudes, feelings, and sensations that are unfamiliar is a way to break the mold.

In Plato's *Republic,* one of the most important texts of Western culture, Aristophanes tells of how human beings were originally both male and female, with two faces, four arms, four legs, and two genital organs. When these considerably endowed creatures, which must have looked a bit like Jabba the Hutt from *Star Wars,* ran afoul of Zeus, the God of thunder and general boss of all bosses on Mount Olympus, the big guy separated them in two with a well-aimed bolt of lightning. From then on the thunderstruck creatures were destined to look for their other half. This story is generally interpreted to point to our desire for a soul mate, someone who will make us feel whole. It's the romantic ideal: Out there somewhere is the one—the very one and the only one—who is for me. Nice, though somewhat impractical and rather limiting.

Another interpretation of this myth might be that human beings have been torn asunder, yes, but this reflects not simply the need to find a mate. It points to the fact that our society as a whole has been torn apart, with "male values" and "female values" organized in such a way as to be seemingly irreconcilable. The legend may also imply that psychologically men have been split from their self that is more feminine, and women have been split from their masculinity.

In the first part of this century, Carl Jung, the great Swiss psychologist, held that we each have an aspect of our psyche that is of the other sex—a female part in a man, and a male part in a woman. He called them the *anima* and the *animus,* the soul, and taught that through the spiritual union with the man or woman within we grow and develop into full human beings. (This does not mean that psychological wholeness will turn us back into some kind of self-contained creature with four arms and legs having sex with itself.)

Shamans often conduct imaginal weddings with gods or goddesses, psychologist Stanley Krippner told us, as symbolic attempts to balance their own sexuality. On some occasions they also wear clothes of the opposite gender. Certain forms of Tantric yoga involve exercises in which one is expected to visualize oneself as a member of the other sex. These aspects of ancient practices indicate a profound awareness of psychological principles and the importance of achieving an inner balance.

We're not suggesting you cross dress to achieve inner harmony, although of course you're welcome to. We're merely proposing that characteristics stereotypically associated with either gender exclusively may not in fact be gender-specific at all. Exploring those behaviors and feelings and thoughts may be a step toward wholeness and away from the caricature that the dominator system has tried to foist on us.

Like a multifaceted diamond, the characteristics of the creative person reflect one another. Androgyny requires independence of judgment and tolerance for ambiguity: "I'll decide what being a man or a woman means, and, in the process, I'll cross over into territory that I don't know." Androgyny involves no specific sexual orientation, but it does mean moving into territory commonly inhabited by the "opposite" sex. It means men can explore emotions other than anger, jealousy, and joy, and women can be assertive and critical thinkers.

The Tiruray Construction of Gender, or Stuart Schlegel Attends an Unusual Concert

"The Tiruray consider whether you're male or female to be a personal choice," Stuart Schlegel told us. "I was interested in a small project on musical instruments and musical traditions. The Tiruray are very musical. In the evenings they dance and they play musical instruments that they make out of materials collected in the forest. They sing long epic poems, or they sing love songs, or they sing riddles. They have a wonderful musical tradition. I was interested in listening to and recording examples of all their musical instruments and songs for my project.

"They make a kind of bamboo zither with eight strings, which has a beautiful sound, like a harp. They call it a *togo belotokan,* or *togo* for short. I asked them to play it for me, and someone said, 'It's a great pity that this woman who lives several mountains away isn't here to play because she's the great virtuoso, a great specialist in *togo belotokan* music. She can play better than anyone else.' I said, 'Wow! I wish I could go there sometime,' and he said, 'Well, maybe she'll come here sometime. I'm going to be there in a while and I'll invite her to come and play for you.' And sure enough she did. She came and played for me and I have pictures of her playing, and recordings.

"As she was playing away, I was very interested in her and I asked, 'Is she married?' They laughed. I said 'What's funny?' They said, 'Well, she's a *mentewalay libun,*' which in their language means one who became a woman. I had never heard that expression before and I said, 'Oh, you mean she's really a man?' since I didn't have a word for transvestite. They said, 'No, she's really a woman, she's a *mentewalay libun*, she's one who became a woman.' Now, they have a perfectly good word for 'really and truly': *tintu*. And I said, 'Then she's *tintu lagey* (man).' They said, 'No, no, no, Moléni,' they call me Molé ni, father of my eldest son, Lenny. They said, 'No, no, Moléni, she's *tintu libun* (woman) but *mentewalay libun*. She's really a woman, but she's one who became a woman.' Well, we went on and on about this. I was extremely confused, and what I finally learned, to make a long story short, is that Tiruray believe if you're born with a penis you're a male, and if you're born with a vagina you're a female, but that's not what determines your real gender. If you live your life as a woman, you're *really* a woman. If you live your life as a man, you're *really* a man.

"If, in growing up as a boy, you decide you don't want to be a boy, you want to be a woman, then you can dress like a woman, take a woman's name, weed instead of cutting down trees, do the things that women do, and you are really a woman. What I realized was something I'd never investigated, something I had never formalized in my mind. We Westerners think it's your plumbing that makes you either truly a male or truly a woman. The Tiruray don't. They think it's your sociological role. In the language there is no *he* or *she*. The language doesn't commit you to a gender in pronouns. There's just a pronoun for the third person. But I have to use *she* or *he* in English. I said, 'Does she have a penis?' And they said, 'Oh, yeah, of course. She was born *lagey* but she's a *mentewaley libun*.' I said, 'If she has a penis, then she's *really* a man.' 'No, no, can't you understand? Look at her, she's really a woman!' Finally I realized that for them what really makes you one gender or the other is the sociological role you play. So then I said, 'What you're saying to me is you can choose either to be a male or a female,' and they said, 'Of course, of course. How could it be otherwise?'

"I told them that in my society you couldn't do that. If you were a male and wanted to be a female, and dressed as a female, and acted as a female, many people would hassle you. They would give you a bad time. And the other way around. They thought that was outrageous. They said, 'Why do you do that to people? If people want to be female, why shouldn't they be female? If someone wants to be male, why shouldn't they be male? Why are you so mean to those people as to make them unhappy if they follow their wishes?' I've not been able to think of a good answer."

LOVE

What It Is

Art and Elaine Aron fell in love while studying psychology at Berkeley in the late 1960s. They were so overwhelmed by their feelings for each other that they decided to study the psychology of love. Art spent several months in the Berkeley library working on his Ph.D. dissertation on love in 1970. He looked for anything remotely scholarly that had been written on the subject. He found twelve books in the entire library.

This was a bad sign. But then most of his dissertation advisers thought he was pretty far out, and the track record for people researching love was not good. In the seventies, social psychologists Ellen Berscheid and Elaine Hatfield had received a grant to study love but were then blessed with a Proxmire Golden Fleece Award, which basically made them lose the grant and receive death threats for wanting to study love. The Golden Fleece Award is given by Senator Proxmire to expensive research that in the eyes of the committee is considered a colossal waste of taxpayers' money.

Research on love has had a tough time, Art told us, and for several reasons. First of all, love and close relations are not serious, male, public affairs, and in the eyes of many people, they simply do not qualify for scientific scrutiny. Studying love is not quite acceptable because it's feminine and private and fundamentally *frivolous*. Now, aggression, there's something worth looking into. It seems more relevant. It's certainly easier to get research funding for.

Some people believe that by studying love we will somehow make it evaporate or disappear in a puff of smoke under the clear light of reason. Studying it doesn't seem to have bothered Art and Elaine much, though, and given the poor rate of success we seem to be having with love, it could certainly use some outside help, some understanding.

Elaine thinks that underneath their veneer of science and respectability, the people who call research on love frivolous fear exposure in this highly sensitive area. It's private. Every man's home is his castle, and we can't have people poking their noses in to find out about love (or the lack of it) or how my wife or husband really feels about me. It's taboo.

Sex, interestingly, has been studied far more than love. This is probably because it has obvious physiological dimensions that can be scrutinized, labeled, measured, compared, and drawn up statistically.

99

Sex may be naughty, but it is still a more "manly" topic to study than love, since it has that hydraulic-engineering-plumbing dimension that makes it seem a merely mechanical act.

This academic neglect, which Art and Elaine Aron and a handful of other researchers have tried to correct with a number of thoughtful scholarly books and articles, is counterbalanced by an enormous amount of literature discussing love *outside* of academia. Virtually all great plays and novels revolve around the theme of love. Movies and television shows almost always have a love interest. Soap operas explore the bizarre behavior they call love in titillating and painfully elaborate detail. Women's and men's magazines discuss love with great abandon, teaching us how to "find that special one" or "what men really look for in a woman." Almost every pop song ever written is about love. People clearly want to know about love, and academia just isn't going to tell them—or it wasn't, until very recently.

"To travel the world singing love songs, and making a living out of it, is fantastic. I like to think it's the greatest thing you can do," rock singer Roddy Frame told us. "Singing love songs makes you feel good. When I first started, I believed in catharsis; I believed that expressing my anger was a way to get rid of it. But now I think it just makes people angrier. If you have to go on stage every night and sing about hate, it's not a very nice environment to be traveling in." One of Roddy's albums is called *Love*.

But what is love? "Love is the desire to be in close relationship with an other," Art told us, which hardly seems an explosive definition. We don't think he'll get any death threats for it. But it gets really interesting when Art and Elaine start talking about love as an "expansion of the self," the topic of one of their many books.

When we fall in love, they remark, our self is expanded, our identity enhanced as we include the other as part of the self. In romantic love, whether heterosexual or homosexual, this happens very quickly. It is not simply a metaphor. Very rapidly our self reaches out to the other in an effort to unite emotionally, physically, intellectually, and even spiritually with our love.

The Arons mentioned a fascinating piece of research. Not only people in love but also mothers and best friends react to events that happen to their loved ones as if they had happened to themselves. The self has therefore expanded to the point of including the other. We care deeply for the person we love and are as concerned for their well-being as if they were part of us.

Making love is perhaps the strongest way of feeling this union of self and loved one. But the Arons' research focused on far more prosaic instances of everyday life, in which people literally treated the person they loved with the same concern they had for themselves, showing the same kinds of automatic, instinctive reactions we might have when we raise our arm to protect ourselves from a blow. The Arons showed in their research that people who have just fallen in love spend more time when asked to describe themselves than people who are not in love. The self of those in love seems literally to be expanding.

Love, Creativity, and the Expansion of Self

The expansion of the self, Art and Elaine claim, is a primary motivation in life. We instinctively want to grow, expand, be all that we can be. But the crucial question is, how can we expand the self? For the sake of brevity, here are three ways, two dominator ways—and a partnership way.

The two dominator alternatives are a variation on the domination-submission dynamic. The first one is, obviously enough, the strategy of domination. If I want to expand, I'll become powerful and conquer territory, land, nations, women, men, booty, today the world, tomorrow the solar system. Upward and onward! He who dies with the most toys wins.

The expansion is taken literally here. It becomes a perverse kind of gluttony. We want the world to dance to our tune. Most men barely manage to make their family dance to their tune, but it's the first place they try. Sometimes the roles are switched, and it's a woman who dominates the family, becoming a control freak, just like her male counterpart in the domination game. Everything has to be more like me, the way I want things to be. The self expands through power over others, power to dictate the ground rules. In this configuration, it is preferable to be alone than not to be in control.

"I have friends, beautiful, successful women in their forties," Isabel Allende remarked, "who go to these agencies or these clubs where they get blind dates. One friend had something like a hundred and fifty dates in the last year, and I witnessed it. A hundred and fifty, and she wouldn't get one that was worth writing home about. What happened there? What happens generally in this case? You are very clear about what *you* want, you don't want to make commitments, you don't have the slightest idea of what you are willing to give. How can it work this way? I think that is the result of a very selfish society where you don't make commitments if you can avoid them. If you are alone, you are safe, you control everything. But life is risk, a tremendous, wonderful risk."

The second dominator routine for expanding the self is by allowing the self to be swallowed up into something much larger than the self. Relinquishing responsibility and throwing oneself into the hands of a "higher power" or an idolized loved one is what drives some cultish phenomena, some pathological religious groups, ideological fanatics, addicted lovers, the I-was-just-following-orders types. This is another form of escape from freedom.

We become so identified with the group, with the symbols and leaders and history of our great and glorious movement/party/guru, that we actually feel part of it. People in love behave as if the person they love were part of themselves, and the same applies if they love a group or a person who has power to abuse them or to "heal" them. They bask in the aura of the fearless leader. In relationships gone wrong, we can identify so totally with the other that we lose our self in the process. We initially worship our lover and invest them with all the power we do not have. We become bigger and better and more desirable just by being around them. Our self-esteem soars briefly. But things don't quite turn out the way we planned. Our whole identity is invested in the relationship, and we do everything we can to make the relationship work, or just bearable. The one thing we cannot do is break it up, because we would be totally lost without it, or so we think.

The partnership alternative doesn't accept this dance of domination and submission. The self expands not through controlling others, or being engulfed within the other, but through understanding and empathy. A subtle realization occurs that involves a greater flexibility, a psychological spaciousness and openness to the other and to the self. There is no need to control or to be lost in someone else for good. Beginning an intimate relationship with a person we love is somewhat like opening a door to new worlds of inner and outer experience. Every meal in a restaurant, every walk in the woods or on the beach has a special glow about it. We seem to be more alive—lost in a dream, yet more aware.

Along with the outer experiences of doing new things together, we discover feelings and sensations we may not have known before or had forgotten. Inner and outer world suddenly seem to have more meaning, and the urge to express this meaning manifests itself in a variety of creative gestures and expressions typical of being in love.

We are motivated to do things for the person we love that we might normally not do, tapping into a creativity we didn't know we had. Falling in love is a creative act, Elaine and Art Aron told us, because it involves a constant restructuring of the self and of our view of the world. As the self expands, it includes more and more of the other's experiences, in an ongoing process of expansion and integration.

This is the same dynamic Frank Barron found in the creative process. Although we are not all philosophers, Barron says, we each in our own way answer some of the fundamental questions that have intrigued philosophers for millennia. What is real? Are people basically good or bad? What is the good life? What is moral behavior? We may not even know what our answers are to these questions, but we have answered them in our behavior. Some people grow and develop throughout their lives and constantly revise their answers to these questions. They are searchers who know that they do not know and are aware that, as Nietzsche said, we are much greater artists than we know. They are open to new influences, they constantly seek out the new and the unknown, they attempt to create their own synthesis out of what they learn and experience.

Creative people question their own and others' assumptions. They don't buy prefabricated answers to the basic questions of life. The self-renewal of creative people involves snapping out of one way of seeing and doing things and creating a new one. According to Barron, the process involves *diffusion,* that is, exploring, expanding, opening up to new possibilities and new experiences; and *integration,* that is, making sense of, digesting, and assimilating the new material. Being in love makes us want to look at ourselves and the other's way of life; it makes us discover ourselves, as we find out why somebody loves us—and also why they may eventually be irritated by some of the things we do. Love opens us to new experiences, sensations, and feelings. It opens our eyes to things about ourselves and about the world around us that we had previously been blind to.

Creating partnership in intimate relationships may well become the developmental task of the next generation, much as personal growth and inner journeys have been for the present one.

The Power of Love and the Love of Power

Expanding the self the dominator way is the ego's time-honored means of gaining control over the other, incorporating more territory, establishing dominion over the environment through force. But this ego is not strong, argues Frank Barron, it's actually brittle.

The "dominator ego" is fear based: Fear that it might not be able to control the situation. It is constantly building walls and fortifications and crocodile-filled moats around itself. If you are not afraid of something, you can let it go about its way. But if you're scared of it, you have to control it. Why else would we put criminals in jail or wild animals in cages?

There is much evidence to show that no matter how dreadful a particular behavior pattern may be for us, we often strongly resist change because we fear change itself. It's somehow safer to keep suffering than to venture into the unexpected. Our very identity, we feel, is grounded in a particular behavior, a relationship, or certain feelings. "What would I do without you?" We believe we'd be nothing without the person we're in a relationship with even if sometimes they're ruining our life. Battered wives are often unwilling to leave abusive relationships because of their learned helplessness. They have been trained to become utterly dependent on their spouses.

In a dominator system, we flip-flop between dependence and avoidance, total vulnerability and impossible independence. We hold on for dear life to people who are making us miserable and who threaten to leave at the drop of a hat. In fact those same avoidant people either stay with us anyway or split and move into a relationship with identical dynamics of clinging and avoidance. As we have seen, in our polarized and polarizing society, men have generally been trained to avoid, and women to cling.

The dominator system has imbued in us the belief that, particularly when things get out of hand, an adversarial model is the only way of surviving: either I win or you do. Relationships are conceived as zero-sum games where one can win only if the other loses, and no other option is available. Don Dutton, a Canadian psychologist who has conducted extensive research into wife assault, reports that in the treatment of wife beaters "we attempt to encourage their thinking of power in interdependent terms. We help them see that by diminishing their wives, they lose a vital partner; whereas by accepting the empowerment of their wives, they themselves gain in the process." Don Dutton's approach to wife beaters brings out two important ingredients of healthy relationships. First, an awareness of interdependence; second, a new understanding of power.

The awareness of interdependence can lead to an entirely different perception of the world, one in which it is always possible for both persons to win. In other words, relationships become by definition nonzero-sum games. The prerequisite to play this kind of game is creativity, based on the belief that if we expand reality, and expand the self, we can make a quantum leap to a higher level of understanding and sharing.

The other vital point Dutton makes is that the nature of the relationship changes drastically when we shift our perspective from one in which either you're the boss or I am, to one where we can help each other grow. The other person is then seen not as someone who either takes power from us or is controlled by us at their expense but as a companion in an evolving system. The partnership way of expanding the self does not involve controlling the other and making the other conform to our regulations and demands. It's not "my way or else!" Rather than seeking to expand the self so as to eliminate differences, the partnership self has the ego-strength to open up and become vulnerable enough to let the other in and to go inside the other. This means letting go of our judgments for a while, accepting the fact that we may not know what is going on, and being secure enough in our self to temporarily let go of it. The philosopher Alan Watts called this the wisdom of insecurity. This is the meaning of ego-strength.

The experience of falling in love, and the experience of being in love for an extended time, can make us aware of how the self is created in relationship. It has often been remarked that people who have been together a long time, or who are really close, mirror each other's body language. Relationships have profound effects on who we are. We are never alone. We are always in relationship with the world around us, animate or inanimate. In a partnership system, relationships are the fundamental way of co-creating our reality.

Sex

Sex is the quickest route to the expansion of the self, or so it seems. Our society is almost overwhelmingly obsessed with sex. Sex is everywhere yet, strangely enough, nowhere. Although advertisers use sex to convince us to buy products and bombard us with images of scantily clad women and hunky men, sex itself must not be seen. Even though soap opera stars in just about every other TV show engage in some sexual act or other, we're not actually supposed to see them doing it. Watching people doing it is dirty. Naked bodies must not be seen in public, since naked bodies are also dirty and smutty. You and I have bodies, we probably wash them every day, we almost certainly catch glimpses of ourselves naked, but we still have to live with the fact that this nudity is somehow dirty.

Underneath our clothes we're all *nekkid,* we assume, which makes it hard to get away from the fundamental cause of nudity: bodies. But only some bodies. We're allowed to see members of our own sex naked, in locker rooms and places like that, but not members of the "opposite" sex. They're dirty. Our system creates an incredible tension between the sexual imagery that floods our consciousness (legally) every day and the requirement that this sexuality at the same time be repressed.

Perhaps there is a good reason for this concern with dirt. Human beings in the Western world were not known for washing a lot until just recently. At the court of Louis XIV, the Sun King, with all the splendid luxury and sophistication of European culture, folks didn't wash but a couple of times a year. Why did you think they were so heavily into perfumes in the 1600s and 1700s? Those attractive powdered wigs worn by the nobility were infested with lice. Baths were considered positively dangerous to one's health. So, really, would you want to make love to somebody like that if you had the choice? Wouldn't you think sex was dirty too if your partner didn't wash but a couple of times a year? So maybe the idea that sex was dirty had some justification. There seems to be no sensible reason, however, to equate sex with sin. Think about it: A society that believes making *love* is basically a bad thing. It makes you wonder how sane human beings are.

The sexual revolution in the 1960s was supposedly all about freeing us from the shackles of sexual repression. In typical revolutionary but basically reactive fashion, we went totally the other way. For a while we espoused free love, which was really about free sex without love. Sex is good and should be engaged in at all times with anyone who strikes our fancy, was the message. "Why don't we do it in the road," John Lennon asked. (But remember, even he added, "no one will be watching us," suggesting the need for a modicum of privacy.)

No matter how well meaning the sexual revolutionaries were (and frankly, we suspect at least some of them were just looking for an excuse to have sex with people who would normally have had nothing to do with them), they were still trapped in a dominator dynamic. Viewing sex as a purely physical act divorced from feelings and spirituality and even brains—"Contraception? What contraception?"—makes little sense from a partnership-system perspective.

Moreover, the guilt factor was still there, but in a different form. Now instead of feeling guilty about having sex, people were made to feel guilty for not doing it at the drop of a hat. "Don't be so uptight."

"You're not free," they said, as if doing what *they* wanted was a sign of freedom. Independence of judgment, that old standby of the creative personality, was not encouraged. This is a typical dominator dynamic: Do what everybody else is doing to show you're free and an individual. It's great if you're giving the orders.

In the final analysis, the true meaning and influence of the sexual revolution had probably very little to do with sex. It precipitated a cultural transition because it proclaimed that sacred cows could and should be questioned. It also helped women to take charge of their sexuality, which in turn gave greater strength and momentum to the women's movement. But the fundamental paradigm had not yet shifted.

After the sexual revolution, a woman who had casual sex would not necessarily be considered "easy," by some people, although for more conservative types nothing had changed. In a 1991 MTV poll—we're talking scientific here, folks—a considerable number of men felt that they had the right to coerce a woman to have sex with them if they thought she had slept with many other men. From this perspective, she's common property. She doesn't belong to anyone, and so she's a commodity. And it's inconceivable she might belong to herself and sleep with everybody except you, just because she feels like it.

The most extreme example of dominator sex is rape, during which a woman's body is temporarily possessed by a man who controls her against her will. This kind of "sex" involves getting pleasure from violence and another's suffering. It is a seething, vengeful resentment taking physical form. Some people think rape, or date rape, which may take the form of having sex with a drunken coed, is a "natural" thing, simply an expression of male sexuality, our bestial instincts, and so on.

If the guys who rape women are examples of "hot male sexuality," as controversial art historian and author of *Sexual Personae* Camille Paglia writes, for instance, then one can only wonder what their definition of "hot sex" really is. It's perhaps no surprise that in San Francisco's *Image* magazine, Ms. Paglia said of her own sex life that it has been "a disaster, an absolute disaster, because I've never been able to connect with someone." Should anyone be surprised by this? She says she is attracted to men, "but I cannot give up my independent power to them, I cannot submit." This is a classic example of a dominator-system dynamic: an intelligent, independent woman convinced that the only kind of relationship possible is a domination-submission one. Who says you have to submit? Buying into this system keeps you trapped so that an intelligent powerful woman can never be satisfied.

Ms. Paglia's message posits the inevitability of the dominator system, hence her tough posturing about women who condemn date rape. She argues that it's impossible to have a world without rape and violence, and chides the women who let themselves be fooled by their own personal dynamics into such utopian dreams. It seems to us that Ms. Paglia's personal dynamics are leading her to believe everybody's sex life should be as disastrous as hers. We'll have to turn down her gracious offer.

Dominator sex is part of a gender dance that has more similarities to the predator-prey relationship than to the courtly love songs of the troubadours. The violence that pervades sexual relations all over the world reflects the fact that for many people the guiding metaphor for sex is war and conquest. The 1991 MTV report on sex revealed some opinions that keep us locked in our present predicament. Some described men as rutting, out-of-control stallions. This view that "men are men" and want sex at all times because it's "natural" for them to be sex-crazed is a pathetic myth. First of all, sexuality clearly does have a physiological component, but the way it's channeled and even the frequency of arousal are socially constructed. This means that in a society where a man's status depends on how many women he has slept with, where horniness is a sign of virility and manliness, and where we are constantly bombarded with aggressive sexual imagery, it's no surprise that men feel they *have* to be aggressively sexual. It's simply not true that men are always sex-crazed fiends. Many men pretend to be sexually aroused—ogling and propositioning—because they're being faithful to their role. If they had other models to follow, they would. Furthermore, there is an enormous variation in human personalities and preferences. Some people always talk about sex, joke about sex, and engage in active ogling; some don't. These sweeping generalizations—not unlike the ones we made about the differences between women and men—are just that, sweeping generalizations. "Real" people tend to fall somewhere in between.

Isolating the sexual act, divorcing it from feeling and connection at anything but the physical level, undoubtedly sits better with men than it does with women, given the general gender differences we have discussed. But it does not reflect fundamental differences in human nature or describe "the way guys are." It does reflect perhaps the way some guys are now and how incredibly diminished our experience of sex, of ourselves, and of other people really is. When pressed in polls, guys—even *Playboy* readers, that notoriously "sexy" bunch—will always confess to preferring a committed relationship with a woman they love above casual encounters.

Sex is undoubtedly a great thing, but that doesn't necessarily mean more is better. It's not simply a physical function, like sneezing (and more sneezing is not necessarily better sneezing). It is a remarkable process that has some very complex psychological repercussions. To call it a bonding process is to put it mildly.

One of the reasons why we are all so concerned with sex, and why it can be such a profound experience is precisely because it is a "whole systems process," because, dropping the jargon here for a moment, it affects our hearts and souls and minds and bodies. And it doesn't only affect us as individuals, because then masturbation would be entirely sufficient. Making love includes an other, a person we love, in the process, and so it literally makes two hearts beat as one. The "system" becomes more than one, and sometimes literally even more than two.

This is what the Arons mean about the expansion of the self. The whole self becomes part of a larger system with the person we love. We don't own them or control them. We *are* them, for a while, or as close as we can be.

Sex can be a battleground, but it can also be a remarkable road to healing the split between men and women. Sex does not have to be a game of domination and submission. Sex is a way of being connected with an other, a physical manifestation of love in which we try and become as close to somebody as humanly possible. This delightful dance requires exquisite sensitivity to our partner's needs, and vice versa, but also an awareness of what our own needs are. The playfulness of sex can allow us to experiment with different roles, literally with different positions with our partner and the relationship. Sex is a place where we can explore the dynamics of relationships and develop flexibility and creativity as we expand our self.

When we talk about the model of partnership sex, about breaking the dominator stereotypes regarding sexuality and gender, we are not awaiting the dawn of a new age or the development of some amazing new technique that will give us a piggyback ride to a higher level of consciousness. Lest we get depressed at the thought that once again the whole of society is going to have to change before we see any real difference, we should bear in mind that we can all begin by looking at some of the realities the dominator system wishes to hide, the blind spots that have been forced on us. We can see how men can be both gentle and caring and strong, "masculine," and sexy; and how women can be both independent and sexy.

The dominator system has had us focus on the importance of orgasm. Traditionally one of the differences between women and men is that women enjoy a greater amount of sexual foreplay than men do. It is not difficult to trace this back to physiological causes, for all it's worth, and one could say that this is just the way we are built. This assumption of fundamental difference becomes outright inequality when we realize that historically men have wielded the power in sexual relations and defined the rules of the game.

In a dominator system, difference is viewed immediately through the lens of domination and submission. Which way is it going to be, yours or mine? By contrast, when faced with a situation of difference, the partnership alternative asks, How can we both benefit from this? From a dominator perspective, this means compromise. The partnership view stresses the importance of synergy.

Prolonged foreplay, for instance, increases sexual intensity for both partners and enhances the feelings of bonding and involvement. Both parties then drop their facades, the roles they have learned, and really begin to explore each other.

Sexual play and enjoyment can be a wonderful way of expanding the self, of playfully integrating new elements into oneself. Both men and women can allow themselves to be both more passive and more aggressive, more sensitive and more forceful. Rather than exacerbating existing patterns, making love can open the way to greater freedom, a freedom created with the person we love.

Making Love Last

"Now that we've found love, what are we going to do with it?" asks the reggae band Third World. They're not the first to ask. Tom Robbins's book *Still Life with Woodpecker* asks the same basic question: How do we make love last? The data show we don't really do a good job, Elaine and Art Aron told us. Most marriages go downhill pretty fast, unfortunately, although a minority of people seem to keep on having a grand old time of it. Love can turn into boredom pretty damn quick. All great love stories are about finding our love, losing it, and getting it back, or some such sequence of obstacles and conflicts. Elaine Aron, who is also a novelist, points out that writing about married sex is a surefire way to lose your readership!

Boredom and lack of basic interpersonal skills are the real killers. Well, maybe we *are* clumsy and know nothing of conflict resolution and the latest communication skills. But how is it that we can get so bored being with someone we once considered a gift from the gods, a creature from the stars we could never get enough of? Is it them? Is it us? What exactly is going on?

"Higamous hogamous, woman is monogamous, hogamous higamous, man is polygamous." This great insight came to William James after he took some nitrous oxide, and sociobiologists today want to prove him right by developing theories about males wanting to "maximize their reproductive efficiency" by generously offering their genetic endowment to as many females as possible. Females, on the other hand, want the man to stick with them and protect them, since this is the right genetic move for them. Women can only have a baby at a time, whereas men could conceivably have a bunch of them at one time with different females.

"All is fair in love and war," goes the saying, and here we come across some of the most explicit examples of dominator dynamics, which operate in love relationships just as actively as in other areas of our lives. Terms like having and possessing a lover reflect the close ties between relationships and the idea of property and, conse-quently, status. Men are under pressure to exhibit their status and manliness to their peers through the women they have. Women, who have historically been dominated by men in almost all areas of life, find that in romance and courtship the tables are often reversed, and they have an unusual amount of power: Men will fight for a woman or otherwise make fools of themselves. Stereotypes such as the temptress emerge from an unfavorable perception of women's power over male emotions. But throughout this, women are con-stantly reminded of their dependence on men. A woman's notion that she has to keep her man once she's got him leads to an uphill struggle to remain enticing and competitive, which clearly puts the woman in conflict with other women.

Men have their own equivalent of the temptress, namely, the Don Juan figure who loves 'em and leaves 'em. Love is seen as a bat-tle for conquest, and the disposable lovers are dispensed with as soon as possible because our hero simply doesn't know what to do with them. So trapped is he in his own shortsighted beliefs he literally cannot see beyond his own nose. Even the dominator ends up by confessing that he is trapped in a vicious cycle and will never be sat-isfied this way. How can he live happily ever after with an object he has conquered and mistreated? And remember, if he gets too close, she'll be able to see through the mask, which the Don inevitably has to drop at home.

One of the saddest aspects of this view of love as battle and conquest is that once the chase is over and the excitement is gone, many relationships deteriorate rapidly. Boredom and routine set in, petty details loom large, and romance is often found only outside the relationship. The dominator system simply does not have a way to make love last, because it is based on a constant process of domination and submission, and dominating the same person gets old after a while. The challenge that makes us feel alive is renewed only by new conquests or in some cases through jealousy—the fear that we have not really conquered fully.

These dynamics as we have summarized them here are exaggerated, of course, but they are a lot more prevalent than one might think. It is important to remember that they make life miserable for both men and women. The dominator system is an equal opportunity oppressor.

The story of the first meeting is always exciting. "How did you meet?" is a sure way to get a couple talking and giggling. "What went wrong?" is unfortunately more often than not the obvious next question. There are a lot fewer stories about how couples lived happily ever after. Few movies or books or plays celebrate couples with a thirty-year history riding off into the sunset to continue the romantic experience of their lifetime.

How could they, though? The dominator system is simply not geared for double features. Can you imagine the havoc too many great partnerships would cause? They would imply that women went along on some kind of exciting journey, be it spiritual or physical or psychological or intellectual, and didn't just cook the grub and mind the kids while the man of the house was killing Indians, discovering a new vaccine, climbing Everest, governing the country, or something equally heroic. Great partnerships would imply that sex is more than just making babies. They would imply that wives are actually sexual beings, that they defy the madonna/whore dichotomy.

Art Aron and his graduate student Charlotte Reissman conducted some fascinating research that sheds light not only on falling in love but also on keeping love alive. When people are in situations that cause arousal—say fear or great excitement—they are more likely to fall in love than when they're just "neutral," or waiting in line to get their driver's license renewed. The arousal gets "generalized," in technical terms, and what supposedly happens subconsciously is something like "Wow, I'm aroused. Gee, it must be her/him. Well she/he is kinda cute . . ." This theory holds that emotions are socially and psychologically determined "labels" we stick on sensations of arousal. Interestingly, couples who do exciting things together for two hours a week are happier than those who are together just for some activity two hours a week. Again, the issue seems to be arousal, and this might even explain why some couples love to fight. The arousal is then followed by the it's-great-to-make-up-again feeling. It's a bit like banging your head against a wall because it feels so good when you stop. There are definitely better ways of feeling good.

The partnership systems seem to offer a wide variety of alternatives. The metaphor of the expansion of the self suggests that love may be a way of continuing to learn and grow, and not just in the waistline. It seems folly to say that only the first moments of romantic love—typically before marriage—have obstacles and conflict, which are supposed to add the spice that makes romance interesting and kindles our love. If there are obstacles anywhere, it's after marriage, after the relationship has been going for a while. There lies the real creative challenge, but we are so blinded by dominator dynamics that we think this part is boring.

Social psychologist Carol Tavris says that in good marriages men have more stereotypically feminine qualities, such as warmth, openness, and empathy, and women are more assertive, confident, and independent. These are also traits that Frank Barron found in creative persons. It certainly seems that people with these characteristics are more flexible, open, and capable of creating their relationships rather than falling victim to circumstances, habits, or patterns and expectations that cause them to move apart. Couples who have these creative traits—independence of judgment, tolerance for ambiguity, empathy, and so forth—may be much more capable of making love last because they see their love as an ongoing creative process rather than as a thing that can be lost or found.

According to Isabel Allende, "The idea of romantic love as it was conceived was possible when people died very young and didn't live until they were ninety. You would get married at fifteen. By the time you were thirty you were worn out by pregnancies, and your husband was going to crusades or somewhere. Life was not so long, therefore you didn't make these terrible demands on love.

"I think that love is possible even now, with long life expectancy and so many factors interfering with it. We should change our demands of love. We shouldn't expect from love what we used to. I am a very passionate and romantic person myself, and I always think when I am in love that it will be forever and it can only grow. But

113

experience teaches me that love is not something already made, like an apple. It's a road, a process. It's not something that you acquire; it's a place where you go with someone, a journey. You *make* love one day at a time, one step at a time, one minute at a time. *El camino se hace a l'andar,*" she sings (the road is made as you travel). "Applied to love it is beautiful: *making* love constantly."

Love and creativity may be seen as part of the expansion of the self, not a military-style, imperialist expansion but a sharing and broadening of our experience to the point that the barriers between self and other begin to disappear. Then love and creativity become more than just ways of expressing or pleasing ourselves. They become something beyond selfishness and altruism so that self-interest is not seen as fundamentally different from the good of the whole, and the good of the whole serves our personal betterment. The emphasis is not on either the individual or the whole but on the relationship of partnership between the two.

This lofty-sounding ideal could just as easily come from a religious dogma or totalitarian ideology. It needs to be "operationalized," that is, defined in terms of everyday behavior.

Several people featured in this book are outstanding examples of partnership at work. Riane Eisler and David Loye, whose work has inspired this book, are partners in marriage and have embarked together on an intellectual journey that has resulted so far in the publication of *The Chalice and the Blade,* the founding of the Center for Partnership Studies, the joint authorship of *The Partnership Way,* and the formation of sixteen Centers for Partnership Education across the U.S. Art and Elaine Aron and John Todd and Nancy Jack Todd (whom we'll meet in the chapter on the environment) are other good examples of the increase in energy, output, and brain power that comes from partnership synergy. And there are many others like them.

Gabrielle is thirty-five years old and exquisitely beautiful. Her man's name is Paul, and they look very good together, not only because they are so physically suited to one another—a classic beautiful couple—but because of the ease and affection with which they relate to each other. Isabella met them in Sausalito, California, where they were spending a few months on their boat before setting sail to Mexico and Central America.

"I went to this cocktail party in Capri," Gabrielle told Isabella one windy day on her boat. "It was a perfect evening, with a warm wind blowing softly. I could still taste the salt on my lips from my afternoon swim. It was the usual crowd, I knew most of the people there. You know how there comes a time at a party when you're just thirsty for some water? I met Paul over the kitchen sink; we were both reaching for a glass of water. We looked at each other. He smiled, and I thought, or better my heart said, 'My friend!' and that's the way it has been ever since. Before being my lover, he is my friend. We've been best friends for ten years now, and I know that no matter what happens, we will be each other's friend for life."

Her words described perfectly the most powerful root of long-lasting love: the friendship born out of absolute trust. It is a dangerous gamble, for what assurance do we have that our trust is well reposed? Yet without that recognition, followed by the connection that is best described as "I trust you completely," there is no foundation for lasting love.

John is a seventy-year-old lawyer who has been involved with Ann for thirty-four years. They are not married and probably never will be. Their story is almost out of a B movie. He came back from the war (we're talking WWII) and married a childhood sweetheart he had not seen in five years because it was the honorable thing to do. They were both from a small town, and everyone had expected that they would get married. After two children and twelve years of marriage (a rather average marriage), the wife had a terrible accident. She became wheelchair-bound and sustained enough brain damage to make any meaningful relationship impossible. He would never consider divorce, John explained to Ann when they met. Ann did not care, she loved him because he was that kind of man. She was probably right to trust his depth of commitment because he has been in love with her for more than thirty years.

"Perhaps because of my past history," he told us holding Ann's hand and smiling affectionately at her, "I knew that what I had found with her was very special. For me, the secret of our love is very simple. I can always trust her to tell me the truth, and I will always speak the truth to her, even if it means telling her that I don't like her new dress or that her article for a law journal needs rewriting. But we know it's a truth spoken from the heart."

"We have a rule," Ann added. "We wait until we are both in a good space before we bring up something that might upset the other. Then we can be sure that we will find the right words, and that the other will be receptive. We get mad, of course. I don't trust those relationships where people never disagree; it's phony. But when we get mad, we look at each other and we say, 'Is it really worth a fight? Let's talk about it tomorrow.'"

"This is very important," John continued. "We only postpone the discussion to a better time, a day or two later at the most. By

115

Relationships

then, trivial incidents are forgotten, but things that matter are addressed. We never sweep things under the carpet."

Maybe Federico Fellini was right when he had the protagonist of his movie 8½ deliver the line "My dearest, happiness consists in being able to always tell the truth without ever hurting anybody."

"Be happy, little one," the old housekeeper told Isabella when she got married. "And remember, never hit below the belt! Giovanni and I fight sometimes like cat and dog, we argue for hours, but we are still together because we fight fair."

Isabella took the lesson to heart. After all, the housekeeper knew what she was talking about after forty years of marriage. Isabella found the same lesson in print when she was studying psychology at the university several years later: It was the main point of a little book called *The Intimate Enemy*.

Andrea has a different story. A strong-willed woman with a lot of spice, she chose to give up a promising career to stay home with her children, who are now in college. She is married to an equally strong man, and that made for a lot of sparks the first few years of their marriage.

"I wouldn't go back even if it meant I could be young again," she states forcefully.

"There were times, back then," comments her husband, "when I truly hated her. It's a miracle we are still together. The crazy part is that it happened by chance. Had I not gotten a promotion that changed my job, we would probably be divorced by now."

"What happened was," Andrea explains, "that he started long-distance commuting. He was gone four days out of seven. All of a sudden, we were in love again! Imagine, we had been too dumb to realize that two personalities like ours need space. We had made each other claustrophobic, and we didn't even know it. We were taking our stress out on each other, resenting the invasion."

"Now we know what our relationship needs, and I don't have to be traveling the whole time anymore to keep us together," her husband said, laughing. "We have time apart when each of us does things we have to do or like to do on our own or with our friends, and then we have the times together."

"It's funny," concluded Andrea, "but as the years go by, the times together are getting better and better. I thought my mother was selling me a bunch of baloney when she told me that her relationship with Dad improved over the years. She even told me that sex at sixty was better than at twenty! But I am beginning to believe her, and I guess it's something I can look forward to!"

"One of the things I like most about our thirty-year relationship," another love veteran told us, "are our dates. This is the time dedicated to us, when the phones are unplugged, the house is empty and all for us, and the schedule is clear into the evening and night, nothing to worry about until the morrow. We visit with each other, we find out where the other is. Sometimes we cry a bit, often we laugh, sometimes we fight. We find each other and we always rediscover. I deeply believe that without this renewed acquaintance and affirmation of commitment to each other and liking for each other on a regular basis, couples become strangers. They keep household together, but they do not share a soul. They may appear to be very successful relationships to the outside world; as far as I'm concerned I see them as successful roommates (no small feat!) but not successful marriages. Our dates are absolutely sacred, and nothing short of an act of God gets in the way." As you might guess, this is a busy professional couple, but that doesn't mean that their recipe couldn't apply in other kinds of situations.

One engineer who claims to be very much in love with his wife of thirty years sums it up: "It's very simple, we have made our relationship our number one priority."

PARENTING

Who's the Boss?

The dominator system creates polarities: male and female, society and nature, natural and unnatural. It also defines specific roles in the home. Some things are women's work—the ones that are never over, because they reflect the cyclical, "natural" rhythms of life. Others are clearly men's domain. Men fix things when they're not working. Women cook, sew, and look after the kids (but this is not called work).

These separate spheres of influence around the home demarcate men's and women's territories, their sphere of competence, the space where each is in control of the situation, is the captain and the landowner. The kitchen is typically mother's territory. She has the technology, the know-how, the skills to operate here in the same way the father has the garage, or his office, from which the wife is barred. Some women do not want men to help them out in the kitchen or with the kids because these are the only domains in which they feel some power. Mothers know that children are often their only real area of authority where they have knowledge and power, so they don't exactly invite fathers to come into this space.

117

The dominator system does not encourage us to cross over those boundaries. A major problem with this division of labor is that it produces fathers who don't have a clue about infants. Babies require a certain amount of playful gentleness, typically feminine behaviors, like nurturing and empathy. In a dominator system these are simply not part of a man's repertoire. Dads don't know what to do and basically they just split ("Daddy's working very hard"). They avoid their children because they're probably embarrassed at not knowing what to do with their own babies, who start crying whenever dads pick them up.

Today, as the spaces become less clearly defined, there's trouble ahead if we keep playing by the same dominator rules. So accustomed are we to one territory, so habituated into certain patterns of behavior that change and disruptions can be traumatic. Paul Watzlawick told us about a friend's dog who was used to finding a bowl of water after he brought in the paper. One day the bowl didn't materialize, and the dog, after a moment of disorientation, ran back out again, repeated the paper-fetching routine, and ran right back in. The poor dog was flabbergasted, operating on a stimulus-response basis that is all to familiar to us in our everyday behavior. Once, Isabella and a colleague of hers, a young math professor whose wife had just had a baby, got involved in a conversation with a venerable university trustee. She had spoken with this man before and found him bright, compassionate, and worldly. This time they ended up talking about women and careers. The trustee was clearly upset about the idea. "If women start having careers," he asked with earnest consternation and genuine concern, "who will help take care of the children?" "The men, of course!" the math professor and Isabella answered in unison. The trustee looked at them with the same expression the dog must have had when he couldn't find the bowl of water.

Partnership Parenting

Scott Coltrane, a professor of sociology at the University of California, Riverside, became interested in partnership parenting when he became a father. Sharing the parenting with his wife raised quite a few eyebrows, those shouldn't-your-wife-be-doing-this? looks. This crossing of role boundaries, and the reaction it elicited from some, spurred him to go back to school to study parenting, focusing not just on the effect it had on children but also on the parents themselves. He found that partnership parenting tends to produce children with a partnership orientation. The partnership approach is "generalized" into other areas of their lives.

Isabel Allende told us that as a result of her involvement in one of Chile's path-breaking feminist groups, "I could raise my kids with very clear ideas. My mother feared that I was making a 'faggot' of Nicolas, and Paula was going to be what in Chile we call a *marimacho,* which is much worse than a tomboy. This is because Nicolas was allowed to express his feelings, to cry if he wanted to, to be weak or sentimental. But at the same time he was expected to be responsible, to work, to study. I did the same with Paula. Of course they have different personalities, but not because of their gender, because they are different people. My son got married, so I have a grandchild now. My daughter-in-law is very much like my daughter, though she was brought up in a conservative family. Somehow she rebelled, and she is very much into the partnership idea. They share everything. It's so wonderful to see them together: Nicolas is always carrying the baby, he feeds the baby, they both work, they share the cooking, the cleaning, everything. Life is so easy when you have a partner!"

Scott Coltrane points out that as men start doing more of the housework, spouses negotiate more about who does what and where. Men and women are talking about the roles in the home, since more often than not they're both working outside the home. They're talking, not shouting or fighting. This is vital, because when we abandon a system where one person gives the orders, we have to find mutually acceptable ways to agree about tasks and roles.

Men's involvement with their children seems to be growing in our culture. Along with the image of supermom, we also now have superdad, (portrayed in ads by handsome, bare-chested men cuddling babies when they get home after a hard day's work). But partnership fathers do not like being portrayed as superdads just because they do things their wives do every day, according to Coltrane. He told us that men involved in partnership parenting do not compare themselves with the men at work, the men who might rib them, for instance. Instead they compare themselves with their wives or with other men who are more involved in their families. Most men, by contrast, compare themselves with their own uninvolved fathers, which they feel lets them off the hook.

When men get involved in parenting on a daily basis, they seem to change. Men see their children as a safe way for them to be sensitive, a place where they can begin to test the waters, as it were. It seems that simply being around kids elicits in men the responses some have claimed were genetically female, the caring, sensitive awareness of others. Coltrane believes that very little is fixed in our genes as far as the capacity for intimacy, caring, and sensitivity goes. He maintains that it is far more a matter of what we've been calling basic training.

Men's capacity for intimacy improves as they get involved with their children, and their emotional antennae get better tuned. They have to learn to read subtle cues to tell how their kids are doing, whether he's depressed or she has a touch of the flu, and so they become more empathic. This new sensitivity is sometimes generalized to their spouses and the world at large. Parenting is a way to activate aspects of men's being that were previously ignored.

This is quite significant, because the same principle applies across the spectrum of activities and shows us that crossing the boundaries which we set for ourselves as human beings can be a most powerful way of expanding the self.

What Children Need

"My first film was nominated for an Academy Award," said documentary filmmaker Vivienne Verdon-Roe, who went on to win with *Women—For America, for the World.* "It was a series of interviews with children ages six to eighteen, asking how they felt about their future in view of the nuclear weapons buildup. It came out in 1983, when the nuclear weapons freeze campaign had just got off the ground, and we were finding that so many people in this country were in denial, did not want to look at this issue. The possibility of nuclear war was very frightening, and they didn't feel they had any way of preventing it. They figured, why get involved?

"Along came this film showing that children were extremely concerned, extremely aware, saying they hadn't spoken to their parents about it because their parents didn't seem to care. The parents were not opening up this issue, so the kids felt that maybe their parents didn't care about the future. They didn't understand that the parents themselves were so afraid that they couldn't communicate to their children. I felt it was valuable for parents and teachers and the general public to know about this incredible lack of communication. I also felt it was important to give young people a chance to speak about what was going on in their hearts. That's why I made that film. I had no idea that I had created a controversial piece. When it came out, I got hate mail. The letters accused me of having no integrity, that I had lied about the way I'd done this film, that I'd done something to induce this response in kids who couldn't possibly understand or fear what was going on in terms of nuclear weapons. Yet children who have parents whom they can really talk to about these issues are not afraid. There's not some big dark secret in the corner."

Talk-show host Dominique DiPrima spends a lot of time with adolescents. She points out that "the level of the discussion on my show always shocks adults, because they don't feel young people think about issues in the serious way that they do. That's because a lot of adults don't ask, or if they ask, they don't listen to the answers. People ask me, 'How can you keep up with what young people are into?' or 'How can you still be trendy after seven years when trends come and go so fast?' This is all about listening and respect, as far as I am concerned. You ask and—it's not a mystery—teenagers can talk and respond."

According to philosopher Mara Keller, "the partnership between adults and children is the new cutting edge, politically. All the horrible realities of abuse, poverty, homelessness, hunger, disease or war impact most harshly on the children. Children are the most vulnerable in all cases. Some of my students were asking, 'Why make a special issue of the children? The elderly suffer, women suffer, men suffer, why single out children for special attention?' The answer is not only because children are the most vulnerable, but also because they are everyone's future. If children have the worst conditions to grow up under, they will not be able to function very well as adults. The ones who survive become somewhat hardened in their humanity. Malnutrition will produce mental retardation, and when survival is a harsh struggle, people lose their sense of relatedness. They grow up with the experience of life being a struggle for survival, a life or death struggle in many instances, in which only a relative few are successful.

"I was just listening to [Vietnamese Zen Buddhist teacher] Thich Nhat Hanh, and he said, 'Well, it's like raising lettuce. If the lettuce withers, or is underdeveloped, we know we didn't give it the right conditions of nourishment.' He said humans aren't all that different from lettuce. If children aren't growing up well, it's not their fault; they're not getting the proper conditions of nourishment and love and care. We need to be very, very careful about the conditions in which children grow up, the quality of life.

"One of the things I focus on in my research, but also take to heart and feel very close to, is the partnership between mothers and daughters. I would also like to see men address the partnership between fathers and sons. These relationships are badly scarred. The

121

love is there, but the parenting model is one of domination, power-ful control of the dependent, of those who are weak. Parents usually feel perfectly right about doing that instead of recognizing children as souls who are every bit as important as every other soul who's alive, regardless of age.

"Women have to go into the heart of this relationship, deal with the pain in there, and heal that relationship and transform it so it's truly beneficial for both the mothers and the daughters. I see this as a crucial point for cultural transformation, because the way mothers and daughters relate will influence the way daughters become mothers."

According to psychologist Susan Hales, "Self-esteem comes en-tirely from your experiences in the environment. If as an infant, for example, you have parents who are neglectful, abusive, and puni-tive, that sets the tone for your whole orientation to the world. The world is a frightening place because there's no warmth, no comfort, no relief from distress. This sets off a snowball effect. Children from these homes are hesitant, cautious, and fearful. They are slow to learn because their natural curiosity and exploratory behavior, which are essential for learning, are significantly curtailed by their fear. Their fearfulness and insecurity also make it difficult to estab-lish friendships.

"If you're born with parents who are responsive and supportive, then when you cry, somebody comes and alleviates your distress, somebody feeds you, changes your diaper. A responsive environ-ment is a warm, supportive environment. You establish a positive re-lationship to other people. You need a positive relationship with other people to facilitate your affiliative need. We're all affiliative be-ings, we need love and support and affection and intimate relation-ships in order to feel good about ourselves, to have a happy life. Children from responsive, supportive homes develop competencies and social skills much earlier than children from rejecting or ne-glecting homes, and these early experiences give them a significant head start in life."

In their most recent book, *The Good Society,* Robert Bellah and his associates focused on the importance of attention, and the role it plays in a good society. They found that in the case of families, it is essential for kids to get attention; not just food and clothes, but love and care and what they call psychic interaction. If human be-ings are formed in relationship, if, as psychotherapist and systems philosopher Paul Watzlawick suggests, life *is* relationships, then to be denied attention, to be ignored, is literally to be considered nonexistent. We all know children who drive us to distraction because they are so noisy and obnoxious. We don't know what to do with them. Ignoring them may well be the wrong thing to do, it seems. "I'll show you," the kids say. "I'll get you to pay attention to me, and I don't care how I do it. The more I shock you, the more grossed out and horrified you are by me, the more you'll pay attention to me."

Later in life we become less dependent on our parents' attention, and we tune in more to feedback from the rest of our environment. As circumstances change around us, as we are changed by life experiences, as we acquire different skills, we interact differently with those around us, and their feedback changes accordingly. This is why, according to Susan Hales, our self-esteem may change significantly in the course of life, but it sure helps to get a good start.

The Future of the Family

In the traditional family, we went from being someone's child to being a parent rather quickly. Nowadays people get married and have children later. We often have a period of ten years or so in which to explore and create our individuality. People then have to negotiate the family-individual relationship when they get married. This means the family is undergoing changes, and people are not buying into the old models. Since everything is up for grabs, we are not surprised to hear dire warnings about the death of the traditional family.

"My stepfather, who is seventy-five," mused Isabel Allende, "says that not only is the family gone forever but marriage is as well, and in the future kids will be brought up in special places away from their parents, and they will be brought up to become certain kinds of people according to the needs of the society. I think that won't happen. What will happen is that we will come back to the extended family, because it has become extremely hard for everybody to live without it. Rich countries thought that the state could replace the family, that if you were pregnant or had a child or were old, you would always have a place and someone professionally prepared to take care of you. You may have to pay for it, or maybe your taxes pay for it. Now it has been proven that it doesn't work that way. After a while there is crisis in the society, a crisis in the values of the society showing that nothing that you can pay for replaces the family. So out of pure necessity we'll go back to the extended family, grandparents who take care of the little ones because the parents are working.

123

"My husband and I are in the perfect position now to be by ourselves, with our children grown up and in college. But we have chosen instead to relate as a family. My son takes care of my bills, they drive me to the airport, I help them by taking care of my grandson, our house is open. There are always people coming in and out, there are lots of things we do for each other. If I am sick, my daughter will take care of me. It's assumed. And I know that I would take care of my mother if she were to become senile or too old or whatever because she took care of me for twenty years. This chain of relationships keeps you going and helps everybody."

"The family has definitely changed. My family is not typical," shared Dominique DiPrima. "Some people trip when I say this, but I think my family is more where the family is going in the future. It's more of an extended, loose network, but we're family. It's no joke—you don't mess with my brother, you don't mess with my sister. We're very loyal, and we're very close in some ways, but it's not a nuclear family. I think there's a lot of concern these days about the survival of the black family, the African American family. It's a genuine concern, and I think it's important for people to nurture that in their art and in their work. At the same time, in my family, my mom has five kids, we have four different fathers, we have various relationships with our fathers, and those fathers have kids from their other marriages. I have a total of thirteen brothers and sisters, and they're all different colors.

"I think that's where things are headed. Not just women heading the household, but more multicultural families, more families that are able to survive because of the extended, communal care for one another, keeping people from ending up homeless and all that madness. We always had that. On Christmas we had adopted uncles and cousins and friends, kids with no parents, and parents with no kids. We kind of mixed and matched, and everyone took care of one another. I think that with our scarce resources, especially in the black community, where we have a war going on, this is one of the things that's going to get us through. People tell me all kinds of little twisted psychological theories about how messed up I should be because of the way I was brought up. But for me the extended family is an incredible support system. It's something I wouldn't give up or change. I don't think I'm all messed up. I think I'm fine."

Royal Alsup described for us the extended family tradition of the Native American community, with "nondescendant, nonbloodline aunts and uncles. A lot of times aunts and uncles are people from the same tribe who just come over and stay. Sometimes when

I do family psychotherapy, I might have fifteen people in one room. I say, 'Are you living in the house?' If they say yes, I say, 'Well, join the group.' So we have to have the whole extended family.

"Once a man went over the cliffs driving along the coast, and they couldn't find the body. So the medicine people were searching for it. They set up camp over by the cliffs. Caucasian people would say to me, 'Why are those Indians going down there? They're not even related to the person that got killed.' I said, 'Yes, they are. It's a tribe.' We have a tribal family, not just an extended family."

These new views of the family are reflected in research, futurist Willis Harman told us. "The Vanier Institute in Ottawa has been exploring this very question for many years: What is the future of the family? They use the term *familial relationships*. They say that, on the one hand, we all need familial relationships; and the big change is we will probably cherish them more and more. We went through a low spot in that regard," he reminded us. "On the other hand, the variety of arrangements that we will allow for securing those familial relationships is going to be much broader. I think that is probably a pretty accurate prediction, that familial relationships will be the core of everything, but they won't all be in the biological family."

Systems scientist Bela Banathy shared his views and his own story: "If you have a strong commitment to your family, and you see it as an association of people who have their own identities but are still bound together by love, the family becomes the most remarkable expression of what a small social system is. Next year is our fiftieth anniversary. We have four sons, and they have their own families. We have ten grandchildren and one great-granddaughter. We have experienced how a small social system works with members of our family, not only within the home but outside it.

"The family unit has many dimensions. It has social and economic dimensions, the dimensions of learning and human development, of governance, ethics, and wellness, which includes physical, mental, and spiritual aspects. All these dimensions are integrated into a pattern. What binds us together is love for one another, respect, and devotion. The family is a system in the sense that you can consciously nurture it and develop it and be aware of it and explicitly build a mutually shared vision of what the family wants to become."

This notion of the family as a system has generated extensive research and innovative approaches to psychological treatment. Instead of treating individual family members separately, as was done in the past, psychologists now approach the family as a unit.

A systems view of the family also has important implications for fostering a partnership approach. As a microcosm of society, the family can act as a crucible for the creation of partnership. It seems the most obvious place to start, with the people we love most and are closest to. In close relationships we let down our guard, and we discover that our less flattering moments can be a source of learning and fun instead of embarrassment.

How we use our creativity may well be defined in these early stages: are we drawn toward creations that will reflect the warm relationship in our family, or will we "heat things up" in a cold family that does not pay enough attention to us? Researchers have found that children from warm families, in which they get a lot of attention, are more sympathetic, helpful, caring, and supportive. The children turn out less defensive and more sociable, cooperative, and sure of their worth. Being ignored by a cold family can do a lot to make a child—and a grown-up—feel worthless.

The researchers point out that until recently most of this attention and warmth was created by the mother. In the dominator family the stereotypical woman's role is to keep the fires burning both literally and figuratively. As the roles in the home change, however, men will take on more responsibility in this area.

Researchers also found that warm families do not have many rigid rules and regulations, but are "practically *invented* by their members." In other words, the family is constantly being created and re-created by family members. The evidence does seem to point toward the importance of nurturing one another, and of co-creating one's life and one's environment.

Creation is not a lonely struggle anymore but a shared project. Because there are fewer rules and regulations to shield us from the threat of having to think for ourselves, we have to acquire sensitivity to ourselves and others and learn to pay attention. We simply become more aware.

Perhaps one of the reasons why the spiritual search in the West often gets sidetracked is because we focus on remarkable experiences, whether it's speaking in tongues or seeing God. These experiences have their place, but by paying very close attention to home we can come to see the remarkable in the ordinary.

Working

Isabella Reports from Paradise

Once there was an island in the middle of the South Pacific, an atoll of white sandy beaches, ten miles long, with tall coconut trees and green waters inside the calm lagoon. The blue ocean surf pounded the coral reef, dissolving into white foam. This island was deserted except for one man, an old man who had lived there alone for twenty-five years. He had visited this island in his youth, and throughout his life he had but one dream: to return and make the island his home. He worked hard, he married, he had children who grew up and went their own way. His wife left to follow her own dreams, and he continued to work hard and save every penny. When he turned fifty, he put together everything he needed, persuaded a friend with a sailboat to give him a lift across several hundred miles of ocean, and settled alone on the island of his dreams. His name was Tom Neal, and as you can imagine, he was quite an unusual fellow. When I met him, he had spent twenty years on the island.

He appeared out of nowhere in the middle of a coconut grove, blue, navy shorts, bare chest, a machete in one hand and a green coconut in the other.

"You must be thirsty," he said.

I was so surprised all I could do was nod. I had forgotten to bring my canteen and had been walking for a few hours. We had dropped anchor in the calm lagoon earlier that day for a week of rest between two long ocean passages on our fifty-foot ketch. It was past noon, and the tropical sun was hot. I was very thirsty indeed.

With two deft strokes of his machete, Tom opened the top of the coconut and handed it to me. Then he stood there, watching me drink the delicious milk with thirsty gulps, drops sliding down my hands and throat. I drank it all without pausing and was out of breath when I finally stopped.

"Thank you," I said. "I was very thirsty."

Tom took the coconut from my hands, propped it up on the ground and cut it neatly in half with one stroke, then he sliced a sliver from its shell and with it made a gesture to scoop up the insides. The meat that lined the green coconut had the consistency of a light custard and was as refreshing as ice cream.

"I must be going now," said Tom after my first bite. "I have so much to do, you know, the chickens to feed, the tomatoes to water . . ." On his last, trailing words he disappeared as quickly as he had materialized.

We ended up spending much more time on Tom's island than we had anticipated, which was good, because I learned some important and unexpected lessons there. I had been somewhat depressed for a few months. As a psychologist, I recognized all the symptoms, but I could not find the cause. After all, I had been living the dream life, a leisurely cruise from island to island, from one tropical paradise to the next. No pressure, no worries, no deadlines, just a few daily tasks interspersed with snorkeling and swimming and reading and lying in the sun. I had thoroughly enjoyed the slow pace and the minimal demands on my schedule. I could feel my body and my mind relaxing after the hectic life I had been leading before departure. Life at sea was like a balm for the soul. Whenever I thought about my friends back home, still trapped in the rat race, I felt sorry for them.

Then, slowly, a malaise had set in. Every day I was becoming more melancholic and less motivated to take care of even the smallest task. From this sort of heavy stupor I watched Tom, wondering how he had managed twenty years of a life-style that had brought me to my knees in eighteen months.

Soon it became clear that Tom's day was crammed with activities. From dawn to dusk he followed a rigid work schedule that left almost no time for leisure. Only at sunset would he sit with a cup of tea on a wooden bench on the beach and watch the sun drop below the horizon. The most fascinating part of Tom's routine was just before teatime: He would spend two hours shoveling sand from one side of the beach to the other. Tom's shoveling style was as efficient and precise as his handling of the machete. In spite of his age and the physical strain, Tom carried on as if he were training for the shoveling Olympics. He would assess with obvious pride the results of his effort, then march off to take a shower and prepare his tea.

As I watched him work from my boat, sitting in a comfortable deck chair, I tried to figure out the purpose of Tom's daily shoveling, but I couldn't come up with a single plausible hypothesis. Finally I gave up and asked him.

"The tide moves the sand to the right side of the beach and changes its shape," explained Tom. "When I sit here at teatime and look across the lagoon, I like to see the beach in the foreground with the shape it had when I first came to the island. I like it better that way."

In a flash I understood that Tom had escaped depression because he kept busy with tasks he liked and he was good at. That, in a nutshell, was the goal and meaning of work. He could easily have exhausted what he needed to do in half a day and spent the rest of the time in complete leisure. Yet he had constructed additional work for himself and restricted his leisure to less than a third of the daylight. Tom taught me that leisure has meaning only in the context of work, and only when the balance is in favor of work. Of course I had heard many times before that "idle hands do the devil's work" and similar ancient and wise proverbs, but I had never believed them until I watched Tom go about his daily life through the eyes of my melancholic apathy. Tom taught me that work is more than providing for our basic needs; it is in itself an integral part of our well-being.

The issue is more complex, of course. I could easily have filled my day with all sorts of activities: sanding and varnishing the woodwork, scraping the bottom of the boat, making necklaces out of seashells. But the truth was, these were not activities at which I was particularly adept or that gave me much sense of accomplishment. I learned lesson number two: The nature of the task and its psychological payback to the individual is another essential aspect to work. In my particular case, I realized that I am very much a daughter of my own age and civilization, because only in "civilized" society do I find the tasks that are meaningful to me. The first few months at

129

sea were pleasant and healing. I found that when I returned home after three years at sea, I had an enormous amount of energy and creativity that allowed me to accomplish everything I had dreamt up during my voyage. My adventure taught me that at regular intervals I had to leave my work life and regenerate at sea, in that very environment that is bound to give me depression if I indulge for too long. To my surprise, I have found that weekends are not sufficient to recharge me completely. I gladly give them up in exchange for an extended time of leisure so that I can complete a cycle that includes rest and detoxification. This allows me to slip into a quieter rhythm of contemplation, communion with nature, and meditation from which I emerge full of creative energy and ideas.

Balance is the key, allowing the different aspects of the self to be listened to and expressed. Even the unpleasant but necessary tasks, the ones that I would rather avoid, have an important side effect: They make the meaningful tasks more pleasurable and keep me grateful for being able to earn my living doing mostly what I find rewarding and creative.

I also learned that for workaholics, who even pack their leisure with all kinds of tasks, work becomes an escape from themselves. They make no time for contemplation and create no opportunity for getting to know their own souls. So lesson number three is that leisure too has different components and different functions, from rest to fun, from adventure to self-exploration and dreaming the dreams that tomorrow will give work its meaning.

Surfing on the Waves of Change

Through the ages, the balance between necessary but unpleasant tasks and meaningful activities, as well as the different kinds of leisure, has been more an issue of class than of individual choice. When the dominator system is strongest, the division of activities is extreme, so that the leisure classes are precisely that, and the serfs (whether slaves, medieval peasants, or migrant workers) do all the necessary but unpleasant tasks. This configuration carries the seeds of its own undoing, however, for the serfs will always struggle to reach leisure. But the leisure class is not that well-off either, as Isabella had occasion to learn from her three years in "paradise."

In a partnership society each person would be allowed to find his or her balance between necessity, meaningful work, and leisure; finding and reassessing this balance would be part of a person's job. As a society we are still struggling with these issues and have been able to consider them only since World War II, when most Western economies started generating widespread wealth. When survival or mere subsistence is at stake, a society can focus only on the overwhelming needs of the moment, and questions of meaningful work and leisure are considered purely academic. But we believe that the world has enough wealth to move all of humanity above survival and subsistence. Even more wealth could be generated if only global priorities shifted from a dominator mode of aggression, defense, and exploitation to education and stewardship, motivated by partnership values rather than fear and self-protection.

More and more workers in the United States are refusing promotions that involve relocation because they would disrupt family life. Many men and women report that they would sacrifice employment opportunities for the sake of spending more time with their children. We personally know of several people who, having achieved a certain level of financial stability, opt to quit well-paying jobs to seek more meaningful though less lucrative work. They want to give something back to society and help create for others some of the opportunities they had available to themselves.

Willis Harman confirmed this trend. "I think you can already see that people, some people anyway, are demanding that work life be primarily self-development, where you voluntarily have joined an organization of other people involved in developing themselves through doing something useful for society. That's totally different from being a paid slave in a corporation dedicated to the enrichment of some small group of people. Qualitatively it's a different setting, and that means that all the details are different as well. A lot of jobs may be essentially the same, mechanically speaking, but they would be in a totally different framework of meaning.

"I have known some organizations that were clearly voluntary associations of people involved in finding fulfillment in their own lives. And to do this, people had to be involved in something socially meaningful, because human beings are built that way. Society offers a tremendous variety of worthwhile pursuits. What's important is to get together to do something you feel is worthwhile, be it through a business or a nonprofit organization. People do get paid, and some organizations make a profit. But that's a secondary consideration.

"We can already see a few examples. The first one I ever encountered was the Rouse Company. The Rouse Company is the company that built Columbia, Maryland, and rebuilt the city centers of Baltimore and Hartford. More than twenty years ago, when I first

131

met Jim Rouse, this was a relatively small company. All the people in it agreed on the mission statement; they had a set of goals. The number one goal, and I have to paraphrase, was self-fulfillment—the self-realization of the people involved. The second goal was to do something worthwhile for society. The third goal was to do those two things well enough so that you just automatically made a profit to stay in business. I think that in the future we are going to see many more examples; organizations of that sort will become predominant in order to attract and hold the most creative people. Then, of course, the question is, what happens to these tremendous corporations that have been built up?"

Futurist Paul Saffo believes that they will be transformed. "A colleague of mine, Richard Adler, coined the term *virtual company*. A virtual company is something that looks like a company to the outside world but in fact may be a loose alliance of smaller companies. Ocean Spray is an interesting example. It's a growers' cooperative. True Value hardware stores, same thing; it's an owners' cooperative of hardware stores. We're going to see companies built on a more organic model, where alliances are made and broken and the arteries and blood vessels of these corporate animals are computer systems."

Through our work as management consultants, we are witnessing firsthand what in other parts of this book we have called the changing of the tide: different currents mix and create whirlpools, with waves going in all directions. At the very top of the most forward-thinking and enlightened corporations, executives not only understand rationally but feel in their guts the sweeping changes affecting economic forces throughout the world. Industries that have dominated the market for decades forecast significant shrinkage in their market shares. They anticipate radical shifts not only in the way they do business but in the kind of business they are in. Industries and occupations that never existed before are springing up almost overnight.

Most executives we talk to see a future where the market pressures are going to dictate a need for extreme flexibility and adaptability. This requires a streamlined, agile, intelligent, and well-prepared work force, a minimum of hierarchy, and a high degree of individual accountability. This also implies considerably fewer opportunities for traditional career paths, advancements, promotions, and openings at the top. It also implies that the higher-level positions will no longer be as secure and stable as in the past. There is no guarantee that the same position will be available tomorrow. To survive and thrive in this different environment, individuals will need to find different sources of satisfaction and different measures of success.

In this changing tide, those who are still motivated by traditional values that describe success as a vertical climb will be disappointed. As the pyramid gets smaller, only a very few can be admitted to the apex; all others will lose out. Thus for those still in the ebbing tide, their careers will necessarily be a losing game, ending in bitterness or resigned acceptance. Most of the complaints we hear from middle management and below have to do with decreasing career opportunities. Clearly people have not yet gotten the message about the vast change that lies ahead. It is as if they were clamoring to have more of a currency that was about to be taken out of circulation.

Relatively few people are now asking for different options, but in these requests we hear the sound of the new wave. For when we look into the future, we see loosely connected teams forming to produce goods or perform services in response to or in anticipation of a particular need or window of opportunity. Once the goal is achieved and the task performed, the teams disband and its members join other teams. In this scenario, the function of the leader is more that of facilitator and coordinator than commander. We will hear analogies taken more from the arts, academia, and cooperative sports and less from war, combat, and aggressive sports. John Sculley, the chairman of Apple Computer, likens the good executive to an impresario or an orchestra director who inspires, supports, and keeps the tempo for the people who are the true performers.

In the new workplace managers may gradually be replaced by mentors, who will guide apprentices. Leadership positions might be temporary and by election or mandate from other workers, as opposed to appointment from above. This is already happening in some form in worker-owned corporations. The circle or the helix will likely replace the pyramid as the geometric metaphor for a successful career path. Breadth of expertise and cross-functional experience will be the sought-after skills in tomorrow's workers. The people called to forge the vision of the corporation of the future will have grown not vertically, within a single function, but laterally. They will have demonstrated the ability to grasp and master disparate functions, perhaps in more than one industry. Flexibility, adaptability, and breadth of experience are already necessary in small companies, which are becoming the economic backbone in more and more countries. Another crucial skill, presently in short supply, is the

133

ability to step down from a "higher" position to take assignments with less glamorous titles, in response either to an organizational or a personal need.

Recently Isabella was listening to the confession of a senior vice-president in a Fortune 500 corporation. For a number of years he had climbed the corporate ladder and had reached a position of considerable influence. But lately, following a few miscalculated steps and a series of internal political maneuvers, he had come into disfavor. He feared he would be asked to resign. Yet he did not want to leave this company, to which he had developed a strong attachment. He wished he had the courage to take a step down to avoid the highly political atmosphere of the executive suite and to heal his wounds yet continue to make a contribution to the company's future. "Even if I found the strength to do so," he told her, "the system would make it impossible for me to do so. A step down is considered a failure; and if you are seen as a failure, you cannot operate successfully."

There are exceptions, however—successful ones. In another company we consult with, a distributorship with a series of branches over a wide territory, the position of branch manager is one of the most coveted and is typically achieved after demonstrated success as a salesperson. Occasionally an exceptional salesperson turns out to be a very mediocre branch manager. These people are strongly encouraged not to leave the company but to return to a sales position. The loss of prestige is compensated by higher income deriving from commissions.

A rather well-known "step down" was taken by Deborah Coleman, "Debi" to the people of Apple Computer. Having demonstrated an extraordinary ability to launch the company's manufacturing facility in Fremont, California, making it a model of flexibility, efficiency, and quality in record time, she took over the leadership of Apple's worldwide operations in her early thirties. At thirty-four she became the company's chief financial officer, the youngest woman and the only woman holding this post in a Fortune 500 company. For a variety of reasons, two years later she decided to take a six-month sabbatical. The price tag attached to this move was a year in corporate limbo, a vague title with vague assignments, a situation known to discourage even the strongest souls and usually leading to resignation. At the time, an article appeared in the *San Francisco Chronicle* with her picture, alongside those of a couple of Apple executives who had recently left the company, with the caption "These executives are out." This was followed by the pictures of three executives who were "in." Debi is not motivated by the traditional values of climbing the ladder just for the sake of climbing, however, and she is keenly aware that the executive of the future is one who has a thorough understanding of the corporation as a system. So she stayed on, and when the company needed someone to accept a major challenge in an area that desperately needed leadership and vision, she was ready. She became vice-president in charge of the company's information system. Her own people marveled at the speed with which she grasped this highly technical subject. By the age of thirty-nine, this remarkable woman was in the process of assimilating experience in three major functions of a six-billion-dollar corporation. In a few years she will be ready to lead a company with an intimate understanding of how a whole system works, by far a more solid background for the corporation of the future than that of the average CEO of the past. (In November, 1992, Ms. Coleman joined Tektronix in Portland, Oregon.)

Lateral moves and rotational assignments, which are still viewed as consolation prizes in lieu of a promotion, will in our opinion become the sought-after career path, bringing fulfillment more than status.

Robert Haywood, vice-president of Power Planning and Contracts at Pacific Gas & Electric Company (PG&E), shared his views on the matter.

"In most organizations, the position you currently hold, or a higher one, will be your position for life. That will not work in the future. There is going to be a lot more flexibility. You may be leading a team in one area and be on another team somewhere else. The need to respond to external forces is so pivotal that if the company is going to survive and succeed, it needs a group who can unite around that need and hold it as the binding common vision. That common ground is so important that it has the power to supersede personal ego. You have to set up systems that are fair, but fairness entails a lot of flexibility; fairness won't mean somebody is locked into a position. The successful group will assume that the need to respond to external forces is greater than the ego need. This doesn't mean we are going to become saints; we are all going to need education to create rapidly adaptable yet fair organizations."

In the past, work has been an economic exchange: money and other perks in exchange for mental or physical sweat. As the paradigms on which the world turns change, the nature of work will also change. It has been known for years that, past the subsistence level, the majority of workers give compensation only third or fourth place in the list of motivators. Satisfaction, a sense of accomplishment, and respect usually come first. An opportunity to exercise and nurture one's creativity will probably become a major motivator for the worker of the future. The urge to create and to be creative is fundamental to human nature, and now people are awakening or reawakening to this reality. The workplace that offers this opportunity and that requires this type of performance will therefore be able to attract and retain the best talents.

Robert Haywood described how the seed of PG&E's innovative energy plan came into being. "We got together smart people who are able to think out of the box. They're very sharp, very positive, very proactive thinkers, and very creative—a great team, top-notch people. We told them, 'You have our total support, go make it happen.' We wanted to see this happen, and we would take care of selling it to top management. So we gave them permission to think differently. To me this is part of the leadership's function: to give people the freedom and the encouragement to think differently, and I believe that is how our Green Resource Plan was born.

"People want to be creative; they have a natural urge to be creative. The dark side of a corporation is when rules and regulations snuff out creativity. In spite of the fact that you are in a corporation, you have to say, 'Make it happen, just let it flow, I want the creativity.' It's not just that creativity is demanded or encouraged, but rather 'Do me a favor, be creative.'

"As a result, some strange surprises occur in a very difficult area, that of reward systems. The reward is in the creativity itself, being part of something that is bigger than you but doesn't work without you. What you put in gets bigger because of what the others put in. You not only feel blessed because of what you gave, you also feel given to because of what they gave, you feel you are on the cutting edge of the wave. The human being's purpose and fulfillment is to grasp reality in a way that he or she didn't yesterday. That, in a sense, is almost Godlike. You feel powerful, you feel good; self-esteem is not an issue anymore. Why wouldn't you feel good? The reward system is built into that. You create a positive-feedback loop.

"This will get better business results than you can possibly get in any other system. People will have a high morale, and they will be fulfilled. Once this starts, you can't stop it. Once you teach the bear to dance, you can't tell it when to stop. It will decide. Once you open up that sense that this is where we're going and people start trusting it and doing it, it will have a life of its own, and that's the good part."

Debi Coleman is an enthusiastic believer in creativity. "This is the spirit of Apple: it's the Apple slogan, 'the power to be your best.'

That's what living is all about, testing all your limits—physical, intellectual, emotional. All those limits are set by society, by your parents. I don't think you are really living unless you are testing those limits. One of the best ways to challenge me, personally, is to tell me that it can't be done. I just don't accept that."

How Will We Work?

The mental model of work in corporate America is changing, and with it, the skills and behaviors that workers and employers are asking of each other.

"Communication consistently emerges as the most important skill," Robert Haywood told us. "Certainly you have to be technically smart. That is essential. But better communication, better ways of working together, better ways of sharing information are equally crucial. In situations where you need to anticipate incredible change in every area, the old models have become quite anachronistic: Paper, mounds of paper, command and control, rigid systems, hierarchical communication that trickles down with all sorts of filters are deadly. They don't work. By the time it gets down to people the message is lost anyway. What works instead is a minimum of paper, getting everybody involved, building consensus. This is what people mean when they talk about communication: real time, get everybody together, no hierarchy, we are all searchers for truth. As each person brings to the table his or her piece, a lot of communication goes on. Suddenly a statement made by the chairman a week ago is put in a context and makes sense. If it had been read in a memo on a Monday morning, the meaning would have been lost."

Teamwork is emerging as another major shift in the structure of work. It is as if corporate America had suddenly awakened to the fact that when people work together, they are more effective and creative than when they are set up to compete against one another. The CEO of a major corporation that produces goods you probably have in your refrigerator, told us the story of how the former chairman had set up the succession to his job.

"He had three of us competing neck-and-neck. All we could think about was who and how we could get to the top. This almost destroyed the company. It was the worst period of my life."

As the emphasis shifts to teamwork, people are scrambling to adapt, making mistakes, and falling into old traps. Yet they are becoming aware that an organization is a web of interdependencies and that the cost of ignoring this reality could well mean the end of a business. Workers are asking for the means to implement this

137

change. They are clamoring for more and better communication, for the breaking down of walls that keep the organization of work stovepiped, and for tools to help them work together. Training in communication and listening, conflict resolution, negotiation, and similar skills can facilitate the transition from a competitive environment, where the push to prevail over others is a primary motivation, to one that puts a premium on the ability to work with others. But these tools can be effective only if they are used in the context of a deeper mind shift. As long as the dominator paradigm shapes the goals and structure of the corporation, these efforts will be only marginally effective.

At the core of true teamwork is a vision that fires the imagination and that allows each person to do her or his best for a common effort because each contributes to, understands, and believes in the vision.

"I was first introduced to the embryonic group that became the Macintosh group in 1981, when I was being recruited by Steve Jobs," Debi Coleman reminisced. "There were only four or five people hidden in a building called Texaco Tower, and they didn't have any official status as a separate division or as a product line, but they did have Steve Jobs, and they did have a vision, and they did have a dream. These four or five people whom I initially met truly believed they were going to design, build, and sell to *the world* a desktop information appliance, the moral equivalent of the Cuisinart. Actually, to Steve it was more like a bicycle; he wasn't building a minivan, and he wasn't building a Cadillac. This information appliance was conceived of as 'wheels for the mind,' and that was Steve's analogy, by the way. He saw that very powerfully: That even without steam and jet engine fuel you could still go pretty far just on a bicycle, and a bicycle is portable; in China it's the main form of transportation.

"I'm sure you have heard the story of when we occupied a building on 'Apple Boulevard' and we hoisted the pirate flag! We were not bad pirates, we were good pirates. We were not in the official navy, we didn't have to follow military rules and procedures, but we were world-class sailors and were on this voyage. The journey was the reward.

"I have a picture hanging on the wall where I am with many of the original team. The tag line is 'We did it for us,' and we did! We were basically designing an information appliance that we could use in our job, in school; a lot of the people who were on the team were just barely out of college or in college at the time. They were students, and we conceived this notion that the education we were addressing was C through D: College through Death! (The Apple II group of course had the K through twelve educational market).

"When we introduced the Macintosh our idea was to have in a booth a span of ninety years, from a five-year-old to a ninety-five-year-old, each in this booth using the Macintosh. I think this is vision! I thought that was powerful and very audacious, and we were thinking that way all the time.

"I'll never forget a dinner we had with some of the women in the group; one of them had the audacity to say, 'But after all, it's only a computer!' The rest of us jumped on her. 'What do you mean it's only a computer?! We're going to change the world! We are going to save the world from the dark ages of computing! We're going to bring the power to individuals!' We really did think that we were going to change the world. We really believed that we were going to change the way people learned, worked, communicated, maybe even the way they had a good time . . . and we did."

Bob Haywood described the process by which he worked with his people to establish the business objectives for the year. "We had done a terrific job in the previous year. We had well-thought-out objectives and plans. We could have dusted them off a little bit, changed a few dates, and had it done. But I said, 'Wait a minute, what a trap! This assumes status quo, and this may not be the case.' So I said, 'Let's just forget about last year's goals. Blow them up. If we come up with the same ones, we verify that it's all right to implement them very quickly. Let's set aside a day in which we all come in as managers of our departments and talk about the industry as it is today and where you think it's going. I'm not looking for overheads or presentations; any way you want to do it, verbally or otherwise, is fine.'

"We went away from the office, got out of the daily pressures. We went as seekers of truth, with a pact to challenge each other. Of course each of us is thinking about these issues all the time, but when we go off-site together, five very smart people, who know about each other's business, we help one another develop our thinking. From this a mesh slowly emerges, a common model that evolves in the mind. This is not a computer model; it's in the mind, and it's powerful because you can change it instantly. You can test assumptions, you can test scenarios, you can discuss what-ifs together, and you don't go far off because the others will push you along or pull you back.

139

"In one day we had this incredible feeling that we had gotten hold of a crystal ball, almost, of the truth built on the best information available in the market today. We had a sense of power and understanding, and if someone came in whom we needed to convince, we could do it. An intellectual bonding took place. People were energized. They enjoyed it so much. Although it started with, 'I've got a busy agenda, I've told you all this before, there is nothing that we don't really know, but I'm on the spot and let me do it,' we moved to an attitude of, 'Boy, this is the best thing we could be doing! I have a list of changes I'm going to make immediately, but more than that, I now have a sense of this market.'

"Since then I have been taking this process to every part of my organization. I meet with all the people at every level of my organization in groups of fifteen. I sketch down ideas as I talk, making them see certain comparisons and asking what would happen if our industry got restructured. In this way I get a debate going, I get people's ideas going. This gets people charged up, and the discussion can go in a lot of directions, including how we manage our own department. But the important point is that they start building their own mental model about these changes that are about to occur. It's almost like a recruitment process. Even those who come in with the attitude 'What am I doing here? Here goes another day, and I have so many things to do,' all of a sudden wake up and get involved.

"The whole purpose in this exercise is to make people aware of the fact that we live in a world of incredible change, of uncertainty, and we need to watch out for our assumptions, our biases and mental models. Unbeknownst to us, they can lead us to the wrong place. Then we move from the intellectual debate, from talking about models, to talking about how this makes us feel, living in this world of uncertainty. The objective here is to deal with the emotional aspect of the change, which on the one hand is cause for anxiety but on the other offers many opportunities. At the end of the day we focus on personal vision. Individually we look at our life's vision. Take away all the shelters and hurdles and the I-couldn't-do-that-becauses. Take them away and forget current reality. Envision the best that you can possibly be. Just let your mind go with it. What is your vision for your life?

"People need this vision. There is a gap between the vision and the current reality called creative tension. The more you can direct every ounce of your energy toward closing that gap, the more creative you are, the better you are. We are all just a sum of energy; my whole life is so many ergs of energy. The more I can direct it, so that it doesn't get dissipated having arguments with the wrong people or simply getting lost in trivia, the more I can focus it toward closing that creative tension, and the more fulfilled I become."

Once again, it is important to stress that partnership does not mean a utopian community where people live in harmony ever after. This is precisely the misconception that guided the early work in organizational development, which gave team building a bad reputation. As traditional hierarchical authority was eroding, organizations tried to substitute it with the ideal of one happy family working together in harmony. The consequence is that many of today's managers have grown up with the idea that disagreement is bad, and they shrink from any kind of conflict. In the partnership paradigm, conflicts are part and parcel of life, and efforts are directed at finding creative win-win solutions. It's only in the dominator system that conflicts need to be avoided, because they imply a confrontation that results in overt or covert warfare with lots of casualties along the way.

"There were some good things and there were some bad things about the experience of the original Macintosh team," according to Debi Coleman. "The pirate flag was a bit of flipping our nose to the rest of the organization and setting us apart. We were known for calling the rest of the organization bozos. In retrospect, we would have done better to have identified the 'enemy' as an external force, such as any of the big companies 'conspiring' to keep personal computing power out of the hands of individuals. I think that would have been a more enabling vision. Doing it internally, within Apple, caused a lot of problems. We had tremendous success, but we created this tension within Apple, when actually Apple was our banker. It put up the funds for the development work and put up with our numerous antics, including the pirate flag and delays on delivery.

"In retrospect I don't feel that this attitude was very healthy. It set up an unnecessary us-versus-them mentality. If we had the concept of total quality management that we have today, we would have done it differently. We would have identified the processes in the rest of the company, such as designing a product, marketing it, pricing it, et cetera, and we could have worked with those appropriate people. Then we could have been iconoclastic and challenged the way they did things and try to create new processes. If they did not adapt to what we thought was necessary and essential, we could have created another model. But we didn't do that. We just assumed

141

that everything they did was wrong, and we reinvented the wheel constantly. That, I think, led up to the disillusionment of business and to the management and economic crisis that the company faced in mid-1985."

The authors have witnessed corporations go through traumatic and disruptive reorganizations because one executive could not sit down with a colleague and say, "We have a difference of opinion" or "I am losing confidence in your plan to handle this situation." Instead of open dialogue, they prefer to skirt the issue; through reorganization they decrease the other person's responsibilities, until that person feels obligated to resign. In the process scores of people throughout the organization are subjected to unnecessary pain. This would not happen if conflicts and differences of opinion were seen as opportunities to work through differences and evolve creative options.

Of course this behavioral shift takes honesty and courage. It requires that people in positions of power open themselves to questioning. It entails the willingness to take substantial risks.

"In a few days we are going to have a department meeting with all two hundred people," Robert Haywood told us. "Ross McGowan and Ann Frazer of the TV show 'People Are Talking' will run it, and we are going to have open and honest dialogue. This couple has a way of working with the audience so that in one and a half hours you can quickly get to the heart of the issues. They are able to keep the conversation going and the energy high. Although the mood is light, the issues are serious, because people want communication, real gut-level, face-to-face, two-way, honest communication. This idea of putting the entire system in one room is very powerful, because you can actually experience all the feedback loops that happen in a system. You start with one issue, which then leads to another issue. The danger is that today's solutions become tomorrow's problems, so you don't want to misquote people trying to get out of an issue. If you don't know, you say you don't. On the other hand, if you've got a real sense of why you're doing something, say you're doing it even if others disagree. If you're trying to stonewall somebody or cover up something, setting up a feedback loop will cause you far more problems. Most organizations have rules that specify what you can and cannot tell people and how you should manage them. But the truth is, you can't manage them anymore. Instead you've got to free them. The workplace of the future is going to be a much nicer place to work, a much more humane and healthy place. A lot of the stress caused by dishonesty and covering up will heal.

"At this session all the managers will be lined up on stage. Then we let all the people go at us. What are your questions? What is going wrong? What is going right? What do we celebrate? What are our values? If they do not wish to ask their questions directly, people can write them on cards and pass them to the facilitators. I have learned that you do not need to worry about being crucified. If someone gets off base, others will intervene and say, 'Wait a minute! That's not right.' They value this type of communication. They start to treasure it, and they don't want to see it violated."

"Everyone says you're either part of the problem or you're part of the solution. I was definitely part of the problem sometimes," Debi Coleman acknowledged. "I definitely made decisions that contributed to problems the way they are today. You have to acknowledge that, understand what you did wrong and why. After you acknowledge that you're part of the problem, go and fix it. Do something! A day doesn't go by without something that I believed to be true being shown to be wrong. So what? I don't think you have to get your ego too tied to what you believed or implemented in the past. Everything gets challenged over time; systems are known as error-correction cycles. It comes to a point where you have to make a leap of faith; even with everything all laid out, you still have to make a leap of faith, you have to want to be part of the change and help manage it and not have too much tied up in the status quo or what the ultimate result is."

The Changing Nature of the Corporation

Futurist Paul Saffo traced the origin of the changes in corporate structure and philosophy to the technological changes that have taken place over the last one hundred years.

"We're in the middle of a real pattern of change, particularly in technology. The PC [personal computer] was the horseless carriage of the information revolution. I think the PC is the start of the revolution, not the end of one. The information revolution is only about ten years old and is just now picking up steam. I think we're in a thirty- to fifty-year period where we are actually witnessing the move to a paperless society. I qualify that: We're not going to abandon the use of paper, but we're going to do more things with electronics that we once did with paper. We will someday become paperless the way we once became horseless. Commuters did not give up their horses to drive cars; commuting didn't exist until we had automobiles. The new technology won't replace paper technology directly. Instead it's going to displace it with new activities that will keep us from using paper the way we do now. That's a big change. If you look at the impact of information technology in organizations, the notion of the modern corporation is changing very, very rapidly. Looking back, we will say the modern corporation was invented in the 1870s in Germany, reached its high point with General Motors around 1965, and went into a long, slow decline, then was replaced by a new model sometime after the year 2000, with information technology playing a big part in that change. It has eroded the traditional corporate barriers.

"Before the 1870s, the model for companies was the monarchy. There was a great man, like Andrew Carnegie, at the center, and everything flowed in and out of his office. The arrival of reliable postal service and telegraph caused events to start moving so quickly that a monarchical organization couldn't keep up with them.

"A couple of German businessmen borrowed the German army staff command model and created an organization around a command-and-control hierarchy. This was the genesis of the modern corporation. When telephones arrived in the 1930s, corporations changed yet again. We may think other technologies moved us out to the suburbs, but it was the phone that made the suburban metropolis possible. Before the telephone, an executive had to work within walking distance of the factory. The moment you had telephones, you could create these white-collar executive ghettos dozens of miles from the factories so all the white-collar workers could go work in vertical villages like Manhattan. Then computers allowed more complexity. The apotheosis of the command-and-control hierarchy was General Motors in the mid-1960s. But after that, events started picking up even more speed.

"Peter Drucker wrote a brilliant article titled 'The Coming of the New Organization,' where he said that white-collar executives are disappearing because their function was to move information around within the organization, and that function will be taken over by computers. We're seeing a shift from the individual to the business team as the basic unit of productivity. Drucker observed that the structure of organizations in the future will be more like symphony orchestras—bands of high-performance, semiautonomous people, violin section, horn section, who are coordinated by central management rather than controlled by central management."

Traditional organizations have been struggling with the issue of centralization versus decentralization for many years. In classical reductionistic fashion, these two concepts have been seen as antithetical, and companies typically have moved from one to the other without ever seeming to find the optimum point of equilibrium. From a systems perspective, this juxtaposition is unnecessary. It is not a question of one or the other but of how we can learn to do both simultaneously. The environmentalist motto Think Globally, Act Locally, which is, by the very nature of the movement that has generated it, a systems application, serves us well here. It is not an easy lesson to learn, nor an easy concept to apply, particularly when those who must apply it have spent their entire careers within an either/or model.

"The change is phenomenal," said Debi Coleman, "and it's happening right here, right now, in this organization. In the old paradigm, the model was decentralized versus centralized. I claim that is not even relevant anymore. We have to create a highly networked, interdependent organization where pieces of the puzzle are worked on or parts of the systems and services are handled by various competency centers and groups that are united by a global strategy and by a plan that is locally implemented. Because we're highly interdependent, highly networked, communication becomes the big issue. We have to do much more with less money and fewer resources. We have to be more responsive. We have to build systems that are more flexible and scalable. We have to improve our time to market. This is going to take tremendous discipline, and we have to leave the old behind."

More and more companies are realizing the strategic importance of their information systems. In a world of fast-paced change, the speed, accuracy, and user-friendly format of information is essential for steering a course in treacherous waters. If the slow-moving vessels of ancient times could find their way through underwater ridges with slow and methodical soundings of a lead weight attached to a line, modern vessels require the speed, accuracy, precision, and readability of sonar. But information systems are much more than that; they are like the impulses running through the nerves and giving the brain the information needed for any activity, from the simplest to the most complex. Information technology also implies that many workers will become teleworkers, performing their tasks from homes or locations other than the workplace, sending in the fruit of their labors as bits of information transmitted over long distance.

145

"Organizations and companies are going to be much more amorphous, and defining our jobs will be much more difficult," Paul Saffo continued. "We're seeing everybody becoming more like consultants. Ultimately the line between work day and personal day will disappear completely."

Another important change made possible by the information revolution is the global nature of corporations. They transcend national boundaries and will eventually force the issue of an international currency. Corporations, even more urgently than nations, have to deal with the awesome challenge of a multicultural workforce. They have responded to the need with massive training in diversity, courses that explore the nature of prejudice and train people to interact across cultural, racial, and gender barriers. Again, all this is setting in motion forces that are bringing the new paradigm to the fore, and we find partnership, creativity, and systems thinking at work.

As perceptions about fundamental aspects of the work environment are changing, as more and more corporations are asking themselves, What business are we in? and How do we want to do business?, some are taking unprecedented steps.

"We live in a world that has dynamics that are much more powerful than one corporation's particular needs and desires," Robert Haywood told us. "What makes you successful is looking at those dynamics or trends and tapping into them and making them part of your business. The common mistake is to extend the present way of thinking into the future. Things are moving so fast that the major question for an executive is, have you moved your thinking process in the same direction of the change? The only way you can free yourself from current thinking is go through the process that I described before and tap into the best brains; and not only in your industry, because you also need to learn from the mistakes made in other industries.

"Psychologically this is not comfortable. Everything that you want to protect is threatened by the change. If you come up with a scenario that is plausible but devastating, the danger is that you may make it implausible because it's devastating. You may deny it because the cost is too high. This is a big mistake. Instead, by accepting the idea that it is plausible, you become motivated to deal with it in a strategic way that may cause pain, but you decide to take the short-term pain for the long-term gain.

"In Electric Resource Planning we have devised a strategy based on efficiency, competition, and renewables, which means we do not necessarily build new power plants. Instead we get efficiency and 'negawatts' (negative watts); we have made that a viable resource strategy in a profitable business. The electric utility industry has been built on the building of power plants, of course. That's the business you know, and that is what you're used to. Consequently there is some resistance to this idea of efficiency. But the business you know may not be the business in which you can make money anymore, and so we may need to change our business. We are going to be in a new business, the business of energy efficiency. It serves the purpose as well as building power plants and is acceptable to the public, regulators, customers, and environmental groups, so it makes sense on many fronts. This is what we need to do nationally and internationally because every time you go for efficiency versus generation you are reducing pollutants.

"Competition is the second part of our strategy. Competition is a new paradigm for utilities. We've noticed that if society has a choice between competition or monopoly, it will choose competition because that means freedom of choice, and it tends to lower prices. So PG&E is learning to support a competitive environment because it is good for our customers. They can get the benefit of our buying power from whoever can produce it the cheapest.

"Renewable resources is PG&E's third foundation cornerstone of our electric resource power strategy. We see a future when we'll come off fossil fuel, so we at PG&E support renewable resources.

"Customers and regulators we talk to about this say, 'Terrific! What a great strategy!' You don't make enemies with this strategy. In fact you become a hero. We have been invited to give presentations to Congress. We got an award from the President for our Green Resource Plan, and I was in the room when that idea was born. It makes you feel good. Talk about trusting the process! Examples like that tell me to trust the process absolutely because good things come out of it, and in a short time—one year. Having thought the unthinkable, we now have the 'greenest' resource plan in the United States in an industry that has notoriously been on the wrong side of the environmental equation. We have become part of the solution."

Putting Empathy into Economics

Along with business and industry, sweeping changes are occurring in economic theory. We asked Hazel Henderson, an economic analyst at the cutting edge of the new vision, to give us her perspective. An Americanized Englishwoman living in Florida, this renegade analyst seems infinitely more pragmatic and down-to-earth than any graph-wielding, back-off-I'm-a-scientist economist we've ever met; and she makes a lot more sense.

In order to appreciate how fundamentally different and creative her approach is, we need only to remember that economics is based entirely on the assumption that human beings are motivated exclusively by self-interest. This is the premise on which the economic system of the world is based today.

Hazel Henderson describes how economics became a way of life, a way she calls economism.

"On the macro level, the most noticeably pernicious and troublesome assumption of economism is that human activities take place in a vacuum and don't account for the operation of the biosphere. We see ourselves as above the workings of the biosphere rather than embedded in and part of it. That's the overall problem. The secondary problem that flows from this is a linear approach that goes from extraction to production to consumption to waste rather than looking at the whole chain, at what really happens to the whole material flow.

"There is also the problem of having a mechanical model of locomotion. Economies were simple models of locomotion. We saw that operate a lot in the 1980s, where Reagan decided to make the dollar his policy. This meant either running a high or a low dollar rather than dealing with any of our significant problems, whether external problems or problems of restructuring. Whole business sectors were destroyed when the dollar was so high. Economists assumed that when the dollar fell, all of those factories that had closed down would magically reactivate themselves. They would magically find themselves with employees and managers in them again. But these economists did not realize that such activities are subject to the second law of thermodynamics. When a factory shuts down, the workers go away and get other jobs, and people start vandalizing the building. So it doesn't suddenly start up again just because one of the variables has changed.

"The concept of irreversibility finally seeped into the economic literature. Even the mainstream economic literature began to include that by the end of the 1980s."

She explained the concept of reversibility, a perfect example of how our thinking is shaped by an age's metaphors and methods. In classical Newtonian physics, time could go backward and forward. It was reversible, like some jackets. Either way was OK. This made sense when you were dealing with machines, which you could construct, take apart, and put back together again without getting a peep out of them. But it doesn't work for humans, and it doesn't work in biology and living systems in general.

Physics, the hardest of the sciences, provided the foundation on which all other sciences were built, including economics. Physics, meanwhile, went through major revolutions around the turn of the century, but none of them were incorporated in the thinking of economists. Stuck in an outdated way of thinking, economics is now trying to inch its way out of it, with the help of brilliant mavericks like Hazel Henderson, who are systematically deconstructing its assumptions and reconstructing a more human edifice.

"The model of human behavior in economism is so simplistic: We are all competing individuals, all rationally maximizing our self-interest every minute. If we do anything kind or cooperative or, God forbid, unpaid, then we are per se irrational.

"On the national economic level, we measure progress and success on the basis of macroeconomic money indicators. The problem is that they leave out much of the real world and at least half of all economic productive activities that are not in the money economy, like the use of natural resources.

"Economism is obviously very linear, mechanical thinking. Its main idea is that societies are hydraulic systems or simple systems of automation that can operate in reverse. More recent models, based on systems theory, are a huge improvement because they allow you to deal with feedback loops, circularity, mutual causality, and all of these concepts that didn't fit with the Newtonian mechanistic model of how the world worked. I think systems theory is the bridge between economism and what I call Earth ethics. We cannot live by the left brain alone. We need to incorporate Earth ethics, which I believe will be our survival strategy, because it incorporates empathy. Empathy is really a survival instinct that human beings have; it must be just as much a survival instinct as any other, like fight or flight.

"The concept of empathy is to put yourself in the other person's shoes. This is going to be our most useful natural-instinct equipment. We need to cultivate it. Altruism is the same survival instinct seen in a larger systems framework. Those who are altruistic know they're working on a sort of cosmic accounting system. They know that in many cultures there are old folk laws, and folk wisdom, incorporating the idea that you cast bread on the waters and trust that it comes back. This is the absolute opposite of economism. This sharply illustrates the difference between the ethical approach, or

149

empathy—what we hope will be Earth ethics—and the economism approach, where altruism per se is considered irrational.

"I remember reading in *Time* magazine a few years ago a rather sarcastic article written by their resident economist, Robert Samuelson. He was writing about him and his wife, who had just had a baby. The article complained about the ecologists who demanded that he and his wife give up the convenience of disposable paper diapers for ecological reasons. Samuelson said they were totally illogical. He said that if he and his wife were to take the trouble not to use paper diapers, they would be irrational unless they could be sure everybody else would do the same thing.

"I thought this was a perfect example of how economics has created this excessively 'entropic' society. Because the other point of view, which luckily so many people who are not trained economists instinctively take, is that I will do the right thing, regardless of whether anybody else does it. That's a totally different approach. And thank God we aren't all trained economists!"

Hazel Henderson's example illustrates well the paradoxical nature of economic thinking based on pseudo-individualism. I can make my own decisions, it says, but basically I am powerless to make a difference in the larger picture. Pseudo-individualism is presented as empowering, but really it is still a cage that forces you to conform. This story also shows us the importance of independence of judgment and echoes Isabel Allende's metaphor of the pebble effect.

"And of course," Hazel Henderson continued, "how can we live together if we don't have faith? Even a thing as simple as standing aside for somebody to get by on a narrow bridge, trusting that they're not going to push you in the water. The whole thing is about innate trust between people. If I go into a store and buy something, and I get back too much change, I tell the cashier. I do that automatically, because I automatically assume that she would tell me if she had charged me too much. If we ever lose that innate trust when we encounter another human being, we're all lost. So it is quite extraordinary to have had a discipline, which ended up ruling our societies, that actually bred that survival impulse out of people."

For Riane Eisler the role of women in business is vital in the creation of a partnership society. For her this is not a "women's issue," confined to ensuring that women are fairly rewarded for their work, for instance. Rather it is the beginning of a complete transformation in the way we think about work and the values that inform our decision making. It's not a question of allowing women to play by the same rules as the men, but of re-envisioning the game itself, of working and thinking differently.

Hazel Henderson concurs. "Some things give me hope, like women running businesses. In the U.S. something like two thirds of all of the new small businesses that have been formed in the last ten years have been run by women. And as women run more and more businesses, men get more experience with the fact that women are good employers, and they're nice people to work for, and they give more credence to needing time off for child care. And maybe men have to have more experience of women's competency in running things.

"Whenever you have a country's or a city's decision-making body made up of half men and half women, the formerly degraded issues—like childhood health, Headstart, housing, and the home-less—suddenly become more important. I think that really is the bottom line. But the human species doesn't yet understand that we come in two different varieties, that we have two different kinds of experiences. If we don't have gender neutrality in all of our decision making, from top to bottom, from the family all the way up through the nation-state and in the United Nations—which is still one of the most sexist organizations on the planet—there's absolutely no hope.

"You cannot just have one or two token women on these regulatory bodies and governmental bodies; they cannot function that way. One or two loners don't have the ego-strength to hang in there, month in and month out, having their issues ridiculed. I experienced that myself when I was at the Office of Technology Assessment, one woman with twelve men. All of their issues were the 'fun' ones, like weapon systems and all this big-bang, exciting technology. It almost made me ill to have to go to those meetings because of the amount of effort I had to make to hang in with those issues. If I'd had one more woman, could I have managed? No. I realized even one wouldn't help. I would probably have needed three or four other women, and then they would have needed to have a lot of ego-strength. We would have had to get our ducks in a row and be good politicians and work on these issues in a very conservative sort of way.

"But it's all got to take place very, very rapidly, that's the hell of it. And when you look at the commanding heights of these agencies that are purporting to run the world, the World Bank or the United Nations or the G7 or even the G15, and the alternative economic summits I've been working with, it's still absolutely male dominated."

151

How Do You Measure Success?

Our idea of progress, and consequently how we measure progress, is changing. In economics, the Gross National Product (GNP) is a measure of a country's success and progress. This economic indicator is at the heart of economic thinking, it's the bottom line in judging how we're doing. But economists like Hazel Henderson argue that it's a profoundly flawed measure.

"GNP takes only a very few variables and equates them with the success of the whole society. They are mostly variables that are quantified by economists in money coefficients. I believe instead that a scorecard of a country's progress must be put together by a multidisciplinary group of people, and they're not going to use necessarily economic numbers, money coefficients. We need statistics from the health area, and statistics from the environmental area about the parts per million (ppm) of carbon dioxide, for example, hectares of land lost through desertification or deforestation."

A country's success and well-being measured by the GNP are like an individual's success and well-being measured by how much money she makes. We know that money cannot be the only indicator of an individual's quality of life. It is one of them, but there are rich miserable people out there. Things like happiness and success are difficult to quantify, so we use simplistic measures because they make it all look neat and tidy and scientific. On the other hand, many and more complex indicators are left out of the picture.

"If you look at the various agencies of the American government, you find that the Environmental Protection Agency puts the price of human life at four hundred thousand dollars. For the commerce department a human life is about a million dollars, and some other agency has a money coefficient for human life as something slightly different. The utter absurdity of trying to reduce the multidimensional qualities of existence into this one set of money coefficients is the major, major error," Hazel Henderson continued.

"One of the most appalling implications of doing that is the conclusion that rich people are more valuable than poor people. It's all based on your imputed salary over your life span. So if you are a humble laborer, your life is less valuable than if you're a manipulator in the stock market. These are the absurdities you get into with that kind of a scale."

As with all the other people we spoke to, Henderson believes we need transformation, not just piecemeal change. She believes countries should show statistics "unbundled," so we can get a good idea of the specifics.

"You'll be able to say, 'Country X is number one in biodiversity, and country Y is number one in literacy.' I fully expect that some of these indicators will eventually drift up and be broadly comparable, as literacy and infant mortality rates already are. More and more as we move toward democracies, governments are going to be held accountable for what their voters have decided is important. You're going to find that the goals of one country are not comparable with those of another, and there's no reason why they should be. What I'd like to see eventually is every country's scorecard so clearly detailed that people can vote with their feet. They can find a country that has just the right kind of menu for them, that supports the arts, for instance, that has a good universal health care system, or whose value system makes music a highly rewarded activity. There's really no reason now why politicians shouldn't be held accountable along all these quality-of-life indicators.

"If George Bush says he's the environmental president, we'll know by the scorecard whether he achieved that or whether he didn't. That's the whole idea. It's a natural coalition-building device. Better health, better housing, higher literacy rates, longer life expectancy, stabilized population, well-managed resources, and clean water are totally nonideological, and they're what most people in all countries want to achieve. They get you right out of this left-or-right economic framework."

Adam Smith, the father of capitalism, who coincidentally produced his magnum opus, *The Wealth of Nations,* in 1776 (the closest thing capitalism has to a Bible or what *Das Kapital* is for Marxists), said that it's not from the kindness of the butcher or the baker or the candlestick maker that we get what we need; it's our own self-interest that leads us to buy and sell. But wouldn't it be nice if that self-interest were tempered with some human decency and neighborly love? Leaving them out of the equation so completely in the development of capitalism has led us down the wrong path.

Adam Smith himself was a profoundly moral man concerned with the role of feelings in human life. In 1759 he wrote a book entitled *A Theory of Moral Sentiment.* But we must acknowledge that Smith, Marx, Darwin, and most if not all the other greats have been misinterpreted, or at least read with a jaundiced eye.

Joel Federman, educator and activist, former coordinator of the Peace and Conflict Studies Program at the University of Southern California and board member of the Martin Luther King Center for Nonviolence, believes that the movement toward a partnership society involves, first of all, breaking down the dominator assumptions

153

we hold in economics and politics. For instance, our conception of human nature rarely pays sufficient attention to such features as altruism and cooperation. As we learned from Art and Elaine Aron, it rarely deals with happiness or love.

This is important because our definition of what it means to be a human being, our conception of human nature, has been a crucial factor in all political theories, not just our behavior. If we assume that human beings are inherently—or genetically—selfish and callous, we will create a theory and subsequently a social system that institutionalizes this "reality." Likewise, Federman states, if our view of human nature is such that we cannot imagine ourselves as having the potential for universal kindness and compassion, then it will be impossible to imagine the end of hunger or the beginning of disarmament.

Machiavelli stated this clearly in *The Prince,* a book that was meant not to be mean or cruel, just "realistic," getting beyond the pious smokescreen of religious lingo. People are basically selfish and malicious, so it just makes sense to do the "natural" thing and act selfishly and maliciously. We'd be damn fools if we did otherwise.

Political scientists and politicians of the *realpolitik* school maintain that power is the defining term in any transaction. Human beings end up portrayed as stick figures with a calculator in hand, furiously maximizing their self-interest. For a while, most social scientists enthusiastically bought into the scientific veneer of economics. They applied a mechanistic, selfish, and utilitarian perspective of "rational economic man." But that is just not acceptable anymore.

The realpolitik view is a simplistic way of thinking about human beings. It leaves out most of what is interesting about humanity in an effort to quantify what little is left, so it all looks scientific. Never mind that both economists and politicians have no clue where we will be six months from now. The whole idea of quantifying stuff is so you can make predictions about it. Power may be the defining term in a dominator system, but it's not the only possible system. Federman finds Eisler's work important precisely because it shows that, as he put it, "what is, is not all that can be."

The fear-based dominator system is also kept in place by a continued belief in scarcity. Sociologist Todd Gitlin concurs that the belief in scarcity is a powerful way to maintain a fear-based system. But "scarcity is a political phenomenon, not a physical one," Joel Federman stresses. "The problem is not production but distribution, and that is really a problem of political will." As long as we believe life to be a dominator game, we'd rather watch food rot than give it to someone who cannot repay us for it immediately. Giving is losing, in this view. Federman is proposing a radical alternative to this view, which, as we shall see, resonates with the spirit of partnership.

It has been suggested by a variety of people, including Buckminster Fuller, who was very vociferous on this subject, that scarcity should really be a thing of the past, that there is no need for us to have to worry about basic human needs anymore. But we're just not used to this recent concept of abundance, and we cling to our well-worn ways.

Novelist and futurist Robert Anton Wilson also believes that scarcity is not a problem of production anymore but of politics. Science is managing to do more and more with less and less, and Wilson is optimistic about its role in our future. It is the belief in zero-sum games and dominator transactions that keeps the scarcity going, he insists. People who see the world in this way believe poverty is a given of human existence. They cannot conceive of transactions where both parties get what they want. It is interesting, though, that two hundred years ago the people who believed in this theory of scarcity and inevitable inequality would not have believed that one day so many people would have indoor plumbing, running water, central heating, and so on. Wilson believes our remarkable capacity for wealth creation is driven by human creativity, and in most cases scarcity is indicative of a lack of imagination. Creativity makes it possible to improve our collective standard of living. We just have to learn to use it more often.

If and when a society does not have to focus primarily on technological and economic production any longer, what does it do with itself? "There seems to be only one satisfactory answer," writes Willis Harman, and that is "learning and human development, in the broadest possible sense." Indeed, if we are going to change, we're going to have to learn how to change and what we want to change into. A whole-system societal shift into partnership is a learning challenge because we have to create partnership as we go along, in myriad forms.

This process of ongoing creation requires an accompanying process of ongoing learning. If we are simply to reproduce that which already is, all we need are certain existing skills and competencies, some memorized routines, and off we go. But if we are to create new worlds, and new relationships, we need more than the existing stockpile of knowledge. We need to learn how to learn. We

155

need to figure out what is useful to us and how to get the appropriate knowledge. We need to understand how to deal with the unforeseen. We need to develop sensitivity to our surroundings.

In new situations, facing problems and potentials we may be unfamiliar with, we cannot simply try to apply the tried and tested ways. In new situations it becomes necessary simultaneously to draw on all our resources and to let go of preconceived ideas as much as possible.

Stanley Krippner told us that by the time Cortés and his men attacked the Aztecs, the latter's system had become rigid and inflexible. As they were being ravaged by imported European diseases and defeated in battle by the few hundred men Cortés had amassed, the Aztecs decided to make more human sacrifices to the gods. Toward the end, they were sacrificing dozens of their best and brightest each day. This was clearly a case of more of the same, when more of the same was definitely not what was needed.

What are we going to learn in a learning society, and how are we going to learn it? We would suggest that it's important to learn how to learn together. We might learn what assumptions we hold to be true, assumptions that we have learned from the culture and society around us. Questioning assumptions, Frank Barron reminds us, is one of the ingredients of creative thinking.

Willis Harman is part of a larger movement that is attempting to reconceptualize work, to rethink what work means to us. He focuses these efforts through the World Business Academy. "The World Business Academy is a very simple concept," he explained to us. "It's just a network of people who are beginning to see this new picture, this new responsibility. They need to talk with other people and bolster their own confidence by discovering that others are also beginning to share these views.

"It's not just people in business, although there is a particular role for business. As this network gets larger, it will help midwife the rebirthing of the whole system. It's hard for us to capture that vision and hold it, even with a network, but we keep trying.

"The World Business Academy came out of the conversation between myself and businessman Rinaldo Brudico," Harman continued. "We both had been running into people in the business world who were either shaped by the sixties or were somehow seeing a different kind of future. They hadn't really thought it through in terms of world economy. But in terms of their own private lives, everything was different because their value emphases were different. If enough people make that kind of change in their lives, then all the institutions will have to change too.

"Business, being the dominant institution on the planet, has to take some responsibility for the whole system, which it certainly has no tradition for at all. The tradition in business is that the business of business is business, and somebody else takes care of the planet. That's the real challenge. The private sector has a new responsibility. We've always given it to the public sector, and they certainly have a role to play in regulating the system and making sure that everybody is in sync; but the initiative has to come from the private sector. It's going to come from all these people changing their minds. Furthermore, in this transition period it is absolutely critical whether the power structure understands why this change is necessary. If those in power lack that understanding they will try to get in the way of it. That will make all the difference in the world in terms of how much human misery comes along with the change.

"I do think trust is the key issue. We've been putting our trust in technology, in politicians, anywhere but ourselves. If we put our trust in our inner knowing, then we'll know what to do."

Community

GOVERNMENT

Democracy and Repression

The image of a lone Chinese man stepping in front of a row of tanks during the Beijing student uprising of 1989 has remained etched in the minds of many. His valiant attempt did not stop the so-called People's Liberation Army for long, and eventually the tanks rolled on into Tiananmen Square, the Goddess of Democracy fleeing before them.

This incident captures the essence of some of today's most important issues: The quest for freedom and democracy, and the authoritarian backlash; the attempt at discussion thwarted by dominator tactics: no discussion, just obedience; the revolt by ordinary citizens against a tyrannical government.

Isabel Allende, a native of Chile, knows very well what a militarized society is and what it means. "It's absolute power with impunity, no questions asked, blind obedience, everything is allowed as long as you have power. The principle is obscene! The idea that a civilian society would give these people immensely dangerous toys to play with, risking that one day they might turn against you in the name of God or the fatherland, is crazy. I think it's crazy that we have been supporting this kind of structure for millennia. I feel very strongly about this because I know its reality very well. People tell me this is in our nature, that men are soldiers or hunters and so on. It may have been true long ago but not now. I am sure my great-grandchildren will see a world where militarism has been abolished, and they will look back at our times and say, 'Those people were out of their minds!' It is true that violence is probably part of our nature, but it is also true that we can control it."

While he was teaching in China, Alfonso worked with married students whose husbands or wives lived at the other end of the country, assigned to a different "work unit." They saw each other only twice a year. The government assigns jobs, and if husband and wife are separated, it's just too bad. In the old days, some couples got to live together only when they retired. In 1985 it generally took at least five years of red tape and backdoor deals to be reunited.

This kind of invasion of one's private life, ostensibly to serve the people's revolution, would not sit well in Western countries. In the United States democracy means freedom from government interference. It means the freedom of mobility (in theory, at least)—just getting in the car and driving, settling wherever one wishes. This freedom—and it is essentially a psychological and social freedom rather than a legal one—is envied all over the world. From Bangkok to Bologna, from Buenos Aires to Bangui, young men and women look longingly to the freedom they see in the American life-style.

Until recently paranoia permeated the lives of Soviet citizens, particularly older intellectuals. The fear of speaking too openly, of attracting too much attention, the constant low-grade alert were disturbing signs of how effective the all-seeing eye of the government was. Stalin himself wanted files on everyone and regularly had his chief spies eliminated because they knew too much.

In Greece, after the coup of April 21, 1967, Alfonso's father, then the Italian cultural attaché in Athens, used to invite opposition intellectuals and politicians to the concerts and conferences held at the Italian Cultural Institute. Since they had been forbidden to see one another by the junta, this was one of the few ways for them to meet and discuss the situation undisturbed. Political prisoners were allowed to study Italian at the Institute, where they would quietly make contact with one another and receive small care packages from relatives. The U.S.-backed junta stayed in power long enough to torture political prisoners and create a regime based on fear. Like so many other authoritarian regimes recently, it was eventually thrown out by people power.

Authoritarianism has a long and nasty history, but there are encouraging signs that we seem to be moving away from it on a global scale. Countries everywhere are trying to move toward some kind of democracy and away from authoritarianism. From Bulgaria to Chile, from the Philippines to South Africa, something is afoot, and it has to do with democracy and with the Greek roots of that word—people and power, *demos* and *cratos*. The power of the people is displacing the power of authoritarian rulers.

A Primer in Authoritarianism from Philip Slater

Authoritarianism, or what we're calling domination, is kept in place, according to Philip Slater, by four pillars. They are (1) deference or submissiveness, (2) systematic oppression through brutality and terror, (3) deflection, and (4) secrecy.

Deference or submissiveness involves the maintenance of a hierarchical order of dominance and submission, whereby anyone lower than you on the totem pole is automatically submissive to you, just as you are to those above you. The habit of bowing to the will of others makes it difficult for us to stand up to them, Slater points out, since the habit becomes profoundly ingrained. We can almost see the look of defeat in some people, the slouched posture, the lackluster eyes. In the worst cases this becomes the reflex gesture of the perennially scared person, shielding his or her face with the arms.

Systematic oppression through brutality and terror is the second pillar, closely connected to the first. Hit quick and hit hard, and occasionally throw in some random violence to keep the population terrorized and a little paranoid. The arbitrary yet systematic nature of this violence makes it particularly painful to bear.

This kind of violence is depicted well in Martin Scorsese's powerful movie *Goodfellas,* which follows a group of mafia hoods over a period of twenty years. Their excessive use of violence reflects the power of the mob, its ability to enforce its rules by scaring everyone so much that no one dares oppose them. One of the characters, played by Joe Pesci, is definitely a borderline psychotic, and yet his out-of-control moods initially serve him well in building his reputation as a powerful figure. One can well imagine not wanting to mess with anyone like that, capable of anything. Particularly frightening is the disproportionate use of violence, shown by Pesci's character,

161

for instance, when he shoots a young bartender to death simply for talking back to him.

Most dominator systems have an unspoken code regarding what amount of violence is appropriate. Some insults, for instance, warrant a fistfight, but no more. Children—and adults—are punished based on the severity of the crime they have committed. Even in wars the use of nuclear weapons is generally considered acceptable only in the case of a superpower conflict, and not appropriate, say, for the U.S. invasion of Grenada or the Soviet invasion of Afghanistan.

In one of his more whimsical and conspiratorial moments, sipping coffee with us in his living room, Robert Anton Wilson wondered aloud whether meanness was not a value in some circles. "From a dominator perspective it makes sense. Just entertain this idea for a moment," he proposed. "American presidents have taken to staging a little invasion a year or so after they've been elected. 'Look how mean our alpha-male is,' we seem to be saying, 'you'd better not get in the way.' [The alpha-male is the leader of the pack in a group of animals.] Displaying meanness is a way of scoring brownie points in the pecking order. It's almost as if by doing something really mean we were climbing up the ranks and leaving behind those without the stomach to act."

It certainly works for neighborhood hoods and death-squad-wielding tyrants. You certainly wouldn't have wanted to mess with Joe Pesci's character, right? Sound farfetched? Yet when we look at those who've made it—politicians who win an election or heads of corporations—we often wonder how many colleagues they had to walk over to get there (whether they really did or not). We often suppose that to get anywhere we will have to be pretty ruthless, otherwise somebody else will walk all over us on his or her way to the top. True or not—and it is not, in many cases—this is the heart of the dominator system, the foundation of the fear-based paradigm.

The most extreme dominator systems adopt a tactic of arbitrary violence in order to ensure that submissiveness becomes a reflex action. When faced with any kind of authority, the oppressed instinctively submits. Some suspected that the Russian people had in fact been brutalized into a permanently submissive stance, one that said "Do with us what you will, just keep some bread on the table." Fortunately they were wrong, and Gorbachev's *glasnost* let in the glimmer of light long enough that going back became simply unthinkable. Humans are extremely adaptable, and no matter how submissive we may be for a while, our spirit has been able time and again to find sources of courage and strength. The question is, after all the heroics, can they sustain the democratic impetus, or will they clamor for a strong-man rule, as people tend to do in times of trouble?

The third pillar is *deflection,* directing the people's hostility toward anyone but us. Let them beat each other over the head, then we can make them look like fools who are not trustworthy and mature enough to participate in the political process. How can we possibly let blacks participate in South African politics, for instance, when their way of debating is to throw tires around each other and set them on fire? Divide and conquer is an age-old strategy, which in the case of South Africa was fueled by *agents provocateurs* and other attempts to discredit the people.

Secrecy is the fourth and final pillar. A variety of secret codes, languages, and symbol systems are used to keep the population ignorant. This is ultimately the reason for secrecy, to keep the other party ignorant of your doings. When the other party is the people a government is supposed to represent, then some extremely bizarre verbal dances go on to assure the masses that they are better left ignorant since there is not a need to know, and we wouldn't want to endanger national security now, would we? If you only knew what we do—and you don't and you never will if we can help it—you'd clearly see the wisdom of our actions.

From the perspective of systems science, secrecy has the effect of making an authoritarian regime a closed system. This type of system, by definition, does not allow for the free flow of information within the system or the exchange of information between the system and the rest of the world. If you keep a population ignorant and feed them propaganda about the rest of the world, they will not have any criteria with which to compare systems. If they're told theirs is the greatest, they just might believe it. It was very hard for people to leave the former Soviet Union, for instance, or for them to get information that had not been sanitized by a bureaucrat with the subtlety of a sledgehammer.

In 1985 some of Alfonso's Chinese university students confessed that they knew virtually nothing about Confucius, whose teachings had been banned while they were growing up during the Cultural Revolution. They were also totally ignorant of ways of life outside their own country. They found it hard to believe that it would be at least theoretically possible for the Italian Communist party to come to power if indeed it ever won an election, which it threatened to do several times. The idea that capitalist governments could allow themselves to be ousted in an election blew their minds. These Chinese students had little if any access to information outside government propaganda. Their enormous desire for knowledge was matched by their quiet and thoughtful determination to learn and—in those pre–Tiananmen Square days—to look forward to the hopeful unfolding of change. They are still waiting; as of 1992, even the *I-Jing,* or *Book of Changes,* is banned.

Dominator systems such as China cannot allow information from other countries in because these systems work best when they can shape and create the reality the people live in. This makes it all the sadder when we in the West, who have access to so much information, use so little of it and remain just as ignorant about the world as those in closed systems are.

Closed societies tend to be highly centralized and homogeneous, even if they are racially or ethnically mixed. In China the most striking example of this homogeneity and control is the Mao-suit, so popular in the sixties and so profoundly unpopular in the eighties and early nineties. In 1986 the *People's Daily* reported that a factory in Shanghai had twice been stopped from making shirts with lively patterns. Only the standard gray, white, and blue were acceptable. The paper complained that it was time to stop this "old thinking" and give the people what they wanted. They clearly liked the new shirts, since they sold out in a matter of days. China's government strives so vigorously for homogeneity that it has only one time zone, whereas China should technically have four. Everyone is on Beijing time.

Historically there have been some strong arguments for this kind of centralization and homogeneity. This is not just Marx and Engels and Lenin and Mao talking, but the same machine metaphor that drove the West for so many years. In the beginning of the nineteenth century, the so-called American system of manufacture was started at the Lowell Mills in Boston, putting all aspects of production under one roof. Workers were easily controlled and scientifically managed, thanks to Frederick Taylor, on the basis of time-and-motion studies performed with a stopwatch to see how efficient they were. Taylor was in fact motivated by the good intention of saving the workers unnecessary toil. Yet his thinking and actions were shaped by the prevailing paradigm of the Industrial Age, which equated the workers with machines. Some business and government organizations today still look an awful lot like centralized megamachines.

A democratic system is an open system, which means it allows a free flow of information, ideas, opinions, goods, and people within its boundaries and in and out of the system. An open society is radically different from a closed society. Open societies tend to be less centralized because the vast array of influences going in and out of the system and the mixing and matching within the system cause different pockets to form, all with their own life-styles, values, and beliefs. These pockets can be sources of strife and conflict, but they are also sources of enormous potential creativity, which gives the system greater flexibility and vitality. As we have seen, complexity fosters creation, and this applies to human beings, nations, and natural systems alike.

It is a peculiar characteristic of open systems that the more open they become, the greater the degree of interdependence they develop. This is true in international economics, for example, where the U.S. goes to war in the Middle East, among other reasons, to ensure the free flow of oil. Japan, at the other end of the world, is also dependent on this oil to build the cars it exports to America. Even at the personal level, we would find it difficult to function without this constant interchange. If we live in a big city, unless we grow our own veggies and keep chickens in the condo, we depend on others for food. Services we take for granted, like running water, electricity, and food preparation (cleaning, freezing, packaging, and shipping), are all performed by other people, some working an ocean or a continent away. We depend on them for trade and entertainment and basic living needs.

As the world becomes smaller, we absorb more and more influences from the four corners of the globe, whether ideas, food, fuel, consumer goods, people, or cultural traditions. Technology is making it easier and easier to maintain and develop this interdependence, and, barring a major catastrophe, the interdependence is likely to increase.

Futurist Paul Saffo believes that "we're into the first couple of years of a fifty-year period that will see the eventual end of the nation-state as a meaningful distinction in global affairs. The decline of the U.S. right now is an example. I think you need at least two superpowers to have any superpower at all; in the absence of Russia, the U.S. might be the most powerful nation on Earth but it is not powerful enough to have more than a limited impact on events. The full force of American power and might landed on Iraq, but Saddam Hussein kept his a job. It's probably a dangerous notion for us to

165

think of ourselves as a great nation able to solve all the problems. We are redefining ourselves in a fundamental way.

"It's happening in Europe as well. The nation-state is really a construct, it's a real latecomer on the scene, and it's a construct that caused cultures to submerge themselves within the state. What we'll be seeing in the future is not a melting pot but a cultural minestrone where people's cultural identity reasserts itself.

"Technology is proving to be a force for diversity as much as for homogeneity. Put another way, Marshall McLuhan once forecast that the world would be turned into a global village by information and technology. He only got it half right. The world is turning into many global villages, and we're using information technology to assert individual cultural identities. It started happening in Europe first. Ask a Belgian whether he's a Belgian and he'll say no, he's either a Fleming or a Walloon, and he's also a member of the European community. We are deemphasizing our national identity as we reach downward to our cultural unit and upward to regional units. The evolution of the European community and the reassertion of cultural identities within Europe and the Soviet Union are absolutely consistent with that. Yugoslavia, which never really became a nation-state, was the first to fly apart. Now the nation-states that continue are the ones where national statehood is a perfect overlap of cultural identity, and that's why Japan is so solid.

"In the United States, we're heading for devolution of power from the federal to the state level. We are headed toward more power at the periphery and less power at the center. It will be more like Europe, where the states still exist, but nation-states no longer have complete authority and autonomy within their boundaries. The United Kingdom doesn't have complete military autonomy because it is part of NATO, and doesn't have complete economic autonomy because it is part of the European Community, and doesn't have complete cultural isolation because it has to let EEC members in.

"A nation-state is really just a bundle of rights and powers, and nation-states have been conferring these powers more and more to international authorities. We are slowly chipping away at the nation-state. Nations won't disappear completely, but they will become just another one of many boundaries on a map. Imagine how complex Europe would look on a map if you actually drew in physical boundaries for the European free trade zone and for the various overlapping treaty obligations."

The More It Changes, the More It Stays the Same

"Already in Plato's *Republic*," anthropologist Stuart Schlegel reminded us, "you find the statement 'I thank God I was born a Greek and not a barbarian, a free man and not a slave, a male and not a female.' Here's an example in Western roots of not only categorizing but ranking. It's better to be this than that. Americans, and Westerners in general, have a great tendency to break everything into twofold judgments and to rank them. That's the critical thing, that we rank. It's the same for good and evil. Hindus have destruction, regeneration, and creation, in the form of Brahma, Shiva, Vishnu. Yet the forces of destruction and the forces of creation are not ranked. It's not better to create and bad or evil to destroy. All of life simply involves these processes, these forces. We Westerners rank our dichotomies: it's better to be good than evil, it's better to be right than wrong, it's better to be just than to be unjust and so on."

Philosopher Mara Keller rightfully pointed out the problems inherent in our dualistic way of thinking. "In my philosophy courses," she told us, "I teach about hierarchical dualism, about the dualistic hierarchies that humans create that generate many unfortunate social dynamics, whether of gender, race, age, class, nationality, or religion. Hierarchical dualism sets up relationships of superiority and inferiority between persons or groups of persons. When people develop a mindset where one thinks certain people are absolutely superior and others absolutely inferior, then it becomes almost impossible to make any changes in relationships, and the suffering—actually of both parties—will be perpetuated. Everybody suffers in this setup, although we don't usually see it this way. The person in the one-down position suffers more, but the humanity of the person in the superior position also suffers.

"The way beyond absolute hierarchical dualism is to have a holistic philosophy that recognizes not only that there are polarities between, for example, women and men, but that we all have our uniqueness and individuality as well. This realization brings a recognition of pluralism, and with it the understanding that dualism is not the ultimate category of cognition. At this point, however, something is still lacking philosophically: it is the unity, the oneness. Dualism isn't the ultimate point of understanding, but neither is pluralism," she feels. "Our culture is beginning to shift away from dualism toward pluralism. I think that if we really want partnership we also need to understand unity as well, the unity that comes from mutual benefit."

167

This is why, in spite of the enormous changes and upheavals that civilizations, governments, and nations have experienced in the past five thousand years, the dominator system has remained unchanged. It varied only its historical manifestations, and there is little hope that we can break out of this vicious cycle unless we change the fundamental paradigm and, as a whole, switch to a partnership system.

How Systems Change

"Societies, like people, can change their myths," psychologist Stanley Krippner mused, "but it requires considerable effort, because social myths are the result of so many different influences over the years. It usually takes a catastrophe or a cataclysm to bring about this type of change. We are seeing this in the former Soviet Union right now, where social myths are undergoing drastic changes.

"Look at the demise of the Communist party, where a very important, very powerful social mythology has capsized, and capsized quickly. One wonders what will take its place. It's completely conceivable that something worse will develop. Let's hope not. Let's hope that this shift opens the door for opportunities. Let's hope that from the chaos some positive forces can emerge that will construct social and cultural myths to ennoble and empower what used to be Soviet society."

Frank Barron also discussed with us the dynamics of the breakup of the Soviet Union applying the same basic notions that exist in creativity and in psychology.

"The country has gone from almost perfect rigidity, simple symmetry, with repression of anything that didn't fit the idea of balance and order, to a gradual breaking with that. The first point of breakage was analogous to the beginning of a breakage of repression in an individual's psychic system. In other words, if you've repressed a lot of feelings and then for some reason some of them break out, you don't know what to do. At that point, you can get very confused. And the more leakage in your repression system, the more that leakage doesn't know where to go. It's like a hydraulic process that has been contained but is now seeping through the system. When that happens, it begins affecting all the structures. That's what happened in the Soviet Union.

"My judgment is that when Gorbachev started on *glasnost,* he unleashed an extremely powerful force. It wasn't just a little change in the rules about newspaper publication or radio or TV. It was something entirely different. I don't think he reckoned with it. I don't think he understood the extent of what could happen. The system began getting completely out of control, and there was no way to contain it again. He desperately kept trying to contain it, by asserting his personal dignity, his sincerity, and his honesty, for instance—trying to get rid of all the old icons and throwing it all back on the ability of the people to regulate themselves mutually. He was asking too much over the short term.

"He wanted to maintain a center. He didn't want to just kill communism, he wanted to change it. But he wanted to change everything gradually, not realizing that it was a flood, and so it all broke apart. Through the folly of people who didn't grasp what he was after, and thought they could reinstitute the oppression, the so-called coup was staged. When that failed, it was too late to resume the desired pace, and the whole thing fell apart. The former Soviet Union is in a very dangerous situation, in my opinion. They're out of the arms race game, and everyone's counting them out, not realizing that they've got all this power still there, uncontrolled."

In chaotic, unstable situations like these, characteristics like independence of judgment, tolerance for ambiguity, and a preference for complexity (the traits that Frank Barron identified in creative behavior) play a vital role. Unfortunately these are precisely the characteristics a totalitarian regime does not want its people to have, so the people of the former Soviet Union have not been educated in these skills.

One learns to develop independence of judgment by becoming more and more aware of what the consensus story is, where cracks may appear, and where the assumptions can be challenged. Tolerance for ambiguity allows us to wrestle with a difficult situation without immediately wanting a strong hand to decide for us, but it requires a certain ability to thrive on chaos and complexity. No matter how orderly and even boring our lives may seem in capitalist countries, the predictability of communism was in many cases simply crushing. Not because of the welfare system, as some gleeful right-wing Western apologists for capitalism suggest, which guaranteed everyone food, housing and health care, no matter how poor the quality, but because a frighteningly hierarchical system of bureaucratic domination did not allow people avenues to make their own choices.

Domination Switch or Transformation? David Loye Explains How to Get out of the Left-Right Loop

For David Loye, the Russian context reflects the "typically tangled situation of our times. The people who attempted the coup supposedly represented what used to be the communist left. But actually, by the time it reached this stage in history, they were clearly identified as the conservatives. Communism started out originally in the hands of people who wanted to change the existing norms under capitalism. Ironically, still earlier, the capitalists had been the norm changers, wanting to change the existing norms of feudal aristocracies. By our time, however, the communists had become entrenched. They were the norm maintainers, or those who want to hang on to existing norms.

"In contrast to them, Gorbachev represented the forces of liberalism. Yet the irony is that what Gorbachev represented—the idea of shifting to the market economy—is what has been identified in this country as conservatism, though it started out as liberalism in the time of Adam Smith. The shifting labels can obscure the real dynamics of what happens underneath. And what is happening underneath is really very serious. I like the terms *norm changers* and *norm maintainers,* as they are forceful, reliable guides to what is going on. Still more powerful for analysis are the dominator and partnership models, which get at the truly fundamental struggle underlying the terms *conservative* and *liberal,* as well as *authoritarians* versus *proponents of democracy.*"

Loye has provided us with a reconceptualization of the old left-right dichotomy, which in all this change and confusion is losing meaning these days. In the movie *Bananas,* the hapless hero played by Woody Allen ends up in a small Latin American country that is in the hands of a somewhat dyspeptic dictator and his cronies. Through the usual series of mishaps, our man Woody ends up fighting on the side of the rebels and eventually helps the rebel leader take over and rid his country of the evil dictator. Then Woody witnesses a remarkable spectacle. Before his very eyes, the rather chubby, bearded, and benign rebel leader suddenly becomes a raving authoritarian loony, who orders his people to wear their underwear as outerwear, and then begins a stream of demands that put him right up there with the old dictator. Kinky underwear fetish aside, like much good comedy, this is almost too close to the bone.

Why does history repeat itself in this fashion? Can we find a historical equivalent of Alka-Seltzer? Let's try and look at it another way. With a very uncharitable eye, what we see is the norm maintainers naturally enough wanting to keep their power, and whatever else it is they have struggled to win over the years. We suspect the Soviet *nomenklatura* would privately not have disagreed with this interpretation.

In the context of a dominator system, the basic assumption is that the way to do this is to keep the have-nots under control and relatively poor. If they start getting things, they will presumably get things that the haves have, and we wouldn't want that now, would we? Of course, should the present norm maintainers be thrown out, they'll dutifully become norm changers. "This is unfair," they'll shout. "How come you've got everything now?"

The norm changers, on the other hand, feel bad about being have-nots and want to get the present mob out of the way so that they can become haves. They want the norms changed in such a fashion that they benefit. The minute they get to power, they'll become norm maintainers.

What happens, therefore, in this admittedly simplistic and highly uncharitable interpretation of politics is a domination switch. From this perspective, it can be said that there is little difference between extreme left and extreme right: Both favor explicit domination, be it of the Nazi or the Stalinist variety.

But let's not get too smug here and suffer from delusions of the it-can't-happen-here variety, because the exact same process is in action in our own backyards. Incumbents have been known to do anything to stay in power, and challengers, likewise to obtain power. But when the challengers get the power, they start behaving a lot like incumbents, which of course they are.

"In partnership systems, as once existed and are spreading once again," David Loye proposed, "there were and are partnership norms. They maintain and protect norms of gender equality, norms of peaceful interaction rather than violent interaction, norms that foster creativity.

"The partnership society is an open society, open to the inflow of information, tolerance, and interesting diversity. At the same time, all norms set constraints. In partnership systems, norms set limits to discourage and if necessary to repress sexual inequality, violence, war, hierarchies, and brutality. One idea that keeps cropping up in this confused time in history, however, is that the alternative to the big, bad, brutal system is to have a completely tolerant and completely nonjudgmental attitude. That is not the partnership way

171

at all, in my opinion. You cannot have no rules, you cannot have no norms, because that invites the dominators and the dominator system to take over again.

"For five thousand years now, every historical situation that has attempted a so-called laissez-faire type of social, business, or governmental operation has very quickly been taken over by the dominators and has been reincorporated in the dominator system because it offers no firm alternative. Social psychologist Kurt Lewin made the point in his analysis of social change. He proposed three steps: You have to unfreeze the prevailing norm-maintainer mold. Then, in tune with liberating goals, you move to new levels and set up greater equality and greater freedom. But he pointed out that then you had to 'refreeze' the norms at the more advanced levels. You had to build them into the society with more progressive, advanced laws and institutions. Otherwise it all slips back. You regress to the earlier stage."

How Fast Do Systems Change?

"It takes us about thirty years to absorb any really new ideas into a culture, and for the most part that has been a constant for at least the last four centuries," Paul Saffo told us. "It took about fifty years to go from the technology of movable type to the medium of publishing, with the publication of Virgil in 1501. It took us about thirty years to go from the primitive technology of movies to opening night of Al Jolson's *The Jazz Singer.* It took twenty years to go from the technology of the wireless to the medium of broadcast in radio. The reason it takes thirty years is that technology does not drive change at all; technology merely enables change. It's our collective cultural response that drives change.

"Change occurs at the speed of thought, not the speed of electrons racing down circuits or bouncing off satellites. And in a world of stubborn people, thought can be slow indeed. At times I think that perhaps we don't change at all—we just grow old and die. Thirty years is a generation and a half. We form our ideas between the ages of thirteen and seventeen, and we carry them along with us like a turtle shell on our backs. Then we get about twenty years to implement them on the management stage before we're thrown off the stage by the next generation carrying their own ideas.

"This also sheds light on the process of paradigm shifts first articulated by Thomas Kuhn. According to Michael Rothschild's recent book *Bionomics,* for example, classical economics was built on a Newtonian model, and Newton is out. So why are we still doing classical economics? We need a new economics based on the biological model.

"We've discovered that part of the problem is something that biologists and evolutionary theorists realize about evolutionary change, a phenomenon they call punctuated equilibrium. For a long time nothing happens, and then all of a sudden a bunch of things happen at once. I think that's how society evolves as well. We go through these periods of absorption and then periods of expansion. The periods of expansion are the paradigm shifts, or what biologists call periods of rapid change and evolution."

Willis Harman shares similar views. "When I was still with SRI and trying to get corporate clients and government clients to look at some of the issues coming up in the future, I became more and more aware that a fundamental mind change was taking place. It probably started in the sixties, or became visible then, anyway. It essentially was setting aside conventional religion and conventional science and saying neither one of these describes a worldview that we can really live in. Something new is happening, and it's a totally different mind-set. We began to see that picture by the late 1960s.

"The emerging global problems were symptoms of a sick global society, and they were all related. This transformational force was building up until eventually things would begin to happen very suddenly. We wrote about that almost twenty years ago, or maybe earlier. The point is that when people begin to question the legitimacy of a system, they take the legitimacy away, and then things change in a hurry. What takes time is for people to change their minds, but once we reach critical mass, once a sufficient number of people has gone through this transformation, then the change happens with a dramatic speed. We've seen recent examples of that, but we have some more coming."

William Irwin Thompson is a bard, storyteller, and cultural historian. He is president of the Lindisfarne Association, which has brought together scholars like Gregory Bateson, James Lovelock, Lynn Margulis, Francisco Varela, Hazel Henderson, and John Todd to explore the boundaries of the old paradigm and the vision of the new one. Although a native of Los Angeles, Thompson spends his time between Zurich, New York, and Colorado. He has developed a theory about cultural change, and in his view it's the artist who is the shaper of things to come.

"Marshall McLuhan said that artists are the early-warning system of society; they see the invisible environment and render it. They themselves are often not visible until their process is over, and then

173

they are turned into a commodity. The moment they get turned into a commodity, it's a signal that their periods, or *kairos*, are over. A classic example of that is Joseph Campbell and what happened to him as a cultural phenomenon in the eighties. By this time he was no longer intellectually alive and creative. He had crystallized twenty years before when he and Jung and all the people of Jung's circle were having their Eranos meetings in Ascona. He became a popular American phenomenon in the eighties, but all the stuff he was dealing with was a good twenty or thirty years old. There's always this kind of lateness phenomenon, like the interval between the lightning and the thunder.

"There is a sequence for decoding the cycles of cultural change," William Irwin Thompson told us. "A new vision is enunciated by the mystics, by an Aurobindo or a Teilhard de Chardin or a Steiner. Then it's picked up by the artists and elaborated by the Stockhausens and Doris Lessings and Philip Glasses and Gary Snyders. And they influence their followings, and through them younger people who are brought up on reading Doris Lessing, influenced by Philip Glass, or whatever. In the last stage, the message is finally picked up by the politicians. The politicians are still invoking the America of the Eisenhower days. Sooner or later they're all going to look around and realize that the actual people who are out there and who have inherited the wealth are all the people who grew up in the sixties and are now, at forty-five with their parents dying, in charge of America. They've done Zen and meditated, and they're not from the Eisenhower era. That's going to be apparent around the middle of the nineties."

William Irwin Thompson makes the interesting point that politicians seem to be the last to catch on. This may sound depressing if we are hoping for the charismatic leader who is going to bring us all the solutions. If we look at it from a different angle, however, it may mean that government, albeit slowly and reluctantly, is being led rather than leading. This may be the pace of democracy in the next century. We simply need a way to make the process more efficient. In his book *Megatrends*, John Naisbitt spoke of a trend from representative democracy to participatory democracy. Instead of having someone you may or may not have voted for make decisions in your name, you participate in every decision that will affect you. With the electronic revolution, this may become extremely easy. People could vote from their homes through computers or interactive televisions.

Perhaps we, the people, will become the deliberating body, and the politicians would execute our directions. In which case we probably wouldn't mind if they kept their jobs a long time, provided they were competent workers. We wouldn't even have to wait for everyone to be connected to Washington via electronic mail. For starters, along with our income tax return we could send in our instructions on how to allocate our collective tax dollars. Then it would be a question of tallying the country's priorities and getting to work.

No matter how this is done, it requires a mind-set very different from the one we have now because it requires participation. It means people have to become involved in local and national government, and not just when things get completely out of hand, either.

Leverage

Since we have been waiting for several thousand years for the system to change, thirty more years might not seem such a long time. We can also take heart from the fact that when a system is on the brink, it takes only a gentle push to get things rolling. The whole principle of leverage revolves around the (systems science) notion that it's possible to make enormous changes in a system using small interventions. It is not necessary to have a cause that is as strong as the effect. Who would have guessed the changes in the Eastern bloc in 1988, or the Soviet situation in 1990?

During the August 1991 coup in the Soviet Union, and long before that, one would often hear people pontificating about the amount of blood that would be necessary to effect "real change" there. The communist regime seemed to have become such an intrinsic part of the country that to eradicate it would require a massive effort, involving perhaps as much fighting as the original revolution, and perhaps as many deaths as the pogroms of Stalin's era.

Isabel Allende used to believe in this same action-reaction law. She told us the story of Chile's change from dictatorship to democracy. "I used to say that the only way we are going to get rid of [Chilean dictator] Pinochet is with violence. We have to fight violence with violence. Against the violence of the military we need the violence of the people. I was an extremist, and I would have taken a gun and gone out shooting if I'd had one."

When confronted with the horrors of domination, we tend to assume the only way to make a change is to match the dominators blow for blow, or even go one better. When we take this stance, we are still acting, unconsciously, from the dominator paradigm, which says that we can only fight force with force, that we have to resort to violent approaches.

"After seventeen years of dictatorship," Allende went on, "I learned the hard way that violence only brings more violence, that violence comes back against you sooner or later. In Chile people got rid of the dictatorship without violence. All the violence came from the military, from the government; they committed all the atrocities. The people didn't. They defeated them in their own field with patience, endurance, courage, and organization.

"A wonderful, solid organization was the basis for this. Against this organization the government couldn't do much. It was defeated in its own territory. It was defeated in a plebiscite despite the fact that it had all the press, all the economic apparatus, and the military repression at its disposal, so it could do all it wanted. The government had only one candidate, and that was Pinochet. It had all the media, and yet it lost. The people had organized silently, discreetly, and when the time came to be alone to vote, they voted against Pinochet. They didn't say anything, but very quietly they voted against him in such overwhelming numbers that it could not be hidden. The government couldn't cheat on the plebiscite because the numbers were so overwhelming. So Pinochet was forced to call elections, and again the candidate was Pinochet himself.

"The rest of the country had not had political parties for seventeen years, but they were still organized, and they knew exactly what they wanted. They chose one candidate only, instead of one for each possible party who would have probably been defeated by Pinochet. He was a Christian Democrat, hated by the left in Chile, where the left is very powerful; but the left knew that they were not stronger than the Christian Democrats. If they wanted to defeat Pinochet, who was the common enemy, they had to get together, so they did. Everybody thought, OK, after the elections, after they've won, they will split, and this coalition that they formed for the election will be lost the minute the elections are over. But it didn't happen. We've had several years of democratic government, and we're still doing well, very well, and the coalition is still there. So you can do it without violence. When you do it with no violence, there is a solid organization that has been building up in such a way that afterward it won't be destroyed."

Quo Vadis, America?

Twenty-five years ago, Philip Slater and Warren Bennis wrote an article for the *Harvard Business Review* in which they predicted democracy would triumph over communism in the next fifty years. The day we spoke to Philip Slater, on a sunny August afternoon on the patio of a distinctly multicultural Santa Cruz restaurant (the menu changes from Middle Eastern to Southeast Asian to Indian depending on the day of the week), Mikhail Gorbachev and Boris Yeltsin told American questioners via satellite in a televised town-hall meeting that communism was finished.

But today Slater worries about the future of democracy in America. "It's an illusion that we're so democratic here," he told us. "There's a great deal of denial going on about some fundamental issues in our society. Education is falling apart, crime, homelessness, drug abuse are all increasing. Powerful conglomerates are dictating American policy, with the excuse that it's for free enterprise from which everyone will benefit." These are issues that, according to Slater, were swept under the rug by the Reagan-Bush administration with its don't-worry-be-happy mentality.

It is no coincidence that the issues just mentioned are ones that in the home are generally taken care of by women. They are to some extent *women's issues*. Who takes care of the house, of food, of education, of cleaning up the mess the boys make? Good old Mom. So perhaps it is "natural" that men should not be interested in dealing with these issues and would much prefer to fight a war or confront some fierce enemy. Even communist governments, supposedly concerned with providing their people with security in exactly these areas, were ultimately more concerned with foreign policy, wasting all their money and resources on foreign escapades and on maintaining their own power at home.

Philip Slater wrote that stereotypically feminine traits, "flexibility, sensitivity, understanding, emotional honesty, directness, warmth, realism and the ability to mediate, to communicate, to negotiate, to integrate, to cooperate . . . *are precisely those most needed to successfully maintain a democratic society.* But they are traits that must be developed in the entire population, not merely in half of it. You can *stand* on one leg, but you cannot *walk*, and while authoritarian societies are designed for stasis, democratic ones are designed for movement."

In our society, pollsters have noticed that women candidates fare badly when issues of war and defense come up, since women are perceived as less authoritative on those issues. When the issue is education or health, women candidates are generally viewed more favorably than men, who seem to inspire more confidence when it comes to bottom-line issues like getting out of a recession. In times of national emergency, then, when there seems to be an external threat of some kind, all these "feminine" traits and values fly out the window, because they become equated with weakness. Slater goes to some length in his book *A Dream Deferred* to point out the error in our belief that when the going gets tough, authoritarian measures are needed. Democratic systems function much better even in times of war because they have greater flexibility and collective intelligence.

We're not lumping all men into one category. Clearly a large number of men think domestic issues are the only reason for fighting a war in the first place. In other words, we would defend our home and our country because we like them, we're happy here, and we have an obligation to our fellow citizens.

Ironically, however, when we get ready to fight, we actually start tampering with the very principles we are eager to sacrifice our lives for. Civil rights, human rights, women's rights, education, the neighborhood, economic opportunity, free speech—all lose ground when we get closer to feeling threatened and embark on a foreign-policy adventure. In the interest of national security, of unity and strength, we are supposed to rally behind the flag and fight unquestioningly. The more uptight we get, the less dissent we want to hear. Criticism of the government becomes "unpatriotic." This kind of militaristic authoritarianism is exactly the opposite of democracy.

For Philip Slater, partnership involves not splitting the world into good and evil, either/or. He sees "conflict as an avenue toward movement," where the "opposition forces you to jump to another level" of understanding. It is potentially a source of creativity and synthesis rather than violence. How we choose to view situations, then, is fundamentally up to us. Creativity involves the ability to see a situation from many perspectives.

Slater told us that according to organizational theorist Mary Parker Follett, we generally assume that peace is passive and war is active. She believed it to be exactly the other way around: war is passive and peace is active. Peace is something that requires continuous creativity; indeed it requires more action than war. It's certainly much easier to destroy a Monet or a Picasso than it is to paint something quite as beautiful.

Democracy is a challenge, one that requires much more than blind obedience from us. It is a constant process of co-creation, of maintaining relationships and changing them, of dialogue, dissent, and agreement. Democracy is the soil in which a variety of understandings of the world can grow and different ways of living can co-exist.

CULTURE

Is It a Melting Pot, a Cioppino, or a Wonton Soup?
In San Francisco you can walk from the slightly tacky tourist traps of Fisherman's Wharf (where you can nevertheless pick up excellent crab and sourdough bread—a complete meal, really), walk up Stockton Street, and arrive at Washington Square, where mass at St. Peter's and Paul's church is held in both Chinese and Italian. In the early hours of the morning, older Chinese people will get together in the square to perform their daily t'ai chi, while old and young Italians drink their espresso and pore over the pink pages of the *Gazzetta dello Sport* to find out the latest soccer news from Italy. Nattily dressed Chinese children in plaids and rich blues and greens play baseball in the playground of the Salesian school of St. John Bosco. The old geezers at the Italian Athletic Club seem anything but athletic as they organize another lavish dinner with *baccalá* (dried codfish) and pasta with pesto, the latter betraying their roots in the Italian region of Liguria. And the best espresso is served by a Greek at the Lebanese-owned *Caffe Greco,* named after the famous café in Rome's Via Condotti.

Chinatown in San Francisco is big and reminiscent of certain areas of Hong Kong. Different generations of Chinese all seem to work with the same Confucian determination to make it that is often so overwhelmingly lacking in mainland China, where store clerks might walk out or simply turn their backs on you.

In San Francisco, young and old, Italian and Chinese, but also Mexican and Vietnamese and Thai and Brazilian and gay and lesbian and black and brown and beige and white all mix it up, like they do in so many other cities around the world. In Bangkok you can eat a pretty decent pizza these days; Maxim's pricey French food is a hit in Beijing, and so is McDonald's in Moscow. In Tokyo, an Italian dessert called *tiramisú* is all the rage at Kentucky Fried Chicken.

Despite all these superficial signs of integration in the global village, are we getting rid of prejudice and discrimination? Is the fact that one can eat great sushi in El Cerrito in any way a sign that racism or prejudice is on the decline?

Prejudice, Who Me?
Prejudice (also known as prejudgment) is a statement about a person or a race or a gender that is made without checking first. Blacks or women or WASPS or Irish or Poles *are* a certain way, and every single

179

one of them is lumped together in that category. A person is not there, just a label. The group is simply a mental category, not individual human beings.

African American novelist Ishmael Reed, author of pioneering novels like *Mumbo Jumbo* and *Yellow-back Radio Broke Down,* feels that black men, for example, are increasingly subjected to this kind of negative labeling. What is particularly distressing, he notes, is that white feminists have often singled out black men as a particularly pernicious and sexist variety of male. Nobody disputes the presence of misogyny among black men, he says. But it is no more present there than in any other group. To generalize about all black men and cut off all discussion on the issue, as he claims occurs to him when he voices his disapproval of such blanket generalizations, is dominator strategy pure and simple. It's the technique of picking on those below you on the totem pole, and then preventing them from replying through normal channels and making all the comments that do get through appear like the hysterical ravings of a lunatic fringe. This is precisely what some feminists argue is happening to them in the national media, according to Susan Faludi's book *Backlash.*

Perhaps it is true to say that we do unto others as we think they do unto us. Doing unto others as we would like them to do unto us still seems a very respectable—and eminently sensible—goal.

Novelist and futurist Robert Anton Wilson has gone as far as inventing the admittedly unsightly word *sombunall,* meaning "some but not all," which he suggests we use to replace the word *all* in some (but not all) cases. Particularly unfortunate are statements beginning with "All women" or "All blacks" or "All white males." He is equally insistent that the word *is* does little good in public discourse. "We live in a postquantum, post-Einsteinian, transactional, holistic world," he told us. To say anything *is* this or that without regard for context usually leads to dominator thinking. We are all dumb sometimes. We go to a room to get something and then forget what we want. We may be clumsy and oafish early in the morning. That doesn't mean we *are* imbeciles. We simply *act* dumb occasionally.

This may seem insignificant or inconsequential until we realize that sexism, racism, and prejudice of all shapes and sizes are based in part on this kind of thinking. It is surprising how often we judge a whole people on the basis of one unfortunate representative we may have bumped into at some time. Or we might see people in one situation and generalize wildly about them.

Alfonso once saw some tourists board a London double-decker bus and hang around at the foot of the stairs waiting for the conductor, looking lost and clearly unsure about whether or not to sit down. A young man sitting next to Alfonso shook his head and said, "Bloody foreigners are so stupid they don't even know how to get on a bus!" This guy went on to reveal that he thought the foreigners were stupid because, he assumed, they didn't know how to travel by bus, not because they didn't know how to travel by bus *in London,* miles away from home, with different procedures, and in a different language.

Growing up in Greece, Alfonso was brought up with a strong dislike of Turks. Whenever an earthquake would hit Turkey, his Greek nanny claimed it was an act of God, a punishment for all the atrocities Turks had committed against the Greeks. She would remind him regularly that a nearby street was named after a martyr who had been skewered—like souvlaki—by the Turks. Alfonso remembers rooting for bad things to happen to Turkey, and he certainly hopes he is forgiven now for the bad vibes he sent that way. He didn't start meeting Turks until he got to graduate school, and of course realized that they're people just like everybody else.

It's quite unsettling how arbitrary this whole process is and how easy it is to fall into this trap. It is an unfortunate fact that, no matter the group or its good intentions, in the attempt to throw off oppression, the very strategies and tactics of the oppressor are often used. The efforts to get rid of the dominator system can take on dominator characteristics, as we have seen. There were reports that some of the prodemocracy students in China were organized in a highly hierarchical, authoritarian way. This should not surprise anyone, since the students had never been exposed to anything but hierarchical, authoritarian systems and could not be expected to create a democratic structure out of thin air.

Democracy requires a certain amount of education in democratic principles and also a certain amount of practice in them—like thinking about who to vote for and then voting, or allowing other people to express their opinions freely. Creative chaos is part of democracy, says Philip Slater. People who are not used to this will quickly imagine that the world is going to hell in a hand basket, particularly when people "don't know their station" anymore.

If we truly believed that our mission as human beings was to be creative, prejudice would automatically decrease. When we're being creative, we display independence of judgment, that stubborn tendency to want to make up our own minds. When we think of creative individuals, we often name figures like Einstein, Freud, Darwin, or Picasso, who had a singular vision and made up their own minds,

181

going against the grain of established ways of doing and thinking. This characteristic can express itself in the form of originality, rebelliousness, or simply in a quiet unwillingness to accept much of anything at face value. Creative people search for alternative interpretations to events and situations—they create their own meanings.

As we have seen, we live in a consensus reality, a world shaped through stories we tell ourselves about who we are and what we do, where we have come from and where we are going. Like it or not, we are all philosophers to some extent. We have all answered some of the basic questions of life, like why are we here, what is the good life, what is beauty, and so on. We may not have written big books about it, but our actions reflect a certain understanding of those issues. We have our own ideas of beauty, even if we've never studied esthetics. We demonstrate them in the objects we buy, the things we appreciate. We make choices about where and how to live and how to treat others. We answer with our actions questions about "the good life," even if we've never read Plato and Aristotle.

Most of the time we'll find that habit and tradition account for our choices and decisions. Independence of judgment doesn't always mean bucking the trend and being a pain to everyone else. It just means we ask basic questions, look into things, and make up our own minds.

Prejudgment is based on received wisdom. We don't need to think or look at the person, or the issue, we simply know it's this way, and we don't like it, or we do. "My country can do no wrong." It doesn't matter if we end up using the same tactics as the enemy, the very same tactics that prompt us to call them uncivilized animals. We're the good guys, and this is war.

Prejudice does not like to be questioned. Authoritarian individuals tend to share a characteristic known in the trade as anti-introception, which in English means they do not care to look within and question whether what they are doing is right. They just know it is. Because no questions are asked in this prejudged world, nothing new can come in. This makes for a claustrophobically closed system.

Some people refuse to notice that things aren't working out until it hits them in the face. It's a generic psychological mechanism called denial, which appears across the board in people and families and countries. Nobody likes to be criticized, of course. Sometimes criticism—no matter how "constructive" it tries to be—sounds like "You're a bad person." It sounds like an attack, and we need to act.

As we all know, sometimes criticism, although painful, is valid and useful.

Families that have an alcoholic member tend to be "in denial" about the problem, as the pop psychologists like to say, pretending everything is all right and that person just likes to have a few drinks. Similarly we don't like to hear about things that are not going well in our country. People who criticize a certain government policy are often accused of thinking the country itself is somehow bad. These people are called unpatriotic for being critical, especially if they're critical while there's a war going on. Similarly, when a country's economy is heading toward a depression, presidents like to give optimistic-sounding speeches, so people don't worry too much, or start wondering whether it's time for a different president. When we are in denial, we end up believing our own lies, and we fail to act even if our survival depends on it.

There's an oft-repeated story about frogs that's worth repeating. If you chuck Mr. Frog into a pot of boiling water, he will leap out before you can say "ribbit." But if you put Mr. Frog in a pot of cold water and then heat the water up slowly, Mr. Frog will boil along with the water. Careful, Mr. Frog. One can imagine some of Mr. Frog's friends standing around the pot, warning him that things are changing all around him, that the water's getting hotter and hotter; look, steam is coming from the top of the pot now. But Mr. Frog thinks they're silly worrywarts, and he keeps splashing around in the water singing, "Don't worry, be happy."

We all share these moments of prejudice and authoritarianism when we refuse to look within or to observe without. It's not just them, those dominator folks out there, who keep the dominator system going. We all play our parts, and maybe it's time to stop sending in our contributions.

Our educational system is structured to encourage prejudgment, apathy, and the development of a closed mental system. We are fed predigested facts, which we are told to accumulate and memorize, because the more prejudgments we have, the quicker we can come back with the "right" answer, without thinking. The system of debate is based on this ability to be quick with a judgment. Our way of "resolving" issues still follows this confrontational model.

Fortunately a strong movement toward a partnership orientation is afoot, stressing dialogue rather than debate. In politics, face-to-face diplomacy is emerging as a powerful force for conflict resolution, an approach that stresses nonviolence and resolutions that bring mutual satisfaction. A movement is developing in schools, universities, and citizens' diplomacy groups, that values listening and empathy and recognizes that human beings can solve their differences in nonviolent ways.

Listening is one of the simplest lessons to learn from the practice of conflict resolution. In practice this may mean really listening to the person you're arguing with and repeating back to the person you're arguing with what you hear them saying, what their position is. Seems simple enough, to be sure, but it has made an enormous difference in countless situations of vehement—and apparently irreconcilable—disagreement.

University and school programs in conflict resolution, like the Peace and Conflict Studies Program at UC Berkeley, stress another important lesson. In a dominator system, difference and conflict are to be avoided, unless one is actively looking for a fight. Conflict is swept under the carpet, and the existence of real differences is denied until a fight erupts. Then one must *confront* and create a standoff where somebody has to back down, because "this town ain't big enough for the both of us."

The dominator system has a strong tendency to create oppositions such as pleasure and pain, good and bad, as we have seen. In a partnership system, these oppositions are transformed. Some people mistakenly believe that this means there is no good and evil anymore, that nothing matters and we either become nihilists or pretend we're enlightened, beyond dualism, or something equally vapid. In the partnership paradigm, conflicts are an inextricable part of life. If we are imagining a world without conflicts, we are behaving just like our Mr. Frog. Where diversity is cherished, differences are bound to arise. What we need are tools to deal with conflict, tools that already exist but that individually and collectively we do not have much practice in using.

The Wages of Fear, or I'm Hurting and I'm Gonna Find Someone to Blame

If one fuel for prejudice is the unwillingness to question our thoughts and actions, fear is the spark that ignites the flame. In threatening or alarming circumstances, human beings have often shown a tendency to want to find a place to lay blame—a scapegoat. It's *them*. Get rid of *them* and everything will be all right. Almost inevitably the scapegoat is a group that is different: immigrants, blacks, Asians, women, Jews, men, you name it.

The dominator system thrives on fear, because fear is what justifies and inspires many of the typical dominator behaviors. "It's a jungle out there," and I use survival to justify my behavior. Fear is marked by feelings of separation and isolation, an impulsive desire to control and dominate the cause of fear—or what we think is the cause—and an inability to be in control of our lives, a feeling of being adrift without a rudder, without the capacity to create. Fear is exploited ruthlessly by leaders of all kinds, from corporations to countries to new age ashrams. The us-versus-them mentality that lies at the root of prejudice makes us want to eliminate all differences in life-styles and races and cultures, so we can return to the homogeneous, safe, familiar things we know.

Robert Anton Wilson pointed out to us that anxiety-prone people tend to stay in the same place, eat the same food, and think the same thoughts over and over again. They're basically afraid of anything different. The authoritarian personality, in a classic 1950s study, was defined as "highly susceptible to situational pressures," which is much the same as saying that these types freak out when there is anything new or different or unusual in their environment.

Wilson believes that a traumatic infancy can leave one anxiety-prone, convinced that the world is basically a scary and threatening place. When one is fearful, one tends to cover up that fear in a variety of ways but primarily wants to control the environment to such an extent that it becomes a totally closed system. The problem is, of course, that by making the environment safe through control, one makes it unsafe for others, who do not necessarily wish to be under another's control. And so the game goes on until somebody literally steps out of it.

Creative people, on the other hand, tend to move around a lot. They enjoy travel, Wilson pointed out. It's certainly true for Roddy Frame. "I can never understand people who complain about having to go on the road for six months," he said, "because to me it's a fantastic place to be. My favorite place is between places." When we spoke to Roddy he was apartment hunting in London's Notting Hill. "You know what it's like walking around looking at this place and that; after a while all these places look the same," he said. "So I decided to visualize the perfect place. I sat down one night and cleared my mind, Zen style, and tried to picture the perfect place. It was the Holiday Inn. And now I take my roots with me, in a way, a kind of troubadour. Quite a romantic way to go."

185

It's not just a traumatic infancy that can leave a person anxiety-prone, afraid of the new, of the thrill of travel that people like Roddy so clearly relish. Other factors, social rather than psychological, can also cause enormous anxiety and stress. Economic recessions, hardship, social disorder—all can make us worry about how to pay the rent, where the next meal is coming from, and whether the streets are safe. We can all become anxiety-prone authoritarians if the right buttons are pushed.

Germany between the two world wars is a classic case. Inflation so high the cost of a cup of coffee could go up by thousands of marks from morning to afternoon; anger and shame about the losses of World War I and the disrespectful settlement imposed by the victors; and social unrest, coupled with a potential socialist / communist threat—all led to the certainty, security, and commitment of the fearless Führer who knew what was wrong with the country and had a patriotic vision of how to fix everything.

Wilson feels that "we should all take a sabbatical every five years and spend six months with people who hold totally opposite opinions." All too often we close ourselves off from people who have different opinions from us and refuse to listen to anything that goes against our own.

"I was talking to my daughter-in-law," Isabel Allende told us, "and telling her that I have traveled so much in my life, and the more I travel, the less I see the differences and the more I see the similarities among people. People get hold of a little difference and make the world of it, out of fear. Why are people afraid of, for example, the Latinos looking for a job on the street corners of our cities? People are afraid of someone because he is black or tall or short, but we are all people! By tuning in to the similarities, you become more compassionate, you lose fear, you become able to relate better, you become part of the chain. If you isolate yourself because there are little differences, how can you have a sense of community?"

From Fear to Exploration

Ishmael Reed grew up in an ethnic neighborhood in Buffalo, New York. For over ten years he has lived in Oakland, California, a "really international community," as he put it. Ever since he was young, he has been struck by the relative harmony and richness that exists in some culturally diverse neighborhoods. This made a strong impact on him and led him to wondering whether what was possible at the community level might not be applicable to politics as well.

Can a feeling of interdependence go beyond our nearest and dearest, beyond family and friends, even our neighborhoods? Can it go beyond who's "on our side" and who isn't? How can we resolve conflicts that emerge because of difference—whether race, ideology, gender, or whatever? Can we extend the friendship and feeling of community Ishmael Reed has experienced in Oakland to relationships among nations? Reed himself explored the sociopolitical implications of what is now called multiculturalism in the early '70s with his classic novel *Mumbo Jumbo*.

Joel Federman is working on a book exploring the political implications of universal love, which he defines as "the human capacity for heightened awareness of solidarity with other beings." This is not just so much wishful thinking, Federman stressed when we spoke to him. The heritage of the concept goes all the way back to the Chinese philosopher Mo-tzu and to Jesus and has reappeared in various guises in the work of William James (who called it neighborly love), the American philosopher C. S. Pierce (who called it evolutionary love), and Mahatma Gandhi, Martin Luther King, and Pierre Teilhard de Chardin. "In fact," he argues, "two of the most important political ideas of the modern era, nonviolence and human rights, are rooted in the universal love attitude."

What is this "heightened awareness of solidarity with other human beings"? Federman quotes Einstein as saying, "A human being is part of the whole called by us 'the universe,' a part limited in time and space. He thinks himself, his thoughts, and feelings, as something separate from the rest—a kind of optical delusion of his consciousness. This delusion is a kind of prison for us, restricting us to our own personal desire and to affections for a few persons nearest to us. Our task must be to free ourselves from this prison by widening our circle of compassion to embrace all living creatures and the whole of nature and its beauty."

During the doomed Soviet coup in August of 1991, when tanks were moving toward the Russian parliament building, the people who stopped them used an old argument: We're your people, your brothers and sisters, mothers and fathers; we can't kill each other. It worked. It did not work so well in Tiananmen Square, of course. The troops there were from different regions of China, and maybe they didn't speak the language, or they just couldn't relate to the students, like the National Guard at Kent State.

In addition to countless recorded instances of successful nonviolent people-power social movements, Federman finds very inspiring the occasional moments of concord in the midst of otherwise terrible warfare. One such instance took place during World War I in the hellish trenches of Flanders. On Christmas Eve 1914 British and German troops began to respond to each other's Christmas songs and eventually rose from their trenches to celebrate Christmas together. Another instance of the same sort took place in the American Civil War when Confederate soldiers did not fire on Union soldiers celebrating Thanksgiving. At certain times it seems we are just pushed too far, and perhaps these men realized that across from them in trenches their enemy must have been going through exactly the same hell.

Paul Watzlawick has written about these kinds of events and their significance in his delightful and important little book *Ultra-Solutions,* where he mentions a study of non-Jews who assisted Jews during World War II. When asked why they had risked their own lives to help others, many reacted "almost instinctively" with a counterquestion such as "What do you mean?" and generally indicated that it was only normal to help others. It was just what one human being would do for another. People who perform acts of great bravery often explain their actions similarly—"I could not allow this to happen. I had to do something."

In all these cases, the logical, rational idea that it makes sense to help one another and to be decent human beings is matched to some extent by feelings of solidarity, of empathy, which, according to Federman, are the essential elements of the universal love attitude.

Empathy has many definitions, Federman told us, but two aspects are common to most definitions, one cognitive and one affective—in other words, one that is mostly intellectual or mental and the other mostly emotional. Empathy, then, is the ability to see and understand another's position or perspective and to feel for another person. Noted systems scientist C. West Churchland has stated that "the systems approach begins when we first see the world through the eyes of another."

"Empathy is an ability to feel another person's pain," psychologist Susan Hales explained. "If somebody is in pain and you can imagine it very visibly, if you experience their pain, then you have an empathic reaction. If you are sympathetic, you say you're sorry that they are experiencing pain, but it doesn't really impact you. There is a difference between sympathy and empathy. Empathy is actually feeling the other person's pain or happiness or sorrow.

"Empathy is important for moral behavior because experiencing someone else's pain and distress will motivate you to do something to help rather than to go on your self-interested way. You're induced to action either by your belief about right and wrong behavior, and what you ought to do to help somebody, or by your empathic reaction: you experience their stress so you want to alleviate it. It's not as though somebody stabbed you and it hurts me, and so I want to pull the knife out of you to stop it hurting me. It's not the exact same pain. Rather you can imagine what it feels like when somebody is suffering because they, for example, split up with a boyfriend, or whatever, and so you're motivated to help alleviate their pain."

Empathy seems also to be closely connected to Art and Elaine Aron's idea of the expansion of the self: Can I understand and feel what the other person is going through in a way that temporarily transcends our boundaries? Women have generally been trained to be far more empathic than men, which is one of the reasons why we usually think of women as more understanding, compassionate, and sensitive than men.

The arts offer a remarkable entry point into the expansion of the self. By immersing ourselves not necessarily into writing or singing but even just in reading or listening, the arts can open up new worlds for us in powerful ways. It is not necessary to become actors, even at an amateur level, for instance, to be creative. We can learn to listen, to be a good audience, and to respond creatively to a work of art and to life. The domination-system split between artist and public, and consequently between creative and conforming people, is another illusory opposition that must be overcome. As systems theory suggests, it is the relationship between the two that is vital, and the audience has an enormous role in the dialogue that goes on, particularly in live performances, but also, in less immediate ways, in books. We get out of a book, or performance, about as much as we put in. When we read a book, we have to give it our own interpretation and collaborate with the author in creating a shared meaning, one that emerges in the relationship between reader and author. Our interpretation is probably not precisely what the author intended, because the words and sentences trigger meanings and memories that are personal and unique to each one of us.

Robert Anton Wilson explained to us that when he works on the characters for one of his novels, after much research and preliminary writing, it suddenly all clicks, the characters emerge and develop a life of their own. "I learn the most from the bad guys in my

189

books," Wilson remarked, showing how the process of writing is a way of expanding oneself, of creating a context for exploration. It is also possible to learn about what it might be like to be someone we really dislike. What drives such a person? What are their motivations, their fears and hopes?

Do You Know Who I Am?

Federman told us that "what often confounds the development of empathy are misperceptions concerning those with whom we are in conflict." In the Arab-Israeli conflict, for example, the issue is not only territory—who has claim to what, where, and from what authority, historical precedent, and so forth—but rather the views of themselves and of the other groups into which both have been socialized. One of the big problems in conflicts of this kind, whether Arab-Israeli, Armenian-Azerbaijani, or Catholic-Protestant in Northern Ireland, is that the two parties do not even recognize each other as human beings. They see only what are often particularly ugly images of each other socially and historically constructed through years of hatred. As Sam Keen has shown in his powerful book and accompanying PBS documentary *Faces of the Enemy,* we have often gone to extreme lengths to paint our enemies as inhuman.

How much do we really get to see of the Other—he or she or them who is not us, not part of the in-group—beyond our preconceived ideas, even without wartime propaganda? In disputes of literally biblical proportions, like the Arab-Israeli one, are the two sides seeing each other, really seeing each other, or do they see thousands of years of prejudice and hatred?

Our perceptions are often clouded by assumptions that we never examine. Her classmates in Washington state thought Susan Hales was special, as you will recall from her story, because for them she *was* a tanned California babe. The kids in Lindsay totally ignored her because to them she *was* a migrant farmworker. Is our perception shaped and molded by years of history that can stultify us to the point that we see not a live human being here and now but a set of prejudgments and grudges, with no possibility for a second opinion?

Can we even use the word *is,* or do we have to consider the system of events, the relationships and circumstances, that shaped Susan's life? Who was Susan, *really?*

In the many dialogue workshops that he has conducted with Arabs and Israelis, Joel Federman has seen the importance of getting the groups to express their human and national identities. Jews, for instance, trace their names back to the Holocaust and describe the influence that period has had on their lives to this day. Seeing these life stories told by flesh-and-blood individuals is much more real for Palestinians than the abstract manipulations of the media in their discussions of a people's history, and the same is true for the Israelis when they hear a Palestinian's story.

When we empathize with someone else, we feel for them (and it can be joy or sorrow or any other emotion) and temporarily try to see the world from their perspective. But when we become authoritarian, when we switch into a fearful or angry dominator mode, we tend not to allow ourselves to experience a vast range of feelings, and we become threatened by any understanding of the world different from our own. We are therefore blocked both intellectually and emotionally from experiencing the world in anything but a restricted way.

Along with the inability to feel pain, and the insensitivity toward others, comes an inability to experience pleasure. By blocking feelings, we deprive ourselves of the capacity to enjoy being alive, and this is one of the peculiar paradoxes of existence. As we become blocked, we become inhibited and lack spontaneity, we lack a sense of risk and creative challenge. In our effort to exert self-control, we have severely restricted our own freedom.

We can expand the self by experiencing life as others do, by trying to understand what their position is. By becoming sensitive to other people, we can broaden our understanding not only of others and of the world around us but of ourselves.

Connecting and Expanding the Self

When we let our self expand, as Elaine and Art Aron suggest, at times it is possible to experience a deep sense of connection with human beings, a feeling perhaps expressible in poetry, but one that does not translate too well into prose—our prose, at least—without sounding mushy. Human beings do share many characteristics—we all eat and sleep and fall in love and get angry and go to the bathroom and cry, and eventually we all die, and before that we spend time worrying about it. These are all aspects of our shared humanness, some mundane, some glorious, and some terrifying.

When we say "I can relate" to this or that, we mean that we have had similar experiences, and we may not feel the particular joy or pain or anger, but we have some idea of what it's like. Or we can observe and listen closely enough so that we gain some understanding of what the other person is experiencing.

We may never know each other, really, since we hardly even know ourselves. But we can make an effort to acknowledge the other person or group and make an effort not to prejudge them but to listen and to pay close attention to them. Frank Barron once wrote that perhaps we spend too much time stressing the need for love when on a more basic level we need an act of *attention*—we need to be recognized as human beings.

Ignoring someone, or preventing them from speaking, means denying their identity, denying their existence. Any group or person that feels this will attempt to prove that they exist. And they may well do so in very destructive ways, such as terrorist or criminal acts. This somber fact points to the vital nature of recognition, and basic human dignity, as a foundation for partnership.

In a partnership society we remain open to what the Other is saying because we are linked not only by our similarities; differences can also be a source of wonder. Chinese and Africans all share in their humanity, but they're also different from each other, and those differences can be the source of learning, joy, communication, and disagreement, of course.

"One class I teach on the philosophy of art," Mara Keller told us, "is to show an appreciation for what each culture's vision of life and way of life has been and to discover what is of value for us today in each of these human experiences."

Ishmael Reed told us he had been teaching "what is really a 'multicultural' American culture class for twenty years before anybody came up with the idea. I find I have to teach kids about European as well as African ideas and sometimes Native American art and Asian American art." Reed is amazed at how little students know of any culture, including their own. "I think it's interesting that they've never heard of Maurice Ravel. Ninety-seven white middle-class nineteen-year-old college students. That's some chauvinist education they get! I want to do some stuff on Maurice Ravel, because I love his music. *La Valse* is one of my favorite pieces. Back then he used jazz, he also used North African music and Polynesian dancers and musicians. He was into all that stuff, just as the painters were. On the other hand, now you get Afro-Americans like Alvin Ailey in so-called European-American modern dance."

These cultural differences are an enormous wealth for our planet, since they show us different ways of living, of structuring our reality. They show a world pregnant with possibilities, containing the seeds of transformation and change, always in a dialectic with tradition.

MultiKulti

The writer Arthur Koestler developed an interesting and relevant theory of creativity. He coined the term *bisociation* to refer to the bringing together of two previously unrelated ideas, such as automobile and cinema, into a new synthesis: a drive-in theater, for instance. This process also applies to the meeting of different cultures, which makes people and ideas clash, mingle, and generally shake, rattle, and roll. Bisociation has been employed for a long time by Mother Nature herself. The first creatures on the planet simply made copies of themselves by splitting off into different parts, all identical to the original. Maybe a megalomaniac's dream, but not a very effective evolutionary strategy (remember the link between creativity and complexity?). Evolution proceeded in leaps and bounds with the appearance of *sexual* reproduction, which meant every new creature—including the human variety—was the product of genetic mix 'n' match, Mommy and Daddy both contributing to the new and improved(?) product.

This process refers also to a way of dealing with oppositions, polarities, and dichotomies. It points toward synthesis and creativity rather than conflict and polarization. It asks how we can create coexistence.

"It's funny that whenever playwrights and novelists look for something quintessentially American, they tend to pick cowboys and small rural towns or the decline of the West. Well, this is just loony," Philip Slater told us. "Whatever the U.S. is, it sure as hell is not the West and small towns," he added. Tradition is not really the quintessential U.S., but, if anything, second generations are—the flux of conflict between received culture and change. Forging new identities out of this meeting of old and new is what the American experience is about, Slater told us, and great American plays and novels for him should deal with "foreigners."

"I have always been a foreigner," Isabel Allende told us. "When I go back to my country, I have the illusion that I belong, but I know that I am a foreigner there too. I am used to it, and I like it. It gives me a certain perspective that other people don't have. When you belong in a place for too long, you see the trees but you don't see the forest. It's good to be a step away. You gain another vision, another point of view. In my case, as a writer, it's very good for me. By being marginal you can say whatever you want; you have nothing to lose."

Indeed in America we are all foreigners to some extent, some recent, some tracing their roots to the first foreigners. One of the most powerful images of America, for people all over the world, is

193

the beacon that attracts those willing to break from tradition and shape their own future differently.

Isabel Allende feels that coming to the U.S. has been a very important experience for her. "My new book is about these two cultures colliding and blending. This is fascinating to me because this collision happens in large scale, in the scale of countries and cultures, and it is also what has happened to me as a human being. I was on a lecture tour when I met this gringo who had nothing in common with me, but he spoke Spanish. What my husband (the gringo) and I wanted by getting together was to bring our experiences and our cultures together, to see how we as individuals can work for a better understanding of these two cultures."

Like Ishmael Reed, Allende sees her personal experiences of cultural integration and understanding as an example applicable on a larger scale. "It was a tremendous challenge to try to adapt to a country that was to me the Evil Empire," she explained. "We Latin Americans are the first victims of the terrible foreign policy of the U.S. By moving here and learning about this country, learning to understand it and love it, I think I have become a better person."

Cultural intermarrying—sometimes a brilliant new creation, sometimes an awkward mix—is exemplified by Paul Simon's *Graceland* album, an enormous hit, arising out of the interaction of a New York Jewish intellectual singer-songwriter from the sixties with South African and Latino musicians. Not all meetings of cultures are as successful as this, of course. The specter of racism still haunts us, whether it is among whites and blacks, Germans and Turks, Italians and North Africans, Jews and Arabs, or Japanese and Koreans.

Ishmael Reed tends to distrust people who have abandoned their own ethnicity. He feels that people like conservative commentator and novelist William F. Buckley, Jr., who expectorate about single black welfare mothers should look after their own in the Irish ghettos of Boston. Their real problem isn't with blacks or Jews or whoever they happen to be prejudiced against but with their own ethnicity, he says. Their problems stem from their relationships with their grandparents, who couldn't speak English, the ones that made them feel embarrassed to bring their friends home.

Ashamed of their ethnicity, these people wanted to disappear into the melting pot and come out as sanitized as possible, according to Reed. This meant imposing a homogeneous worldview based on an anti-intellectual, pseudo-European set of values. It's interesting to see, Reed continues, that the Europeans themselves are far more open to American culture than much of the establishment here is. This is true in the case of Afrocentrism and jazz, for instance. The latter is revered in Europe. In Freiburg, Germany, Reed came across Cecil Taylor Week, Taylor being an avant-garde jazz pianist few Americans are familiar with.

Dominique DiPrima believes that "we must understand that cultural pride and self-esteem are a prerequisite for any kind of unity and stability." But she knows that cultural pride, pride in difference, threatens many people, particularly older generations. "Young people are more multiculturally oriented. They are raised with it. Youth culture now is almost synonymous with black culture, rap music, clothing, with talking a certain way. Young people see the same music videos across the country, for example, so there are less differences and more uniformity in the youth culture. There is a lot less fear because people know more about each other. I have a lot of hope for this generation in the area of racism and multicultural understanding."

Here Dominique illustrates a seemingly paradoxical movement in two directions simultaneously. On the one hand is the movement toward cultural pride, the search for roots and individuality. On the other we find a certain cultural uniformity, a greater awareness of what is going on in pop culture all over the country.

And Now a Word from Our Sponsor: Media and Culture

The information age brings with it a world in which the transmission of information becomes the lifeblood of society. We create technology but are in turn shaped and re-created by that very technology. Computers were a human invention, but now humans are being shaped by their ongoing contact with this technology. Television and the remote control, sound bytes, our increasingly short attention span, the fact that a deodorant commercial is longer than a news item affecting thousands if not millions of people, not to mention the role of the media in shaping foreign policy, the CNN-ization of the Gulf War—what does it all mean?

According to futurist Paul Saffo, a large part of the transformation we're witnessing "really comes down to the artifacts we create. We invent our artifacts, and then our artifacts reinvent us. The single biggest change in the last forty to fifty years is the shift to information technology. In the postindustrial world, we really are becoming an information society. And of course an information society is not a

195

society that doesn't make things, it's a society that uses information to make things more effectively. So we are informationalizing our products. An automobile from Detroit is lighter weight and more efficient because of the information processes that allow engineers to design better, lighter, more efficient engines. We are in a world where we still make physical artifacts, but they are the end point of an information process. They're less products in their own right than the artifact of the information processed. "

The term *postmodernism* has been invented by intellectuals and appropriated by the media. It's become very popular these days and is used in architecture, music (MTV has a "postmodern" hour), in literature, film, even politics. It's a term that is supposed to describe, in some way, how the information we create has begun in turn to shape us. Like cars made in Detroit, we're also becoming informationalized, shaped by an information process dominated to a large extent by the media.

The term itself is interesting because it means "after the modern." The implication is that the modern age has ended. Now we're *post*modern, in other words, we don't really know where we're going or where we are, but whatever it is, it ain't modern. Postmodernism reflects what happens to us when we begin to remote control reality, when TV becomes more real than the real world, when history is what the movies tell us it is, and the future is created in Hollywood.

There is a certain macabre, even funereal, aspect to postmodernism, largely because it is associated with the *death* of a lot of things. The death of the author, for instance, according to the French semioticist (semiotics is the study of signs, symbols, etc.) Roland Barthes. Interesting questions arising on postmortem: Does the author know what his or her book "means"? Is the author's meaning the only valid one? What if you interpret a book or a movie in a way the author or director never intended? Does that make you wrong? Of course not! Now it's all about interpretation. Getting some kind of agreement, though, becomes tricky.

The Italian Umberto Eco is a another semioticist. He has written hefty tomes on interpretation, a book about America (some Europeans are morbidly fascinated by the U.S.—they look at Las Vegas with the same awe Americans might have for the pyramids at Giza), and a very famous novel, *The Name of the Rose*. The novel was famous because it was an unfinished best-seller—Eco finished it, 95 percent of his readers didn't—but also because each person read something totally different into it. For some *The Name of the Rose* was a medieval spoof on Sherlock Holmes, for others a trenchant observation on modern politics, others again saw it as a meditation on scholarship and knowledge, some saw it as a critique of the church, others saw it as a reminder of how much they hate Latin, and so on. What did the author really mean? All of the above? None? And does it even matter? The days of telling little Johnny or Mary that this or that book means XYZ are over.

In addition to the death of the author, there's the death of history—the U.S.-Soviet struggle is over, says Francis Fukuyama of the RAND Corporation, so that's that, history has ended. The death of creativity, the death of the subject, the death of progress—it's a big "That's all folks!" All gone, all dead. Nothing left. Just play around with it all, pick around the ruins, and parody old styles. Make movies like *Dick Tracy* or *The Addams Family*, plundering old TV shows. Is *Lost in Space* next? Why not *Bewitched?*

Well, what's alive, then, you may ask? With postmodernists proclaiming the death of everything, it's time for us to add our own obituary: Postmodernism is about the death of the dominator system, and about the postmodernists' lack of imagination in seeing an alternative. Now postmodernism itself is dead, and we can begin to move into an age of partnership.

"When I think of postmodern," Paul Saffo remarked, "I think of art and esthetics; the process of informationalizing has been a crisis for artists. The essence of postmodern thinking in the arts is that we're redefining the notion of what's original and the nature of originality. My suspicion is that originality is a phantom, an artifact of our bad memory, because everything's derivative. We just forget that Picasso borrowed liberally and drew a lot of inspiration from African art, and he made no secret of it; but people who were unfamiliar with African art chose not to pay attention to that. Meanwhile, of course, African artists were borrowing heavily from Western values, but they got the short end of the deal.

"Our new information systems make it so easy to copy—just look at the digital sampling of sounds. But they also make it easier than ever to trace the origins of copies. What we're doing is atom-smashing the notion of original. We're going to conclude that what matters is not originality, which doesn't exist, but passion. We will take it for granted that every work of art is additive, that every artist stands on the shoulders of other artists. What we will ask about his or her contribution is whether it adds passion or whether it is merely a copy.

197

"You can go back to the twelfth century in China, where there was a poet who took the poem of another poet, written two hundred years earlier, and added one word to it. Everyone said, 'My God, you really got it!' He was praised and honored. That's what's happening—creativity will be seen as a group process that not only can involve collaborators of the same time but collaborators who died long ago."

Madonna seems a perfect example. She puts on a multimedia show that's definitely not just pop music. In the entire length of her movie *Truth or Dare* you hardly ever get to see the musicians. The music is just a part of the larger show. And when Madonna borrows—from Marilyn Monroe, for example—you know she's borrowing, and you know she knows you know. Madonna samples the past for interesting tidbits to glue together in her postmodern, ever-changing pastiche. No originality in the old sense of the word, just a clever cut-and-paste job. No matter how great a fan you are of Madonna, few people will honestly say she's a great singer, a really great dancer, really beautiful, a great actress, or even fabulously talented—by the old standards. Certainly not original, but she is very original in the way she has constructed herself and the public's image of her. And that, as everyone knows, is the point. The standards have changed, and sometimes we don't even know what the criteria for our standards are, beyond "the bottom line."

Whatever we may think of Madonna, her image is of a woman in control who is urging other women to take control of their lives as well. Below all the postmodern celebration of kinky surface glitz, her songs are filled with down-to-earth messages urging self-respect and freedom for young women. The in-your-face irreverence that aggravates so many upstanding citizens comes with an almost wholesome message of basic decency that would surprise the thrill-seeking, censorious, conservative Madonna-bashers; but then they're only concerned with surfaces too, both visual and moral, and cannot see beyond pelvic gyrations and overt sexuality.

As Paul Saffo suggests, postmodernism is forcing us to take a hard look at what is original, or creative. In the old days, a modern star or cultural icon had to be fabulously "gifted" and "inspired." Both of these terms imply some kind of blessing, and the blessing, we thought, came from the big Creator himself, omniscient and omnipotent. Even if these stars weren't that gifted, they had to at least have the troubled artist's exterior, the kind of furrowed brow you get from delving a little too deeply into life's mysteries, or at least into the bottom of your glass.

He or she had to have the smoldering intensity of Marlon Brando or Greta Garbo, the encyclopedic brilliance of James Joyce, the soul searching of Sylvia Plath, or the kind of borderline and brilliant madness that would make you cut your ear off, like Vincent, or shoot up, drink a bottle of whisky, and eat two Chinese meals before a set of difficult music played at breakneck speed, like Charlie Parker.

The emphasis in the modern was on depth. Artists plumbed the depths of the human psyche to see what they could find, and brought it all back, like it or not. They would shake society up, criticize the powers that be with songs of protest, like Bob Dylan, and be the voice that catalyzed a generation. Artists may have been making art for art's sake, but many were also engaged in political and psychological struggles which they laid bare on canvases, in books, and on stages all over the world. Depth was part of what you might call the vertical metaphor: the gift comes from above, and we use it to reach into the darkest recesses of the soul and of society.

In most interpretations of postmodernity, depth is out, and surfaces are in. Engagement—political, psychological, or what have you—is out, and "detached irony" is in (sometimes mistaken for downright cynicism). If one gets too involved, one becomes committed, and that means the end of detachment, going beyond relativism and having to make real choices.

Depth: The implications are political too. Who bothers to read a speech by a campaigning politician these days? Who has the time? Sound bytes are what make up our consciousness and influence our decisions. Not a lot of depth in a sound byte, but it has to sound good enough to make you skip to the next question with a certain feeling of satisfaction. "Yeah, he handled that pretty well." Reagan was the Teflon president, in what are being called the years of denial, with the media looking the other way. More surfaces, and of a special nonstick kind too. Don't look now, but underneath those surfaces something was going on. Anger and resentment were brewing, along with the revolution of lowered expectations.

Depth: Even economically we seemed to have little of it. The 1980s were singularly lacking in productive depth economically. Surfaces were what counted. Take the fortunes of the Milkens, Trumps, Maxwells, and Keatings. A lot of loans received by men with a lot of surface glitz but no productive enterprises, with real live people actually working and making something.

No industry, no cars, or TVs, or steel. No factories. God forbid! How horribly modern and low-tech, how smokestack! No, this was the era of high-tech computer transactions where junk bonds and buyouts inflated the price of what little depth there was, without there ever having to be a product manufactured anywhere. We sold each other sizzle, but there was no steak. Like the canned laughter of sitcoms, we sold the prerecorded sizzle of a steak that had already been eaten. And the joke was on the taxpayer, eagerly waiting for the wealth, which was supposed to be trickling down from the wealthy, but was really rushing out of the country to be invested in Hong Kong and Zurich.

In postmodernism we don't get into things deeply anymore. We just glide over the surfaces. With our zappers in hand we succumb to the remote-control syndrome and zap into a different TV reality in a split second, from Sting's new video to "Star Trek," from Bill Moyers to "Murphy Brown" to "Bewitched" and back, is the ad over yet on channel 4? With this kind of attention span, who would ever read *War and Peace?* Who has time for a slow medium like literature when we can channel-surf from world to world at the touch of a button? But we have to ask if this process is also changing the way we think in some fundamental ways.

With such short attention spans, can we really tackle the serious issues confronting us without simply getting bored? Will we get sick of the fuss about the environment or AIDS, and move on to something else, something with more immediate appeal? Will we just change the channel to some other virtual reality, until our bodies finally give up on us and clamor for some warmth and food and attention?

God is dead, that trendy philosopher Nietzsche said, and that's why Nietzsche is now seen as the great precursor of postmodernism, which in some respects is the institutionalization of relativism. If God is dead, and all beliefs are relative, then does anything really matter? Well, clearly some things do, like paying the rent, so we have somewhere to ponder these profound questions. People we love matter, so we have someone to ponder them with and to help us when we take a break from our ponderings. Beyond the basics, the bread-and-butter lowest common denominator called survival, what else is there? What can we believe in?

On the one hand we may believe that we know the truth, the way life really is, and it's all very important, because we're right. On the other hand we may believe that all we know is just beliefs, and nothing really matters. The first one gets us all worked up and fighting mad, the second one gets us too apathetic—nihilistic even.

The dominator system is obviously grounded in the first set of beliefs, the one where we all know the Truth. A lot of people have been questioning Truth and reaching the conclusion that more often than not it is a story told to keep the powers that be where they are. Tearing all the stories down and making them look equally foolish, like the deconstructionists are doing, may be a terribly clever—and necessary—intellectual feat, but unless we offer legitimate alternatives, we will ultimately keep the dominator system nicely in place.

The media has been depicting a discouraging image of the younger generation. The eighteen- to thirty-year-olds, shell-shocked by the complexity of events and with few if any role models, seem to be having a moratorium. They want neither the career-track, corporate-climbing life promoted in the 1980s nor the kind of family they themselves grew up in. In 1990, 40 percent of eighteen- to twenty-nine-year-olds had seen their parents get divorced. Not surprisingly, they are in no hurry to marry, have a family, or get a job. This may have been the reason that "Get a life" was such a popular expression for a while.

Young people don't vote, we are told, but have they had role models? Reports tell us they don't know much about politics and don't really care. They didn't grow up during Vietnam and Watergate, these events were not shocks for them, they were history. They're givens. It's easier to get worked up about oppressive dictators, but when you live in the country that in many cases serves as an inspiration for democratic revolutions all over the world where do you go from here?

An article on the "twentysomething" generation in *Time* magazine depicting this generation as somewhat lifeless, ignorant, and generally at a loss drew a flurry of letters from young people who claim they are misunderstood. Nothing new here. Young people of all generations feel they're misunderstood, until they grow up, and then it's their turn to do the misunderstanding. But like every generation, they do have a point. They think their generation should not be compared with the baby boomers, to the '60s youth who so narcissistically idolize themselves in the media through shows like "thirtysomething." They are certainly not as homogeneous.

The youths of the '90s are painfully aware of the enormous complexity of the problems they are dealing with, and their education in no way prepares them to deal with complexity. "It's not as simple as getting out of Vietnam," they say. It seems that the '90s kids, like some of their older brothers and sisters who supposedly think globally and act locally, are going for a much more local approach to problems, trying to deal with issues like pollution and crime in their own neighborhoods and communities. Local action seems to be an emerging way of participating in the healing of a nation. It's as if there were a giant clean-up operation going on, getting rid of a monstrous social, political, and economic oil spill, the legacy of an outmoded worldview.

Dominique DiPrima feels young people are getting a bad rap: "The media keeps saying the same thing over and over, and I don't think it's true. Young people are active, but they're active in different ways. A lot of them are involved with environmental issues, and a lot of them are really concerned about racism. They're thinking about the world. I think that one of the things that happened in the sixties, or early seventies, is that the protests and demonstrations and activist work were widely publicized by the media, which created a snowball effect. I don't think conservative forces in the media today would like to see that happen again. Instead they tend to publicize this supposed apathy of our youth and are constantly harping on how everyone doesn't care and they're not doing anything and they're wandering aimlessly. When they do cover rap music, they depict it as this sexist, misogynist thing. The hip-hop generation is real and very much more politically aware than people know."

Television is a relief, an escape. It's also a drug, an anesthetic, according to sociologist Todd Gitlin. And, like most drugs, it has some side effects, not the least of which is fostering narcissism and undermining the belief that society is a cooperative commonwealth. Television, like much of the so-called information age, makes us feel alone. Americans suffer from a lack of intimacy, some researchers report, a lack of community and connection with others. The TV acts as a substitute for real experiences and real connection with real human beings. We now have phone sex because at least it's safe, although people are already getting addicted to it. But television does not just turn us into selfish little cocoons. It also influences the way we think and act.

Dominique herself is making a contribution with her TV show. Isabel Allende says, "One minute of TV can make a tremendous change. Let me give you an example: Soap operas are a cult in Latin America, and everybody watches at least two or three hours every day. The lives of the protagonists are more important than the lives of your kids. I was living in Venezuela, and there was a place where women could have free breast examinations for cancer. But you could not get women to go because they didn't think it was necessary. There was this huge campaign about the need to have the examination at least once a year. Nothing happened for years, until someone thought of TV. So they had a character of one of the most popular soap operas go to this clinic for a breast exam. The next day people were in lines to have the exam done."

While on the UCLA faculty, David Loye was research director of the first large-scale study of the impact of television on adults. "We spent nearly half a million dollars on it in order to document what most people would have found obvious, but you have to document these things to have any hope of influencing social policy," he pointed out. "We documented that, yes, if you expose adults to a lot of violence, they're going to change their attitudes and their behavior. We found a significant change, both in attitude and behavior scores, in the direction of more hostility and more hurting behavior."

The study showed that adults were influenced by television and were vulnerable in much the same way that children are. "We not only found that violence produced negative behavior in adults, but we found that people who were exposed to a TV diet high in helping behaviors showed significant change in the direction of prosocial behavior and attitudes.

"For violent films we were showing movies like Clint Eastwood's *Hang 'Em High* and police programs where people were getting killed all the time. On the helping side we had programs like "M.A.S.H." which is loaded with helping behaviors, and "All in the Family," which explored a lot of prosocial issues with biting, comic conflict between Archie the dinosaur and practically everybody else on the side of common sense and decency. Contrary to the idea pervading the industry at the time—that people only wanted sex and violence—we were able to show that programs high in prosocial behavior would get very high ratings."

Television can contribute to the creation of open systems. The introduction of television and foreign movies to China was to some extent part of a Chinese *glasnost*, which allowed images of different, unknown worlds to appear in front of Chinese eyes that had been glazed over by years of propaganda about the rest of the world.

Documentary makers Vivienne Verdon-Roe and her husband, Michael, are concerned with reconciling the social and the personal aspects of the global transformation they see occurring. "We can talk among ourselves about this, but how do we talk to everyone else? Instead of complaining about Peter Jennings handling the news in this or that way, we need to try to talk to Peter Jennings, to try to talk to people who are in a position to do something. And not just to argue with them, but to find out what they really believe.

"I know that people like Peter Jennings do shows on AIDS, special benefits, and so on. He's concerned in his own way, and in very powerful ways he's trying to do some positive things. We have to make a bridge to find out where these people are at, and tell them where we're at. Eventually we'll actually make those steps to build the common understanding, and in some way, reach across.

"We don't usually do that. We consider those people inaccessible, or sometimes we even put them up on pedestals and think they're not quite people.

"We need to deal with the personal dimension of transformation. We cannot just work in public space without making a private commitment as well. We need to take the risk of talking to people. Right now with the basic worldview of 'us against them,' we're not going to make it. If we have a sense that we are us, and all of us are us, then we can begin to ask, Where do we go from here?"

Seeing ourselves as part of a larger web, subject to "the pebble effect," feeling a connection with others that translates into basic human caring—perhaps a less exalted form of what Joel Federman calls universal love—also involves an approach to others that is free of the need to dominate them or be dominated. People of different races, different beliefs, cultures, attitudes, and values are a source of rich diversity and provide a fertile cultural soil.

And indeed, all creation is collaboration, according to Frank Barron. In the past, our guiding image for creation has been the hero-creator, the single creator and his creative process. Barron calls this the monotheism-and-the-seven-days approach, and shows us how our conceptions of individual creativity and cosmic creation are linked. The alternative, he feels, is co-creation and mutuality, or collaboration.

If the modern vertical metaphor has been replaced by a horizontal one, it doesn't have to be just about surfaces. It can also be about *connections*. Let's look at another metaphor, Barron suggests. Let's look at the creation of human beings. Can we draw parallels between biological creation and psychological creation? Is there not a need for a father and a mother? A Goddess and a God? The lone-creator metaphor is simply not enough.

In a partnership world, we can begin to pay attention to the meaning of creation in a new way. As Barron has said, all creative individuals have what he calls a cosmological motive, a desire to create their own world of meaning, to create their own world. We can only begin to explore what this new world might be, where we create worlds upon worlds, like different songs and paintings and dances, each expressing our own vision. But we can certainly begin to create it together.

EDUCATION

Concerning the Somewhat Unclear Connection Between Getting an Education and Going to School

When Alfonso moved from Greece to England, he was eleven years old and could not speak very much English. This was the easy part. The difficult part was to make the transition to a totally different educational system. This is his recollection of that time:

Blessed with a good ear, I was always quick at picking up accents, and bluffed my way past various high school teachers who pretended to give me an entrance exam but were really interested in whether I was going to make a nuisance of myself or not.

I was not desperately keen to go to this particular school—or any other school for that matter. This particular building, swathed in London fog and drizzle, looked like it was the inspiration for a German prison camp castle, with its gray and grimy turrets and dank classrooms. And this was a *good* school.

The uniform everyone was required to wear consisted of a black blazer, gray or black pants, gray socks—regulation went all the way down to underwear. I've never been able to wear gray since.

Classes were so boring that among other things I developed a whole array of strange noises I made with my mouth, and other parts of my anatomy, simply to inject some levity into the overwhelming gravity of the proceedings. It would send shivers of delight down my spine when the entire class quietly started humming the same note, in unison and crescendo, the sound slowly seeping into the teacher's awareness until the poor man or woman burst out in some uncontrollable fit. Jibbering about punitive measures, arms flailing, they were restrained only by the fact that corporal punishment in schools had just been banned. Some of the teachers, I had to admit, were in fact very nice people, trapped in a world they did not

205

make, although that does not seem to have stopped them from participating in it to the hilt.

I was advised Latin would be more important for me than math (why? where? how?), which I was encouraged to drop. I enjoyed creative writing in English classes, but that course stopped at age sixteen. English after sixteen meant literature, and that had nothing to do with creative writing. Maybe somebody else's writing, but not the students', God forbid. Who do you think you are, boy? Shakespeare? This kind of intimidation and wearing away of students' self-esteem and creative ability was commonplace.

My happiest day at school was probably when I put my soccer shorts on my head, wore my long sports socks over my arms and my shirt as trousers, and came across the headmaster walking along a hall. Quizzed by the headmaster as to this unseemly attire, I told him I was dressed as an Italian monk, and walked off. I never heard about the incident again.

Yet for all this school gloom and doom, I could not forget the brilliant, rotund, and rosy-cheeked principal at the Italian elementary school in Athens, Professor Alessandro Sarno. In the joyful anarchy of his classroom, we learned more than we ever thought possible, or ever wanted to for that matter. It simply did not seem like an effort. We felt the thrill of competition, yet it seemed we were competing not against each other but against ourselves. It was taken for granted that we were all promising and brilliant, and any failure or doggy-dinner homework excuse was treated with a puzzled look—"what happened?" Multiplication tables were not sets of numbers to be memorized but visual puzzles, with different patterns emerging depending on the way you looked at the relationship between the numbers. There was no jive about maximizing potential or nurturing abilities, simply a lot of love and a lot of humor.

This experience had a profound influence on my life. It demonstrated that things can be different, even things most people give up on, like multiplication tables, or *analisi logica,* a particularly deadly aspect of Italian grammar. Once you see that things can be different, it's difficult to accept anyone's argument that this or that has to be a particular way. Especially if you hate it.

I wrote a letter to my high school paper in London once, asking why Latin class had to be so boring. My headmaster, a Latin teacher himself who knew about these things, replied: Latin, or at least parts of it, simply *is* boring, and there's nothing we can do about it. But by then I could not take that answer anymore. I knew the headmaster was really talking about himself, and not about Latin at all.

Education and Indoctrination

When we put together the comments about education from all the people we interviewed, we emerged with a discouraging list of characteristics. Words like *segmented, decontextualized, irrelevant*, were common. The criticisms of the educational system by far outweighed the positive remarks. What's wrong with our educational system? We have all heard dozens of different explanations and dozens of recipes for fixing it. It's not always easy to decide who's right or what to do to make things better. Should our schools become more demanding and emphasize the three *R*'s? Should we model ourselves after the Japanese system? Should we promote parents' participation, or enforce dress codes?

From our point of view the issues and problems connected with education are more easily understood in the language of paradigms. An educational system is a most important vehicle for acculturating the next generation into the prevailing norms of the society, that is, for transmitting the predominant paradigm from one generation to the next. Education is the process for passing on the cultural equivalent of the genetic code. Therefore we should expect a culture's educational system to embody, more than any other institution, all the characteristics of the predominant paradigm. Exploring these characteristics can be an educational process in itself.

From our interviews also emerged a deep commitment to improving the condition of our schools based on a vision for a learning community in which the structure of domination is not inculcated and replicated in the classroom. A self-directed, self-organizing system, reflecting a variety of cultural and social values, focusing on both autonomy and cooperation, theory and practice, unity and diversity, emerged as an ideal. This ideal is considered eminently practical and possible, but it requires a willingness to accept, in educational researcher and systems scientist Bela Banathy's words, "not just improvement, but transformation."

If It's Eleven O'clock This Must Be Chemistry

Perhaps more than any other place, learning institutions break down knowledge into neat, watertight compartments with virtually no connection with one another. Humanity has made an enormous effort to separate and distinguish and analyze manageable pieces of reality, going into smaller and smaller units of study and specialization. We have seen how this process was necessary for science to emerge. We have also described some of the negative side effects of this way of knowing, on which most educational systems are

207

founded. They are therefore dedicated to defending it and perpetuating it. It is by design a monument to reductionistic thinking and a factory to produce more reductionistic thinkers.

Children go through years of school without the faintest understanding as to why they are learning something and what connection it has with anything else. Much of what is going on in the classroom has no relevance at all to what happens in the life of the student, the real world. They are two different worlds. And inasmuch as it has no relevance, the student is not interested. The way education is structured today, we learn everything as if it existed in splendid isolation from everything else—math plays no role in history, or physics in politics. Philip Slater told us that until he started doing some research, he could see no good reason to study statistics.

For Dominique DiPrima, "one of the biggest problems we have is that people aren't taught that discussion and debate are OK. People take it personally: they think that if you're critical, you're attacking them personally. They don't see that you can have a difference of opinion with someone, and at the same time both of you learn and benefit from it. My friends and I argue all the time because that's how we figure out what our attitudes are, and we learn. But I think critical thinking is a big missing ingredient in the schools. I never could remember anything unless I took an attitude about it. An arbitrary fact doesn't mean anything to me. Kids are taught that they're supposed to learn things as if they were floating in space, and it just doesn't stay with you. That's not right."

The present educational system, just like our basic way of learning and knowing, is profoundly decontextualized. Information is presented in a vacuum, without any reference to the larger context from which it emerged or the reason why it might be relevant. When students ask, "Is this going to be on the test?" instructors shrink and rightly complain about the utilitarian materialism of the kids. But this question—heard often enough—also highlights a much more serious problem. It means that the information the students are receiving makes so little sense to them, and is so lacking in any real meaning to their lives, that the only relevant function of learning is to get them through the test, which will then, they hope, help them get a job.

"I couldn't keep my mind on school," singer-songwriter Roddy Frame remembers, "I just couldn't do it. I had no interest in the academic side of life at all. I suppose I was quite a romantic kid. My father was a really good singer, and all the songs that people would sing in Glasgow were very romantic—sometimes quite maudlin in fact. Music seemed really tragic and fantastic and beautiful, like real life. Sitting in a classroom seemed a sort of dull unreality."

Schools exemplify the predominant paradigm where head and heart are severed by the blade of rational progress. Roddy, like so many other kids, simply rebelled against this unbearable dichotomy. Who could tell him these notions without relevant connections were more real and more valuable to him than his feelings, his dreams, and aspirations?

Philosopher Bruce Wilshire, in a scathing attack on the academy, points out how university faculty members have to go through "purification rites" in which they are purged of any connection with any other discipline. Can the world really be studied from the perspective of a single discipline? Can we teach science without connecting it to history?

"I remember when I was a fresh Ph.D. and went to my first job at UC Berkeley," Ralph Abraham reminisced. "I was riding up the elevator with one of the older mathematicians about to retire, Hans Levy, and he said to me (this was 1960), 'I bet you've never seen a mathematical paper written before 1950.' Well, he was right! I had gone to a good school and had a good traditional education in mathematics, yet there was no mention of history by any professor. History is not taught in science courses, though the history of a subject is important in the teaching process. In teaching mathematics, for example, presenting ideas in their historical order as opposed to their logical order would make it easier for students to learn them. Once I realized that, the amount of attention that I've given to history in my pure math lectures has increased considerably, and I've come to think of it as a really important factor in the educational process."

Can we really understand the economy, or the way markets are inflated, stock markets panic or get bullish, without a basic knowledge of psychology? Can we understand international politics without an awareness of history, and the social, economic, and cultural factors that influence and shape events?

James Burke's television series "Connections" is a remarkable window into the links that tie apparently unconnected events. In his ten-part PBS documentary, Burke shows over and over again how remarkable inventions and events are connected to one another in the most bizarre ways. A linear view of the past would, for instance, place the arrival of the chimney in a sequence of developments related to change in domestic living. Yet the alteration in life-style brought about by the chimney included year-round financial administration and increased intellectual activity. This in turn contributed to a general increase in the economic welfare of the community to a point where the increase in the construction of houses brought about a shortage of wood. The consequent need for alternative sources of energy spurred the development of a furnace that would operate efficiently on coal, and this led to the production of molten iron in large quantities, permitting the casting of the cylinders that were used in the early steam engines. Their use of air pressure led first to the investigation of gases and then petroleum as a fuel for the modern automobile engine, without which, in turn, powered flight would have been impossible.

We need to create an environment in which learning makes sense and occurs within a context that gives it meaning. Many teachers all over the country are making valiant attempts in this direction, but it is a difficult change to implement because it implies a radical paradigm shift with far-reaching consequences for our entire way of life. A change from a way of knowing based on reductionism to a way of knowing based on systems thinking would be as dramatic as the shift from an agrarian to an industrial society. Paradigms are not changed as easily as socks.

At the Other End of Education

Our educational system has all the characteristics of the dominator paradigm. It is authoritarian, it promotes destructive competition, and it pays no attention to social skills such as conflict resolution through a win-win approach. According to some critics, our educational system dates back to the nineteenth century, when people had to be taught how to be good, obedient, and machinelike so that they could be kept at bay and, eventually, be fitted like so many cogs in an assembly line.

"The same mentality has been applied to the education of individuals," Bela Banathy said with a sigh. "Kids get on the assembly line when they are five or six years old, and then they are moved along as if they were machine parts like those they will one day produce. If they cannot perform as dictated by the system, then they fall off, just like products are sometimes thrown off the assembly line because they are not good enough. Today in the inner city, as many as fifty percent of the students do not finish school. It's a waste, such a waste of human potential that it makes one outraged, not just angry, outraged."

Today's jobs require better teamwork, more cooperative behavior, and stronger interpersonal communication skills, but the educational system still favors either/or, antagonistic debate, for example, as a way of displaying one's learning. Rather than model prosocial behaviors where two people are engaged in learning together, we show people trying to one-up each other with snide remarks. This is the epitome of the zero-sum game: either I'm right and you're wrong, or you're right and I'm wrong.

In this system we are not learning together, we're butting heads, using knowledge as a club to hit each other. Unfortunately, this is not just the way pedantic college debates work. We have all to some extent been taught that this is the way to communicate. This is different from discussions and debates of the kind Dominique DiPrima referred to, where friends have differences of opinions and hash things out, or choose to agree to disagree. Whereas friends are careful to ensure mutual benefit and respect, competitive debate does not.

Authoritarian, dominator systems, while very willing to give orders to those below, are marked by their often virulent refusal to accept any real information from below them in the hierarchy. Many great political and business blunders are made by a refusal to listen and learn from others, those "below" who, by the very fact that they are below, are believed to know less than those on top. We cannot expect children to take orders at school like good little boys and girls, being seen and not heard, and then expect them to become self-motivated workers in our labor force. It's the sad law of the dominator system that when the dominated rebel, they turn into dominators, so students have taken over and schools are becoming—literally—a war zone, with kids shooting each other and their teachers.

Creativity and Attention

The kind of education most of us have had is what has become known in recent years as maintenance learning. This means we were spoon-fed somebody's version of the facts, and a specific set of rules and methods to perform existing tasks and deal with existing problems. Some people call it rote learning. Remembering facts and figures is clearly useful in some cases, but most children remember absolutely nothing of the facts and figures they were taught. If they do, it's some weird factoid that pops into their heads while they're brushing their teeth.

Education as it stands is based on the idea that there is a mass of knowledge out there that somehow has to be crammed into students' heads (so they'll be good citizens and workers) and that the

211

students' task is to absorb this knowledge. Little attention seems to be given to fostering other skills, such as problem solving, independence of judgment, and tolerance for ambiguity. It is implied that every question has only one correct answer, and one should consult the expert to find out.

Isabella was stunned when in her last year of law school she was told that this entire legal system she had labored to learn in its most minute details was actually a construct, based on a set of hypotheses that might or might not be true. It was as if, now that she had earned her stripes, she was finally being let into the ultimate secret: There is no Truth. Her initial shock was soon replaced by a feeling of freedom, freedom to make her own constructs. But then a question struck her with equal force: Why didn't they tell her that in grammar school?

It has been suggested that if creativity is not fostered and nurtured at an early age and finds no acceptable channels even later in life, it can at times be turned destructively against society or the group or the individuals who are perceived as blocking it. Constant frustration of our natural drive to create can lead to bizarre forms of revenge, which seem perversely creative because they are novel and unusual although utterly destructive. This suggests that creative expression through the arts and in the shaping of one's life is not a luxury but a fundamental human necessity. The implications are quite dramatic. It is generally thought humans have a hierarchy of needs, starting with food and shelter, then human company, acceptance by others, and so forth. Artistic expression and creativity are seen as higher needs, important to be sure, but less necessary. In this view, crime, for instance, comes from people who attempt to make up for a deficiency, because they do not have enough money or cannot get a job and therefore need to steal to get by.

But what if crime and violence of all kinds reflects a frustrated creativity, an inability to shape one's own life and express oneself as a unique individual? And what if that expression takes the form of anything that draws attention?

"I think what most young people want and need is more attention from adults, and not necessarily their parents," explained Dominique DiPrima. "That sounds corny, but it's real. Because when no one cares about you, you're going to do crazy things. In good alternative programs, like the Omega Boys Club here in San Francisco, the things that are really working are the adult role models, adults who are able to give attention, one-on-one attention to young people. That's what they want and need. It's kind of simple. The Omega

Boys Club is working with young black men and women, and through one-on-one attention they've been able to take people who are dealing drugs and get them interested in going to college. They're taking them on tours of black colleges. They've got eighty kids right now in black colleges.

"I think we need to do these things more and more, because if we don't do them ourselves, it's not going to happen. Even though we hear so many discouraging messages of hopelessness, those types of organizations are providing some hope. That's why I try to get out as much as I can to speak. I'll speak in the schools and juvenile halls because I'm in the position right now where they listen to me. I lay it out, I tell them, 'No one's paying me to do this, and I'm not in jail. I could be home right now eating a nice breakfast and watching some TV. The only reason I'm here is because I care about you. Period. No bullshit.' That works every time, because they know that I'm real. I think that a return of some adults, especially people of color or professionals, to the community, to spend some time with and listen to young people is vital."

Attention, Frank Barron has written, "ensures that the person who experiences it is in communication with other living beings and offers them the possibility of community. Paying attention, caring, and being there yourself is all that counts."

Improvement or Transformation?

The problem with maintenance learning is that it maintains exactly what we don't think should be kept—the dominator system. We're still taught to see the world in a reductionistic, fragmented way; with an emphasis on quantity and not quality; with a zero-sum attitude; with the idea that ethics is pretty much what you can get away with (in one study 65 percent of high school students said they'd cheat if they could); with rote memorization deemed good, and questioning authority and being creative deemed bad. But as the dominator paradigm is beginning to lose its hold on people's minds, the educational system that represents it and has the responsibility to perpetuate it is becoming unraveled as well.

"Our educational crisis has been building for over twenty years," according to futurist Paul Saffo, "and that means it's probably going to take at least another twenty years to solve it. One hopes that our new information technology will present us with possible solutions, but we thought that television would be an important educational tool, and radio, and phonograph records. Maybe this time, hypertext and other interactive media really will. But my suspicion is that we've taken the current educational system right to the edge and probably past the point where it can be resurrected."

"I have many anxieties about the way education operates," Bela Banathy told us. "I make a distinction between schooling, education, and learning. Education is much more than schooling. And learning is much more than education. The first two may be formalized arrangements. But we have lost sight of learning to which there are no limits, and in all the formalized arrangements we create limits by offering a certain prescribed curriculum. And even that is not focusing on the learning; it is focusing on the teaching process.

"The question as it is usually put is, How can I arrange a formalized institution of schooling that will enable teachers who are faced with thirty or forty students to a class to deliver their message? This is the wrong question. The question to ask is how can we arrange the learning environment and provide resources so that students can master learning tasks. Unfortunately in most cases we are just trying to fix the existing system by making adjustments to it. It's like trying to fix a horse and buggy and make it into a spacecraft. It cannot be done, but we don't realize it, because we are so wedded to the existing arrangement, to its bureaucracy and hierarchy. Those who are heading the system are the least capable of effecting the major transformations required to make us a learning society, which we are not but should become.

"My question is, How can we turn this around completely so that the learner performs as the learner and is helped to attain competence by a great variety of resources and opportunities and situations? I mean competence through a learning program that is relevant to his or her life."

Starting from Scratch: Designing Your Own Learning System

In recent years we have seen top-down, government sponsored, million-dollar wars on drugs, wars on crime, and wars against a lot of other problems. There is something futile and at the same time potentially dangerous in these efforts. Futile because the problems are not seen in a systemic fashion and are approached piecemeal. Dangerous because a war is an excuse to call a state of emergency in which basic civil and human rights can be ignored for the sake of victory. The drug war is a particularly apt example of this.

An alternative way of dealing with these problems involves a grass-roots, self-organizing approach, allowing people to figure out their own local solutions to their local problems. We can become learning systems, learning how to learn together, rather than having a government agency present us with a glorified remedial program. We can figure out together how to design a system that allows us to achieve our goals.

Empowering people to create their own learning systems has been Banathy's major concern. "Much of my work is really to propose not a specific system of education but a process by which a new system of learning and human development can be designed by people who are in the community, rather than somebody else designing it for them. The whole community will become, through years of development, a learning community, a learning society, using all the resources that are available. There are tremendous resources available for learning, but not in the formal thirty-kids-in-a-classroom-box situation."

Banathy's work on the systems design of education points the way to communities learning to harness their creative abilities and creating their own learning systems. The design skills are crucial, Banathy argues, because we have to learn how to make our dreams come true. We need not just a vision but the creativity to make the vision a reality.

"We need to address the whole educational system, not just the curriculum. The issue is how to make the curriculum come alive in a community. We can provide resources, arrangements, opportunities, and situations. The learning agenda today, in a postindustrial information society, must be very different from the agenda of fifty to a hundred years ago. Unfortunately if you look at what is happening at the federal level, we are still talking about science, math, geography, and English as being academic subject matters. You can be most efficient in these and still not be equipped with the competencies required today in a transformed society.

"These competencies, that is, the ability to work with a tremendous amount of information, to process information, a strong personal involvement, problem-solving skills, the ability to engage in decision making in a cooperative way, are different from what we are doing in schools today, where we pit kids against each other in a competitive setting. The cooperation they learn as kids in their play groups they lose in the school, because they are forced into the competitive mode.

"When children enter school, they are wonderfully creative creatures. But then we tell them precisely what to do and force them to follow instructions to the point. So creativity is not nurtured.

215

"In our society, the most systemic thinkers are the four- or five-year-olds because they think in the totality of their experiences; they are systems thinkers," Banathy continued. "Then as they enter school they are put in subject boxes, and the further they go, the smaller the boxes become.

"The fascinating thing is that when they enter the world of work, we expect them to be imaginative, cooperative, and creative systems thinkers! They have to be able to cooperate with the people they work with. Yet we forget to nurture this capacity in school.

"Beyond the so-called organizational issue is also the issue of how to organize our capacities. So we have our task cut out for ourselves. It's a tremendous burden, but it's a challenge to help people understand and move away from the 'fixing' mentality."

Banathy does not see schools doing away with the study of math or geography or history. The way he sees it, "You are going to learn all of them, but in the context of real issues, real-life situations. For example, you may think about everyday topics, like how to take care of the garbage in the community. That's an interesting topic that involves not only technical issues but environmental and human issues. It needs math, science, English, geography, everything. This is a community-focused issue here, just one of many.

"I'm talking about learning in the functional context of real life in the community and the family: how to deal with the homeless, nutrition, health care, and so on. These are interesting and exciting contexts for learning. All the other subjects can be integrated into them rather than the other way around, hoping that if you are good in math eventually you will be able to solve some of the community issues."

There is plenty of room for new technology, Banathy asserts, but first we have to create a new design for education. "First we have to create opportunities for kids to work together, as a team, as a learning team. Fortunately very hard-nosed research shows that children in learning teams, learning how to work in teams and how to share responsibilities, have a higher level of achievement than those who are engaging in individual, isolated learning. The new technological learning modalities are unlimited if we are wise enough to think of them as a means rather than an end.

"We must realize that in a rapidly changing society, what has worked for hundreds of years—namely, maintenance learning or learning how to live with the ways already defined by the existing culture in order to maintain it as it is—simply won't work anymore.

It becomes necessary to learn how to design systems, and our own lives. We need to learn how to have shared responsibility for designing the life of our family, of our community, and of our society. This requires what we call innovative or evolutionary learning, a learning that has to do with the whole of our experience. Its aim is to learn how to design an evolutionary image, an ideal image of where we want to go coupled with the skills necessary to make that image a reality. The notion of evolutionary guidance enables us to bring direction to our evolution, not just leave it to circumstances."

Is It Happening?

There are encouraging signs that we are beginning to figure out what we want to learn and how we can do it. Creative new programs are being developed in schools and universities emphasizing a different set of competencies for the next millennium.

In 1982 a professor at UC Berkeley could not find a department in which to teach a course on Gandhi and nonviolence. Much like Art and Elaine Aron, he wanted to research something positive, peaceful, and beneficial to humanity, and there was nowhere for him to go. This intellectual homelessness eventually led to the development of the first peace and conflict program on the West Coast.

"There was a bunch of very dedicated students," Sheldon Margen reminisced about the early years of the program. "They were concerned about their education. Their views as to what education should be all about differed from those of many faculty members. Peace studies was just evolving, no one had defined what peace studies was. You can study any aspect of the individual; you can study the society, the environment, human interrelationships—all of these things are part of the issue. This began and had to remain a multidisciplinary program."

Slowly people began to work out what peace studies should be. Textbooks appeared and a curriculum developed. Now the program is part of the College of Letters and Science at Berkeley, and the number of students in the program is growing rapidly. This program and the few others like it that are emerging in the country—at San Francisco State, the University of Southern California, and George Mason University, for example—mark the beginning of a new era in the way we address problems of a social nature. Joan Levinson, an administrative analyst at UC Berkeley who has recently traced the development of the Peace Studies Program, explained to us how its orientation was different from traditional programs.

217

"Courses offered in areas such as international security, social justice, and regional conflict are fundamentally global and interdisciplinary in nature. They do not take the position that the United States is the center of the universe but explore a variety of global perspectives. This is a marked shift from traditional politics or international relations programs, which in every country tend to be based on a geopolitical, nationalistic perspective."

The program is interdisciplinary because, in Levinson's words, "life is interdisciplinary." The neat little categories of economics, politics, or psychology exist only in academia. They become dangerous when we look at real problems through the narrow perspective of one discipline to the exclusion of others, and even base policy decisions on this limited knowledge. Not surprisingly the program shows a strong systems influence.

The program at Berkeley also integrates theory and practice. Students studying the problem of world hunger not only bury their heads in books to learn data and theories but actually go out into the streets. They work in food pantries and other community-based organizations. Students practice conflict resolution in neighborhoods, and the techniques they learn are applicable from the interpersonal to the international level, Levinson told us. Now conflict resolution is beginning to be taught in high schools and neighborhoods. Interest is growing in understanding communication and miscommunication and finding alternatives to the adversarial arguments that fuel aggression and mistrust in the dominator system. The business world in particular is becoming sensitive to these new approaches to old problems.

The heart of mediation, in Levinson's opinion, lies in people listening to one another. When we get into arguments with people, we literally stop listening to the other and tend to stand by our position no matter what. We think it's a sign of strength to be unmovable, whereas more often than not it's a sign that we have become a closed system. In a recent speech, former Czech president Václav Havel stated, "We must try harder to understand than to explain. Things must once more be given a chance to present themselves as they are, to be perceived in their individuality. We must see the pluralism of the world, and not bind it by seeking common denominators or reducing everything to a single common equation."

Joan Levinson sees some signs of hope on the horizon. The concept of win-win is spreading, along with an understanding that "democracy is more than just material goods and speaking your mind. The vitality has gone out of all systems and ideologies," she said. Society is in upheaval, not just in the former Soviet Union, not just in Germany, or China, but in Europe and North and South America as well—in fact, wherever we go, we can see the stresses and strains of an old system, and the need for a whole-system change. The idea of partnership implies not a new ideology but the coexistence of a variety of ideologies. It involves, as we shall see, the freedom to be what one wants to be, with the responsibility to enhance the system that gave us that freedom.

What Is the Value of Education?

"All we need to create learning environments is the price of one B-2 bomber," Banathy points out. "We don't need more money than that. I use a metaphor to describe the value that our society places on education: It is as if someone went into a department store overnight and mixed up all the price tags so that the high-value items have low price tags and low-value items, high price tags. That is how our official value system works. It's just a very confused, mixed-up set of values."

Dominique DiPrima agrees wholeheartedly. "The biggest change that needs to be made in the educational system is that more money has to go into it. That's just a fact. Schools are closing left, right, and center in the Bay Area. They say you get what you pay for, and what we get is that we are not educating our people. That's just money. We're just going to have to bite the bullet and pay for it because we also need to have arts programs in the schools and we need to have sports programs to keep young people in the schools. And we need fewer students in the classrooms. You can't teach seventy kids; you can't teach fifty kids. Even twenty-five is pretty tough.

"All the young people are really freaked out because they hear constantly conflicting messages. They hear the commercial messages, 'Stay in school, stay in school!' Yet here in the Bay Area, they've cut artistic programs and are even talking about eliminating school sports. There are a lot of young people who go to school for sports, or whose status in school is based on sports. Why shouldn't they drop out if it's gone? I wonder what all those football players are going to pound on when they don't have each other to pound on. There's so much hypocrisy coming from our government. They like to talk about staying in school; Bush is on the United Negro College Fund telethon every year. But then we're seeing school closures and cutbacks."

But money alone is not enough. Paul Saffo believes that "in the short term, only throwing money and resources at it, without a fundamental transformation, is like throwing drugs at a gravely ill

219

patient: you'll just kill him." The point we want to make here, whether or not money is the solution to our educational woes, is the symbolic importance of a society's budget priorities. It seems that education is always the first to get the ax when governments tighten their belts is significant in many ways. It reflects the fact that most elected leaders will not be around to savor the results of good education and will certainly not get reelected for supporting it. It conveys a clear message that our fundamental value as a society is power over others (military spending), while nurturing, caring, and people development are at the bottom of the list. Teachers know this very well as they try to make do with decreasing resources despite increasing need, and when they look at their paychecks. This devaluation certainly does not show young people that we care about their education.

Dreaming About Tomorrow

Because education mirrors the prevailing paradigm and has been the tool par excellence for perpetuating the current worldview, it may prove difficult to change. But once a critical mass of people understands the dynamics of how and why the current system is kept in place, the system change may happen with dramatic speed.

If Paul Saffo is right and it takes another twenty years before significant changes will happen in education, some of us may not be around to see it. "It doesn't matter," says Isabel Allende. "I am not interested in how long the process of change to a partnership society will take because I will not be able to see it in my lifetime. I am forty-nine, and I don't have the slightest idea of where these years went. It happens so fast. I will not be able to see many things in my lifetime. I won't even see my great-grandchildren. But it won't matter; it is not important whether I see it or not." This long-term thinking is for her part of "a sense of being transcendent, which has been lost nowadays. People have lost the sense of sacred. Yet everything we do has the pebble effect. I feel it very strongly. It keeps me going." The ripple goes through time and space and makes us feel part of something larger than just the next few minutes or hours and the confines of our homes, our short-term interests, or even our own lives.

However long it takes, if we could change the paradigm on which our educational system is based, what values would become its foundation?

"We have practically no education anywhere in the Western world," lamented anthropologist Ashley Montagu, author of the best-selling *Touching, The Nature of Aggression,* and *The Natural Superiority of Women.* "Our system teaches children *what* to think rather than *how* to think. The educational system should teach children about the whole of animated nature and that all peoples of whatever sex, so-called race, or ethnic group are simply in this global village together. There are no strangers, only friends that we've not yet met. We should teach them that to be worthy of being a human being we should live as if to live and love were one. And this applies to everything and by everything I mean everything. Not only living things but rocks and rivers and skies and the air."

Creating a society based on partnership involves a process of learning together how to transform all the different dimensions of our lives. "Learning isn't something you do in schools or universities; learning is something you do in life," according to Willis Harman. "The Greeks had it straight when they said that every institution in society is part of where people learn. That's the primary function of any institution, whether it's a corporation or government bureau or whatever. We're learning individually and we're learning together, and we need to be a good deal more humble about a lot of things, including whom we could learn from. If life isn't about that, I don't know what it is about. Learning and relationships are not separable.

"If that's what society's really about, then what should we do differently? The answer is, Just about everything. We would certainly relate to nature differently; the whole mission of the corporation would be totally different. In learning, the curriculum and the core of the curriculum should reflect the fundamental questions that every person asks: Who am I? What kind of society am I in? How do I relate to you? How do I relate to the society? We've all accepted certain answers, and now we're waking up, some of us anyway, and saying, I don't believe those answers. They never felt right. Even when I was learning them in school they didn't feel right. And so we're rediscovering everything, but that's a continual search. You get deeper and deeper answers to those questions, and you get them by inner exploration."

"The only way to really change the world is through education," Isabel Allende remarked, and she wasn't talking about just sitting in a classroom. Being informed, sharing information, learning together through books and movies and discussions with friends and strangers—this is what it's all about. Learning in partnership is not the kind of boring drill or forced march that it is in a dominator system. Learning can be fun, the source of great joy and insight. All the

221

people we've spoken to are driven by their desire to learn and understand the world around them. For them and for us, knowledge is a source of inner power; it is empowering in the sense that it frees us from the established patterns of the dominator system. We can begin to rebuild our world in partnership and use our knowledge to design our lives, our families, and our communities, rather than have our education use us to repeat the old habits of the dominator system.

Although the current state of education presents us with a bleak prospect, the benefits from a transformation in education and in our attitudes about education and knowledge hold enormous promise. All over the world schools are experimenting with different approaches and methods, different forms of classroom relationships and expectations. A gradual consensus is emerging on the importance of learning how to learn, so that we can write our own histories and design our own lives and communities.

This does not necessarily lead to a tower of Babel of conflicting, inimical viewpoints and factions. It can lead to the establishment of a global community in which individuality blossoms in an environment of cooperative learning.

The Environment

Alfonso's Shrinking Village

In 1984 I went back to the neighborhood where I spent many of my preteen years. It used to be a small town outside Athens, Greece, but in the intervening thirteen years it had, for all intents and purposes, become a suburb. Walking past my old house, I began to realize that distances that had seemed considerable when I was a kid where really no more than a few blocks. Everything looked small and cozy, even with all the ugly new buildings that had sprouted like warty and no doubt poisonous mushrooms in every place I remembered as open and grassy, inviting a game of soccer.

Before I knew it I had reached the boundaries of where I would usually go, even on my bike. A street, or a particular crossing, signified the end of my territory and the beginning of an unknown area, where I had traveled to once or twice, usually in a breathless hurry (in an exploratory mode) and with no little anxiety. When my mom and dad and I would go for walks, our cats would only follow up to a certain point. There they would sit down, look at us, and meow, maybe lick a paw or two, and give up on us. Then they would head back home. They had their territory, their boundaries, so it was only natural for me to have mine.

Perhaps long ago our ancestors where a little like me in some respects. They must have thought the world was huge, that the horizon stretched forever, and nature's bounty was endless—unless you ventured so unthinkably far that you would drop off the face of the earth.

If walking were the only way of getting from San Francisco to New York, or from Beijing to Guangzhou, you might not even consider it because the distance would seem enormous. You might not even know that places that far away existed. By horse it's a fair trek, and even on a train it's more than a day's trip. Until the end of the last century, most people did not travel more than forty miles from their birthplace; it took at least seven days to cross the Atlantic, and six days on the Orient Express from London to Constantinople. Today the amazing French TGV train takes you from Paris to Lyon—267 miles—in two hours, at 180 miles per hour.

When Germany invaded the Soviet Union in the Second World War, many German soldiers became "melancholy," as one of them put it, because of the enormous expanse of territory around them. The hugeness of the country was simply overwhelming. Accustomed to the charming, crowded hillsides of Central Europe, the Germans found the plains and valleys of Russia "disconsolate."

Our concept of space and distance has changed enormously over the past couple of hundred years. Now information crisscrosses the globe in a matter of seconds, live pictures of events from the other hemisphere are the norm, and it's possible to fly to any destination in a day or so. The world has become smaller; we're told it's a global village. This is making us more and more aware of how intertwined and interconnected everything is.

In this new open, global system, technology is uniting us in ways both dangerous and beneficial: Acid rain and holes in the ozone layer do not stop at the border, but neither do fax machines and CNN. Images from Tiananmen Square were said to have inspired Eastern European revolutionaries. The transnational nature of nuclear fallout from Chernobyl prompted Italy (and a number of other European countries) to cut its entire nuclear energy program—a drastic step for a heavily industrialized nation with few natural resources. Middle Eastern oil can spill out of Greek tankers in American waters. Italian toxic waste heads for Africa on French ships, to be dumped there along with Swiss baby formula and U.S. medicines considered too risky for Americans.

One of the effects of our changed perception about the size of the world is that a smaller world cannot be the trash can it used to be. No matter how hard we try, the problems we attempt to export end up in our own backyard. Now we can truly say, "It's everybody's problem."

The Big Picture, with Hazel Henderson

"If you look at it in the very broadest possible framework," economic analyst Hazel Henderson told us, "the human species is probably one of the few species in the past hundreds of thousands of years that has overrun the whole planet and is in a position of being actually capable of wrecking its own life-support system. This is not to say that the planet won't go on perfectly well by making sure that we exterminate ourselves. It's no tragedy for the planet. But I think what is really happening is that an entire species is having to learn to change all of its behaviors very rapidly in the face of possible extinction. It's an unprecedented occurrence. When this happened to the dinosaurs, they didn't have any prior warning, as far as we understand. Human beings have had a lot of prior warnings, a lot of feedback.

"We have to change our behavior by limiting our numbers. Population is an important part of the problem. We know very well that we will not control human numbers unless we give women their freedom and give them equivalent opportunities to express themselves without limiting the options to motherhood. Yet most societies that are patriarchal succumb to an incredible inertia about doing anything about that or even facing up to it. Most societies are in full-scale denial.

"We've created the technology, if not the will, to do that. I think we also have to change our behavior by changing our modes of production and consumption. In principle, we know how to do that, and could do it. But the big problem, I think, are the habits of the mind. They are, in many cases, very slow feedback loops. I call them slow-motion bad news. There is also a great deal of slow-motion good news going on, but our mass media, which has become the nervous system of the species at the moment, really is not very good at recognizing these signals. There was Rachel Carson in 1962 with *Silent Spring* and Earth Day in 1970, yet it took twenty years before *Time* magazine and the *New York Times* started reporting these stories. Environmentalists are amazed that these stories that they've been writing about for twenty years are suddenly being reported as news.

"So this is one of the problems about paradigms. A culture has a certain mind-set, and that extends through all its structures and

225

organs of mass media, and its institutions, and it becomes even more difficult when these institutions themselves are part of the problem, when they are, as you might say in psychological terms, in denial.

"We have to change our perception and our concept of what we mean by progress. To me, the next fifteen or twenty years are going to be extremely interesting. We are absolutely going to have to change our perception, our concepts, our paradigms, and, of course, most important, our values and behavior if we're going to make it. It's quite strange to me that it's all now a matter of political will. Almost everywhere in the world there is no reason, in principle, that human beings can't change or don't have the means at hand to live sustainably. The question is, will we overcome our mental inertia?"

The movement toward an ecological consciousness requires at least three fundamental departures from the old worldview. The first one is an awareness of our systemic embeddedness in a larger system, a system comprising people and plants, animals and rivers and roads and mountains. The second is a shift from a desire to control our environment and impose our will on it to a partnership with mutually beneficial arrangements. The third is a shift toward co-creation, toward a contextual creativity.

Putting the System in Ecosystem

Paul Ehrlich, professor of population science at Stanford University and a noted writer on environmental issues, states that "familiarity with basic ecology will permanently change your worldview. You will never again regard plants, microorganisms, and animals (including people) as isolated entities." Instead, Ehrlich suggests, one begins to see them as related elements in a larger system.

This view replaces the reductionist position of one of the fathers—if not *the* father—of the scientific method, Francis Bacon. In the sixteenth century, Bacon said that in nature nothing really exists besides individual bodies performing pure individual acts according to a fixed law.

Not surprisingly, therefore, one of the areas where systems science has had the greatest impact is ecology. The term itself, *ecosystem*, reflects this. Paul Ehrlich defines an ecosystem as "the physical environment and all the organisms in a given area, together with the webwork of interactions of those organisms with that physical environment and with each other." He suggests that "all human beings and human activities are embedded and dependent upon the ecosystems of our planet."

What the environment is, at any given time, depends on your point of view. Some cultures seem to have a different relationship with nature and the environment, one that is decidedly more systemic than ours in the industrialized West.

"The Native Americans knew there was an invisible spiritual essence that rode through both the environment and the person," psychologist Royal Alsup told us. "This invisible spiritual essence was connected to the visible, so there was no dichotomy between the person and the environment. Human life is part of the environment, you can't hurt one part of the web without hurting the other. If I treat the environment badly, the environment is going to treat me badly. I believe, for example, that we have a dramatic increase in cancer because of the systematic deterioration of the environment. It's our patriarchal, conquering, and controlling obsession that has ripped up the environment. Individualism is also not an ecological approach because it doesn't recognize the dependency factor. There isn't anything in nature that isn't related and that isn't in partnership with the other parts of the globe. Nature *is* partnership.

"True environmentalism has to go beyond the subject-object relationship," Royal Alsup continued. "But this requires a fundamental change in attitude, a psychological change. As an environmentalist, you can't say, 'Well, I'm going to set this portion of the environment aside and exploit some other part of the world.' You can't be kind to nature and the environment and be oppressive to your fellow human beings. You need a systemic approach. You can't just be pro-environment, you have to be pro-human too. So it takes a total attitudinal change, a transformation. Yet many so-called environmentalists are oppressive when it comes to racial issues or are really individualistic in their orientation. People get some kind of personal glamour and glory for saving a part of the environment. Again, I think it's all interrelated.

"You can't save the spotted owl and be oppressive toward ethnic groups. This is shallow environmentalism. When we say 'I'm an environmentalist,' is this a persona, a shell? Or is it the core of the individual? I think the individual environmentalists have to ask themselves that question. It's not for me or anybody else to judge; each has to judge for himself or herself. I'm talking about ethical action, where my private life and my public life are the same. This is what Gandhi's whole approach and goal was, to make his private life and his public life the same."

No matter what we say to ourselves in private, and how self-sufficient we believe ourselves to be, the truth is that we are

227

inextricably connected with our environment, just as much as we were to our mother's body inside the placenta. The environment is our life-support system. Even if we are completely alone in our apartment or house, we still rely on electricity and water; and if we choose to be alone on top of a mountain, we are still confronted with an essential relationship in the air we breathe, the food we eat, and the water we drink. We are part of a larger system, a web of relationships that sustains us and allows us to be who we are.

Our environment, furthermore, is not simply birds and trees and plants and lakes and rivers—the environment we're supposed to be saving from our own undoing. It is also our offices and our bedrooms and our neighborhoods. The environment is also other people, and these people are part of nature just as we are. This environment is in some ways not separate from us at all. We all know the saying "You are what you eat," and although we can safely assume that eating pork doesn't turn us into pigs, the quality of the food we eat, and the degree to which it has been altered by various chemicals, makes a difference to who we are, to how healthy we are. The same applies to air and water; even though they may seem outside us, we must begin to question where the border between our self and the environment really begins.

The more powerful our tools of observation and our technology become, the smaller the world, the more we can appreciate our embeddedness in a larger system of relationships that we disturb at our own peril. When we thoughtlessly destroy ecosystems, we are also destroying a part of ourselves. The more the self expands, the greater our relationships with everything that is around us, until soon enough we will feel that we *are* our environment.

John Todd and Nancy Jack Todd Launch Ecological Toilet Training for Humanity

"As you enter the school, you see a series of seventeen glass tanks, twelve feet tall, spiraling downward toward you, shaped like a snail. To your right you see what looks like a marsh, only it has a lot of exotic plants in it. To your left as you stand in the foyer is a little pond.

"This stunningly beautiful sculpture is the sewage treatment for the whole school. The water is sterilized by ultraviolet light, so you could put your hands in the pool as you enter the building, if you wanted to, and chase the fish with your fingers. It has changed the rules. And it could only happen if it was extremely esthetic and didn't stink. That's kind of an exciting project."

John Todd is describing one of his "living machines," a sewage treatment system designed for a school. The playfulness of his partnership with nature is captured as he further explains his vision: "In *Winnie the Pooh*, there's a wonderful game called Pooh sticks, where you drop sticks off a bridge into a stream and run to the other side to see which gets there first. We think this sculpture is going to be the urinary equivalent of Pooh sticks, where the children will pee all at once and run down and watch this cascading water flow through the building.

"This work is being done by a family of technologies that I call living machines. They involve thousands of species of organisms, and they're powered by the sun. These organisms are in combinations they've never been in before. We've brought them from many different habitats, and said, 'Here you are, here's this horrible material, this sewage and waste. We don't know which one of you is going to do the job, but at least we have a concert that is bound to do the job.'"

How does one of these living machines do its work of purifying municipal wastewater and sewage without the use of chemicals or hazardous sludge by-products? By imitating the way nature cleans dirty water. The idea is to use biology as a basis for design.

First the water goes into tanks in a well-lighted greenhouse. The tanks contain many different kinds of life-forms, which literally eat the organic material in the sewage. The water flows along the tanks, and eventually more complex life-forms enter into the picture. Bacteria find the organic matter quite tasty and thrive in one tank. The bacteria produce wastes of their own, which are handled by algae. The whole lot then flows on into another tank, where snails chomp on the algae, and then, as the flow continues through more and more tanks, mollusks, fish, and over a hundred varieties of plants come into the picture, until it all finally flows into a marshland specifically designed by Todd and his associates at Ocean Arks International.

They have already built working models for clients in Indiana, Rhode Island, Massachusetts, and Vermont. "I'm currently trying to put together a project to begin to repair the Love Canal of the South, which is Chattanooga Creek, right in the middle of a poor black neighborhood. It has more deadly poisons in it than any other body of water in the country. It flows a stone's throw from where the kids play in the schoolyard. Seven EPA Superfund toxic sites are right within and around the schools and the neighborhood. So we're going in there to try to clean this stuff up."

229

The Making of an Ecologist

Speaking with biologist John Todd, one senses the excitement of someone who is pioneering radically different ways of creating partnerships with nature. His work has taken the shadow side of modern industry and technology—pollution—and turned it into a magical garden. The EPA gave him its premier award, the Chico Mendez Award, for this work. Former president George Bush recognized him with the Teddy Roosevelt Award for his work, and recently he received the *Discover* Environment Award for 1991.

"I was born and raised in southern Canada, on the shores of Lake Ontario," Todd told us. "I lived right on the edge of the water. My bedroom was literally a hundred feet from the water. My nightmares were about tidal waves, great ice packs coming up and engulfing me, whirlpools, and things like that. I was surrounded by this idyllic landscape, which involved a huge marsh to the east and a stream that wound its way up to a limestone escarpment. Of course the water was filled with all kinds of interesting life. I walked to school each day, a couple miles up these wooded ravines and across some farm fields.

"And then between the ages of about nine and twelve, I watched all of that world get trashed. The Burlington Bay, which was the body of water I was on, was just overwhelmed by industrial pollution. The animals left. The marsh was bulldozed to make a golf course. Some of the streams dried up because the valleys and the farms were made into subdivisions and office high rises. Even the secret Indian caves that I knew up on the escarpment were blighted by the fact that this development practically backed up into them. So the whole thing collapsed. I got very depressed, acutely depressed, for a number of years. I was a smiling kid, shy, and had spent most of my time pretty much alone, in the wild.

"Then my parents gave me the books of the American novelist Louis Bromfield. He had been in Europe until the late 1930s. He was a Pulitzer Prize–winning novelist and wealthy. As the war clouds were building up, he decided to go back to the hill area in Ohio, where he had known villages and agricultural communities as a child. These were communities with banks and schools and markets, and when he got back he discovered that his valley, called Pleasant Valley, was pretty much abandoned. It had disintegrated. The lands he knew as a child had been so badly abused that they had been unable to support these communities. Then, over the period from about 1937–38 to 1954, he wrote a series of books called the Malabar Farm series. They describe how, using ecological knowledge and European peasant knowledge, he was able to re-create the equivalent of a thousand years of topsoil. With the ecological restoration, the whole valley began to come back to life again. There was this whole beautifully written vision of the devastated state being reborn, of it coming alive again, of the laughter of children, the banks opening up, and what have you. That was the story of Malabar Farm.

"People like E. B. White and most of the famous people of the day knew him and went there. For me, as a child of thirteen, this was the beginning of a quest. This visionary landscape absolutely captured my imagination, and I came out of that depression. I thank my very gifted, sensitive parents for seeking out and finding what I needed."

Todd's work is important for many reasons. Todd is a great example of systemic, partnership creativity. He is changing all the rules. As William Irwin Thompson has pointed out in his series of *Gaia* books, which discuss the implications of the new biological/ecological view of the world, Todd is turning the waste, the pollution, the planetary "evil" of the industrial age, into a harbinger of the age to come, an age in which humans work creatively in partnership with nature. Todd is pointing us toward a different kind of creativity that recognizes the intricate interrelationships among living systems and the novel ways they can be brought together.

John Todd's own intellectual journey involved crossing many disciplinary boundaries in a variety of fields, from biology to psychology to oceanography. His example reflects the growing need that many are feeling to transcend established disciplines that rigidly define what questions may or may not be asked and what problems can or cannot be tackled.

A stint working as a consultant for industry increased Todd's awareness of pollution. An important paper he published in *Scientific American* on communication, specifically on the chemical languages of fish, marked the beginning of a new phase.

"I started what I call the doomwatch phase of my work, which was to look at how toxins influence the social organization of creatures. I looked at extremely low levels of toxins in the environment, a concentration that wouldn't kill animals. I discovered that with certain compounds at least, critical signals were being disrupted or destroyed even at these low concentrations. For example, fish that would normally take care of their young in their mouths would lose their ability to recognize their offspring, and would eat them instead

231

of nurturing them. So I began to realize that things were not as they appeared from the studies that had been done in the fifties in toxicology labs in the country.

"At the same time, and we're now talking the late sixties, my wife, Nancy Jack Todd, had been active in the peace movement in Canada, and then in the U.S., and was interested in the issue of science and weaponry, where the nations' resources were going. How much of it involved destruction, and how much of it involved creation? The role of science and society, in other words. There was a trend at the time to reject science. There was a mass exodus among so many of our young from the larger culture. But for me, of course, science was the pigment for this canvas that I was painting, what Louis Bromfield had described in *Malabar Farm*. So I couldn't throw out the pigment if I wanted to be a painter."

Todd did turn down a prestigious university position to set up the New Alchemy Institute, a distinct change from the academic environment. "We were asked by this community who had acquired some land just north of the Mexican border near Tecate to help them with their dream to try and get out from under the exploitive dominance of contemporary culture. They wanted to be able to live on this land, produce most of their foods, and get off the petroleum addiction. They weren't sanctimonious purists; they were trying to move in a certain direction and to live lightly, in the Gary Snyder sense of the word. We went out to help these people, and in this beautiful landscape, standing around looking at everything from the manzanita bushes to the live oaks down in the lower valleys, we realized that despite our boatload of degrees, none of us knew how to make a little piece of the world work; our knowledge had been abstract.

"That fact became the key for us, and unlocking that key was going to determine our future and the future of New Alchemy. Having been so humiliated by not being able to tell them what could be done, we immediately decided to move from abstraction to engagement. That meant hunkering down as students and making the place a kind of living museum. We wanted to learn all its intricacies, from its soil and soil animals to its vegetation, its light, its wind, its seasonal rains. We learned by having that piece of land tell us how to proceed. We had to ask certain things of the land. And it told us extraordinary things about what would be possible there, about the way of living that would be truly possible."

John Todd and Nancy Jack Todd illustrate another important element of partnership, namely, the importance of listening. Despite their theoretical knowledge—their boatload of degrees, as John put it—they did not insist on a one-up position. Faced with a unique situation, they chose to learn instead of imposing their view—the traditional missionary attitude. They used their observation to search for practical approaches. Typically they found them in a combination of advanced science and ancient science.

This search "led us both backward and forward in time. Backward to many of the lost skills of the Mideast, when civilizations of two thousand, three thousand, five thousand years ago had developed very sophisticated and subtle ways of living in semiarid and arid regions. We also pushed further into the field of Taoist science and started poking into the knowledge of Native American populations of the Southwest and Mexico, although never as deeply as we would have liked. Then in the other direction, we looked into the whole emerging field of renewable energy. What can you do with the sun? What can you do with the wind? How can these be linked to ecosystems? That, of course, became the basis of the design of the New Alchemy Institute. But the idea was to create a science of our stewardship, one in which the earth was our teacher. We were not arrogant."

The Todds' quest had by that time, as John puts it, become a sacred journey. "The idea was to see if ecological knowledge could be the basis for sustaining culture. I think that we proved in the seventies that it was technically possible. Soon we could grow foods and heat or cool buildings using engineered ecosystems. We even began to dream of living machines, of a partnership between humans and what have you."

Inspired by the noted anthropologist Margaret Mead, John Todd and Nancy Jack Todd began to work in so-called third world countries. They went to Central America and had projects in Africa and the Indian Ocean.

"What I found working in the third world and Central and South America is that certain things could be done, like agroforestry, and other kinds of things couldn't be done because people said, 'You work with the wind, but do you work with the wind in Massachusetts? You work with the sun, but do they do that in Massachusetts? You use ecologically engineered systems, but do they do that in Boston?' I had to say no."

By the mid-'80s Todd was back in the U.S., faced with the problem of walking his talk. In the U.S. he took another important step. "The more I focused on water, the more I realized the tragic state of the nation's waters. And I realized that my friends, many of whom

233

were younger than I, were dying of cancers. My own town had cancer rates about nine times above the national average. And it could be traced to our water. So I decided to put our knowledge to work repairing and purifying the water. Under Ocean Arks, we created the Center for the Restoration of Waters. We started working with toxic waste sites, industrial sewage, and industrial city sewage, and now we have facilities in five states and are developing them in two more. We have a center at the University of Edinburgh in Scotland, and we are working on the problem of cholera. All the time we are asking nature to collaborate. Some extraordinary things have happened in the last few years. They're almost beyond belief. Compounds thought impossible have been transformed."

Todd shares some more of the beliefs we have seen emerging in these pages, including chaos theory's butterfly effect: It is not necessary to match every action with an equal reaction, or to use force and destructiveness equal to that of your problem in order to get rid of it. The industrial-strength approach to technological problems is not at all necessary, Todd points out. It is not necessary to build extremely powerful technological solutions—with potentially dangerous side effects—to solve our waste problems.

In fact "it would exacerbate the problem," says Todd. "Ecological engineering permits us to *aggregate* our problems. If your sewage plant looks like Kew Gardens and doesn't stink and is beautiful, you wouldn't mind having it in your park in your neighborhood. Especially if it was also providing flowers and trees for redecorating the neighborhood."

Ecological Futures

In the future, Todd sees "a partnership with nature, there's no question on that. I'm the junior partner. I'm beginning to understand what the ecologies need, I think that's what the human steward does. I see the potential for society in the twenty-first century to eliminate inequities between regions and peoples. I think it can be done by living machines that not only treat our waste but produce our foods in a fraction of the space, provide our fuels, heat and cool our buildings, and purify our air and waters. Some of these things can be designed to operate to last for a millennium; they're not like conventional machines. They have the ability to repair and self-organize, and they do require the humans as stewards. That's the long-term picture.

"From a global perspective, theoretically, I think we're getting close to proving that the current human community could occupy, in order to support itself, roughly ten percent of what we currently do. And if that's true, then the dream of the twenty-first century would not be to explode population because of this, but to be able to give ninety percent of the planet back to the wild. That's theoretically possible. We've proven that, but those are knotty social and political issues. As Gregory Bateson put it, 'Well, you know it's really a question of power, old boy.'

"So that's my story in a nutshell. There is a common thread: the partnerships with individuals that have sustained through the years. Nancy and I have been involved with each other since we were children, really, sixteen, seventeen years old. Bill McClarney and I have been partners since 1955. Not all my enterprises have succeeded, don't get me wrong. But the human drive that underlies all of this is very strong and very intact."

Darwin for Everyone, Parsons and Plague Pits, and the Unfittest Surviving

If John Todd and Nancy Jack Todd represent the future paradigm—the partnership of science, industry, and economics with nature—much of the current thinking about these issues is still steeped in the old, traditional worldview. An understanding of its roots helps to expose the underlying assumptions and makes it easier to question them. The latter is an activity cheerfully suggested not only by some bumper stickers but by the results of many serious studies on creativity.

The Industrial Age was profoundly influenced by the new science of economics. As Hazel Henderson showed us, economics provided an entire way of thinking that supplanted the religiosity of the medieval world. It was a major paradigm shift in its own right. Angels and archangels were replaced by bankers and moneylenders, celestial cities became financial institutions, God was alive and well and operating discreetly through the self-regulating market mechanisms of Adam Smith's "invisible hand," and gold was the road to salvation.

At its worst, the economic way of thinking combined a self-serving pseudoscience about the survival of the fittest in the marketplace with the dull mathematics of accounting and spiked them both with a good deal of "realistic" Machiavellian psychology, a twist of greed, and a chaser of lust. The entire effort was marked by the most blatant reductionism in all possible ways, except capital accumulation, as there was never anything reductionistic about that. Social Darwinism became the scientific justification for this brave new world.

235

When Darwin made his profound observations, which led to the development of evolutionary theory, his view of nature was that of a Victorian man who had obviously been influenced by the prevailing beliefs of his time. He had read Parson Malthus's dire predictions concerning the rise in population, exponentially outstripping food production, and they had a strong influence on him—strong enough to provide a vital clue for his theory of evolution.

Malthus was by no means an optimist; in fact he was an archetypal scientific pessimist, a gloom- and doomsayer who emerged from a study of the numbers believing they'd all be in the poorhouse if they didn't do something soon. After him, economics deserved to be known as the dismal science.

Malthus believed that people were driven by insatiable sexual appetites, and that only the higher ranks of society were capable of adequate restraint. The lower classes, being basically dumb and dirty, were considered incapable of submitting the pleasures of the flesh to a higher goal, or sublimation, as Freud would later call it. "Higher" and more moral ranks of people had produced all that was good in society anyway, such as art, music, literature, and philosophy. So Malthus suggested that any attempt to help the masses, by what we might call welfare programs or even common human decency, would not only be futile but would create an intolerable level of overpopulation. His conclusions were that given the scarcity of food in relation to the growing population, the weak and poor should be encouraged to remain dirty, to build their homes by stagnant pools, in marshy and unwholesome areas so as to foster the return of the plague that would mercifully kill them off.

Malthus was not being ferociously cruel, by his own reckoning. He was only helping nature along, as it were, since he thought there was no hope for these people, and he clearly had no intention of going down with them. He was merely helping to further what would later be called the survival of the fittest. (Have you ever heard of anyone promoting that theory who didn't think of himself or herself as one of the fittest?)

We must remember that in a class-based society such as Victorian England—and Malthus was writing even earlier—the Saxon tradition of determining a person's position by his or her worth when murdered was still entrenched. As James Burke writes, "The penalty for murder was either death, or payment of the *wergild,* or body price of the victim. A noble was worth 1200 shillings; a thane, 300; a churl, or free peasant, 200. Serfs were worth nothing, and a man of whatever rank was worth more than a woman of equal social standing."

So poor people were literally not worth a lot. Why waste your efforts on them? Does this not remind us of what Hazel Henderson pointed out about attempts to quantify how much people are worth today with money coefficients?

The combination of Malthus and Darwin entered into the popular imagination and into our lives in the form of two slogans: There's not enough to go around, and The survival of the fittest. These slogans summarized what many felt to be "scientific" opinions about the world, and they were used as rationalizations for all sorts of dubious behavior and economic practices.

The idea of scarcity as a fundamental condition of human existence has been challenged by those who argue that both scarcity and wealth are largely products of the human mind. Wealth is created by human creativity, and scarcity is often the result of an inability to draw on our full human capacities. Part of the dominator scarcity mentality holds that if the poor get wealthier, they must necessarily do so at the expense of the wealthy. The poor have been known to think so as well. This sets up a ferociously antagonistic system of grasping and clinging, a battle for domination. Some, like Hazel Henderson, are systematically pointing out the fallacies in this kind of thinking and are opening up new perspectives and opportunities that could drastically change our economic system and our civic culture.

Just as we created a split between ourselves and nature, between nature and society, or civilization and instinct, we used biology to justify the idea of the survival of the fittest, of destructive competition as the basis for human relations. Our view of evolution has changed, however, from Darwinian to neo-Darwinian to post-Darwinian. These days, evolution is beginning to be understood in a very different light. Gone is the talk of fittest, and even of "optimization." How do we know who's the fittest, the new evolutionists say, or what is optimizing? Sheldon Margen already pointed us in this direction by asking, Who really knows what our genetic or "human" potential is? A statement is always something said by somebody, and who are they to say what's fit and what isn't?

The criteria have changed. They've changed to *viability* and *survival*. As long as the species survives, it's not doing too bad, reckon new evolutionary scientists like Stephen Jay Gould, Mauro Ceruti, Humberto Maturana, and Francisco Varela. We're moving from survival of the fittest to survival of the fit. The emphasis is not on adapting to your environment but coexisting with it. And there are many ways of doing that.

237

Today the brilliant biologist Lynn Margulis, among many others, is championing the cause of symbiosis, showing us a nature very different from the view held by T. H. Huxley, friend and popularizer of Darwin: "The animal world," Huxley wrote, "is on about the same level as a gladiator's show. The strongest, the swiftest, and cunningest live to fight another day. . . . No quarter is given." Margulis writes: "We consider naive the early Darwinian view of 'nature red in tooth and claw.' Now we see ourselves as part of cellular interaction. The eukaryotic cell (your basic building block–type cell) is built up from other cells: it is a community of interacting microbes. Partnerships between cells once foreign and even enemies to each other are at the very root of our being. They are the basis of the continually outward expansion of life on Earth."

As in nature, humans with very different views can live together without either giving up their autonomy and becoming part of an amorphous, homogenized mass or fragmenting into a thousand warring tribes. Startling parallels in biology and politics show an ecology of differences, a unity in diversity.

Cooperation, mutualism, symbiosis, co-creation are areas which have been neglected in biology, since so much attention has been placed on struggle and strife. They represent not just a blind spot which needs to be covered, but the basis for a whole new interpretation of our relationship with nature and ourselves.

Does this neglect sound familiar? Perhaps Art and Elaine Aron, the love researchers, can take heart here, since they also seem to be dealing with an interdisciplinary blind spot. Likewise peace and conflict resolution have been neglected in favor of "strategic studies." Aggression and depression still get most of the attention, but we see signs that indicate a real transformation is under way, led by anthropologist Ashley Montagu.

Economic analyst Hazel Henderson believes that "it is a better paradigm for human beings to see themselves as co-creative with a living biosphere and a living planet, and to realize the essentially co-creative role that we play in nature. We've had this idea that we were outside nature and could dominate it. But all around us we see the marvelous co-creative activity of the entire biosphere. Plants, for instance, are providing us with oxygen, which is their waste product, and we're providing them with what they need, carbon dioxide, which in turn is our waste product. The whole biosphere actually does operate co-creatively rather than competitively, as Darwin thought. Unfortunately the Darwinian paradigm got extracted and put into the social framework very much as an apologist for economic activities."

Willis Harman helps us put things into perspective: "We use two words where we really need three. We have *ecology*, which has to do with knowledge about this interrelated life-support system. We have *economy*, which has to do with measurement of our home, that's what the word literally means. What we lack is *ecosophy*, wisdom about the whole interrelated life and nature system. And the only way we obtain wisdom about it is to become a part of it at the intuitive level. That's why the role of indigenous societies is so important because they've done that more than any other groups of people in world history."

From Economics to Ecosophy by Way of Witch Doctors

The information on the Tiruray that Stuart Schlegel has brought back to the Western world confirms Harman's position.

"The Tiruray think of nature as a living organism, of which *Keilawan*, human beings, are only a very small part. According to their creation story, they were created to care for the forest, which is a source of bounty in the great cooperative venture of life—humans, spirits, animals, and plants, all working together. You grow food, you hunt, and you fish, but the forest is not to be abused. It's to be lived with in a kind of partnership. Nature for them is home, and will always be home. It must be protected for the future generations even if that involves greater labor now, and the Tiruray are unanimous on that. They will put in great amounts of effort to maintain the integrity of the forest. So they have lived for untold numbers of generations in the midst of the rain forest without destroying it.

"When they are planning their cooperative work in the forest, it's long-term work. Their swidden cultivation, the kind of farming where they slash and burn, is profoundly conservative of the environment. It is different when people at the edges of the forest practice swidden farming. I'm talking about lowlanders who are really cutting a garden into the edge of the forest. They'll cut it down and clean it out and burn it over and over again, so the forest will never grow back. Once you've done that, it's much less labor to cultivate the field. But the Tiruray will cut down only a small portion for each family, and they'll burn it only once. Then they'll leave it alone for twenty years so that it grows back into forest.

"This is very labor intensive, so much so that a single family can't cut a swidden, a forest plot for raising crops. It's too much

239

work. About twenty men, from families that consistently work together and form a unit that I call a neighborhood in English, will mark and slash the undergrowth first in one person's field, then in the next person's field, then in the next, all working together. Afterward, they go back and cut down the big trees, again all working together. At that point each person burns his own field, and then the whole community, men and women, go from one swidden to another planting. Eventually they all help harvest. By working together that way, they're able to do the kind of labor that's involved in keeping the forest so it will grow back. I think if you ask the Tiruray 'Why don't you just make a garden?' they would say 'The forest won't grow back, and we need the forest. We were placed here to take care of the forest.'

"The Tiruray can live by hunting, gathering, and fishing alone, so they don't work together in cultivation out of fear of scarcity. They're not afraid that they won't have enough to eat if they don't do this. Life is not a zero-sum game to the Tiruray at all. There's plenty for everybody. And everybody knows how to live perfectly well off the forest and the river. The reason they cooperate with each other is that the nature of the good life for them is people working together and sharing in their work and the results of their work. Life is enhanced by this, and this is one of the main motivators for their work."

Shamans, sometimes known popularly as witch doctors, are another example of indigenous ecosophy. Their origins go back to the beginning of human culture, thousands of years ago. They can be found everywhere on the planet, in different colors, shapes, and sizes, and yet with a remarkably similar view of the world. This view is much closer to nature than our present mechanized, industrialized, televised universe. It is a universe where everything is alive, and everything speaks to us, including animals, plants, and even rocks.

According to Stanley Krippner, who has studied shamans for more than twenty years and on six continents, shamans are "socially sanctioned practitioners who obtain information not ordinarily available and use it for the good of the community." They let their people know about the weather and where to find game. They mediate family disputes, heal the sick, and consult with the spirits. They get their information mainly from what Krippner calls the four D's of shamanism: drumming, dreams, dancing, and drugs.

It is important not to romanticize shamans, to assume that they and their cultures can do no wrong or that they represent some kind of natural state to which we should all aspire. According to historian Mircea Eliade, shamans are technicians of the sacred. Shamanism is seen as a technology, not a religion. In fact, Krippner told us, shamans were also the first scientists, who constructed worldviews in part as the result of trial and error. In order to predict the weather, identify medicinal plants, and locate game, shamans had to develop great sensitivity to cues that others would completely ignore.

The general idea behind the shamanic worldview is that we have something to learn from all of creation, and we must pay attention to and be respectful of the natural world around us.

"The shamanic worldview is that human beings do not hold primacy in nature," Krippner points out. "Human beings are a natural phenomenon, just like everything else. That's why in so many Native American ceremonies I've been to there are prayers to our four-legged brothers and sisters, those who crawl, those with wings, those who swim in the oceans, and even to those who stand and sprout leaves, and those who rest upon the ground, meaning rocks. All of these are nature's creations, and human beings must, in the shamanic worldview, learn to live in balance with the rest of creation and honor the earth. In some shamanic traditions, when you kill an animal, you utter a prayer thanking the animal for giving up its life for your community and promising that the energy derived from the animal's flesh will be used for benevolent purposes.

"The role of the human being in the shaman's universe is much different from that role as commonly understood in Western industrialized societies. This is of course reflective of Western religions, where the injunction is that God gave human beings domain over all the earth and the products thereof. The shamanic worldview looks for balance, looks for cooperation, and does not grant human beings the right to exploit nature. In fact in some traditions, animals are believed to be wiser in some ways than human beings. This is one of the origins of the so-called power animal, who often assists the shaman on the spiritual plane."

Those who scoff at shamanism as primitive gibberish should remember that our own twentieth-century consciousness is constructed and shaped by television and the media rather than by trees and animals and ancestors. The shaman may believe, like Dr. Doolittle, that she or he talks to the animals and that everything is alive. We technologically sophisticated wise guys get our reality from docudramas, and most of our knowledge about world affairs—even local affairs—is secondhand. Research shows that we often believe what is on television to be more real than real life.

241

Shamans provide us with a glimpse into a world in which the assumption, widely held in the industrialized West, that human beings should dominate nature does not hold. Our hectic life in the fast lane, pampered by the latest technological gadget, has divorced us from a direct, intuitive contact with nature. Yet we instinctively yearn for the connection that is the basis of ecological wisdom, or ecosophy, as Willis Harman suggests. This may account for the growing interest in shamanism. It reflects our need to find different ways of relating to the world around us, different ways of connecting with nature.

The element of empathy, of moving into another's world—or at least trying to—links artists and mystics, and in our culture, women. In fact, the stereotypically feminine characteristics of creative people include empathy, as Frank Barron has pointed out. We remember Robert Anton Wilson's description of how he gets into the characters of his novels; the ability of musicians and actors to conjure up moods and images seemingly at will; Scott Coltrane's discussion of the way mothers are sensitive to the needs of their children, and that fathers can also learn this; and finally Joan Levinson's emphasis on listening as a vital ingredient in conflict resolution.

The ability to heighten empathy and sensitivity to the world around them is one of the many techniques shamans develop in their training. Krippner has spent many years studying these technologies, particularly in the area of healing, and believes strongly that we can learn much from shamans. "These are people who have access to intuition," he told us, "these are people who have access to dreams, these are people who have access to imagination, these are people who can tell good stories, who can interpret dreams in practical ways, who have very keen vision, eyesight, hearing, sense of taste, sense of smell, so they can detect changes in the weather or locate game. Their ability to imagine is keen, and practical. In other words, most of them are not psychotics or mentally disturbed people who live in a fantasy world. These are people who have to deliver, who have to come up with something that meets practical needs and facilitates the well-being of their community."

The technologies shamans employ to deliver the services Krippner described are radically different from those adopted by the industrial world in response to the same needs. The issue is not just an obvious one of technological sophistication. The profound difference is one of outlook and worldview. The point becomes quite clear if we compare the two different paradigms within the same technological arena.

Reclaiming Technology: Who's All This for, Anyway?

The science and technology driving the Industrial Revolution were reductionistic. They isolated the smallest possible variable in any situation and experimented with it to see what would happen. By isolating it, they would be sure that whatever reaction they got would be because of them, and not because of anyone or anything else. This reductionism spread to other aspects of life, as we've tried to show. Pseudo-individualism became one manifestation of it, and it applied even to the way factories were thought of, as isolated dots on the landscape, with no relation to anything but economic distribution networks and the competition. The embeddedness in a larger ecosystem was largely ignored.

The Industrial Age drastically changed agriculture, so that now we have agribusiness, a scientific and corporate enterprise, replete with genetic engineering and scientific management methods designed to optimize production and profits. For the sake of efficiency and productivity, enormous monocultures were developed, with only one dominant species, such as corn. Current agricultural practices reflect deeply rooted dominator thinking, with all its short-term advantages and long-term destructiveness. Although much easier to farm, a monoculture is extremely vulnerable to droughts, insects, overuse, and disease. For the same reasons monocultures are easy to farm—they're all identical crops in neat lines—they're also easy picking for your average crop-eating critter, which can, like the farmer, start at one end and chew all the way to the end of the row, and then start all over again with the next row.

The homogeneity and simplicity of monocultures contrast with the diversity and complexity of natural ecosystems. Forests are much more complex and diverse systems better able to absorb changes that could wipe out a monoculture. Once again we find the basic ingredients of creativity: diversity and complexity. Creativity is required to develop ecosystems such as the ones John Todd is creating, particularly since they represent an effort to work with nature rather than to control and exploit her. The monoculture approach arises out of a worldview that sees nature as fundamentally inert and exploitable. Plants are simply raw construction material or vegetables for consumption; animals are milk-and-meat production tools and products. Even today some deny that animals can feel any pain.

The enormous power unleashed by science and technology in its effort to control nature led some people to think of science as a new religion. Science, in other words, told us the truth, and this was apparent because the equations and theories and experiments of

243

science led to the development of things like weapons and cars and medical technologies, which had an amazing impact on our lives. If science can lead to something as incredible as "technological progress," which altered the face of Europe in a century or so, then science has got to be "right," hasn't it?

Mathematician and chaos theorist Ralph Abraham is concerned with this popular notion that science has a handle on reality and that scientists represent a new priesthood. "I think the tendency of science will have to be opposed by lay people with self-confidence, a self-confidence based perhaps on spiritual values. I certainly do not want to destroy science. I just want to remove this ridiculous mantle of wisdom that's been draped on it by lay people who have bought part and parcel the value of the Ph.D. and M.D. degrees and the implication that an understanding of theoretical physics means a superior wisdom in the understanding of nature.

"I think that science deserves a lot of the respect that it gets. I think it's wonderful. I love theoretical physics. The practical accomplishments of science, engineering, and technology, communications, the space program, and so on are really thrilling. I don't want to detract from the accomplishments or the value of science. But expecting scientists to be wise or to be capable of making important judgments in terms of the future of the species and the planet is wrong."

William Irwin Thompson is critical of the way technology is being hyped with a mixture of naive optimism and greed. Much of our understanding and use of technology, he states, still reflects the perspective of the Industrial Age. "Machines are considered superior to nature and the body. There's still a very strong move toward the 'replacement of nature' with technology," he said. Unconsciously this opposition between natural and mechanical, nature and body versus machine, has made us attack the body and attempt to destroy it with a variety of technology's side effects, he believes.

"Technology is a product of humans," astronaut Edgar Mitchell reminds us. "It's not technology that's a problem, it's the value system by which we guide technology; and that comes from humans. We are a twentieth-century technological civilization guided by a twelfth-century morality and value system. Those two systems are based upon entirely different principles. So in a sense we're a schizophrenic civilization.

"Every technology can potentially be used to great ends. It is not the technology, it is how humans tend to employ it. A knife can be used to cut your food or slice up another human being. Electricity can be used to bake your bread or fry you in the electric chair. It's totally amoral in value. The values we attach to it make all the difference. So don't blame science and technology. They are only a way of thinking and do not claim to purport values. The values come out of our cultural tradition. If our value system is flawed, then the technology will be misused."

Riane Eisler told us that in her thinking about technology, she is "starting with Buckminster Fuller's premise, that technology is the extension of human functions, like eyes and hands and feet. But looking at it in a broader sense, I see it as an extension of the function of nature—take flying, for example."

Central to Eisler's work is the theme expressed in the title of her book *The Chalice and the Blade*. The chalice represents what she calls technologies of production, such as farming, manufacturing, construction, and weaving; technologies of reproduction, related to birth, family planning, or birth control; technologies of conservation, such as ecology and art history; and technologies of actualization, such as art and education. The blade, in sharp contrast, represents technologies of destruction, primarily weapons.

Though in some cases the technologies may be the same, their purposes change depending on whether you are living in a time and place oriented primarily to a dominator or to a partnership model. The blade is necessary for a variety of functions, but in a dominator system it is given disproportionate importance. David Loye pointed out to us that in both new age and academic debates about technology, everything tends to get lumped together as all good or all bad, which is not only confusing but gets us nowhere. With Eisler's new typology, which makes it possible to separate the "good" from the "bad" technologies (the latter falling mainly in the technologies-of-destruction slot), everything suddenly clears up. As Eisler stresses, we can then see that how the types of technology are developed, how they are used, and who gets to use them hinge on which model—dominator or partnership—a society follows.

In a dominator system, she notes, technologies of actualization are generally confined to a small elite, which has access to the arts, leisure, higher education, and so forth. A partnership system, by contrast, would stress access to such technologies for all. But the issue goes beyond access for all; it encompasses what we are getting access to. Actualization presumably means fulfilling one's human potential. But in dominator systems, actualization frequently means possession of material goods, a theme expressed in advertisements that suggest we simply need a new deodorant or a new shampoo to rid our lives of trouble.

245

In a dominator system, technologies of production are embodied in the everyday drudgery of labor in offices and factories. In a partnership system, technologies of production reclaim their creative status particularly through the introduction of an esthetic that strives to create a healthy and appealing work environment and rewards creativity while at the same time fostering cooperation and community. Willis Harman has addressed this is in his book *Creative Work.* "The stuff that passes for technology of production in dominator society is really not life supportive," he told us.

In a dominator system, technologies of reproduction are strictly regulated. In the U.S. attempts are being made to restrict abortion; whereas in the People's Republic of China abortion is forced in certain cases. Reproduction—of both women and nature (crops, cattle, etc.)—is in the hands of elites, who dictate the reproductive patterns of both. A partnership system, by contrast, emphasizes self-regulation; in other words, the other would be allowed to speak, nature would be listened to, as would women, and the different voice would be allowed to emerge.

Technologies of conservation in dominator systems consist largely of museums and monuments celebrating war and conquest and the work of men. To a large extent, conservation means keeping the structures that allow the powerful to retain their position. As we have seen, the "weak" actually have a hand in keeping the structures in place, in part because they hope it will eventually be their turn.

In an article published several years ago, Eisler left out technologies of conservation. It was a blind spot that made her aware of how "even I, who am so conscious of how everything has been constructed around the male-centered model, had managed to omit this, despite the fact that it's women who do most of the cleaning and the caretaking and the maintenance of human beings. I'm not talking about maintenance of cars. I'm talking about conservation of humans. This is a tremendously important technology in terms of humans and in terms of the environment."

In a partnership system, conservation also consists of maintaining and nurturing that which nurtures us—our communities, and nature, for instance—and developing new ways to protect our environment.

A partnership approach to technology reflects a shift in values, which are reflected in our allocation of creative resources. How are dominator values reflected in our development of technology? Why do we think of wars as essential for technological development? Why does the dominator system make us believe that struggle and confrontation are the only sources of progress?

These questions have been asked again and again, but without a unified framework to join all the disparate voices clamoring in the darkness and labeled as anomalies in the paradigm of domination. Now, however, these voices, and the alternatives they have occasionally offered, are more than anomalies. Thomas Kuhn wrote that no matter how many anomalies exist in a paradigm, no matter how many things don't fit our understanding, a paradigm shift will not occur until the broad outlines of the next paradigm have been articulated. The concept of partnership can bring these anomalies together, linking the groups concerned with peace, women's issues, ecology—the great diversity of voices calling for an end to domination, until recently on the fringe of world affairs, but now taking their rightful place on the global agenda.

Creativity and Technologies of Conservation

A few years ago, Alfonso taught a course on creativity at UC Berkeley. In the classroom next door, a course was being taught on waste management. This provided an interesting juxtaposition, since the creativity students were discussing glamorous artists and scientists, reaching for the sky with new visions and inventions, and next door the waste management people were stuck with the unglamorous job of figuring out how to clean up the mess made by these creative leaps. Perhaps it is a sign of the times, but there were many more students in the waste management course.

Waste management, sweeping up after progress, as it were, has generally been considered a lowly task, inherently not creative. Yet John Todd has shown that it can be transformed into a work of art if approached with creative attention. Given the extent of pollution on our planet, waste management certainly seems ready for a dose of creativity. Historically, however, the notions of creativity and of repetitive and routine maintenance have been polarized and juxtaposed as mutually exclusive.

The stereotypical everyday activities of women have provided a context from which creativity can emerge, and this in itself is a creative enterprise that has not been recognized as such. It has in fact been demeaned and trivialized as "women's work." Traditionally the role of women has been confined to the realm of the private, to the home. There women have cooked, cleaned, cared for the family, decorated—in short, they have provided a nurturing environment. This

247

work was absolutely necessary to dominator-system maintenance; without it the system would have collapsed. Yet it has largely gone unrecognized and unrewarded.

Our current conception of creativity does not consider these maintenance activities and values in spite of the fact that without them, creativity is impossible. Without the ground of sympathy, the environment from which it is allowed to emerge, creativity could not exist. In his extensive study of creativity, David Loye calls attention to its feminine aspect, as a "nurturing matrix" for art and innovation in all forms. Frank Barron's forthcoming book is on the ecology of creativity, a subject he has pioneered. Barron draws on the poet Yeats, as he is wont to do on occasion, with the image of creativity as "no rootless flower." Creativity's roots need soil in which to grow. Our present vision of creativity has focused exclusively on the flower, and in the process we have damaged the soil, both metaphorically and literally.

Society has long viewed woman's role as essentially supportive—necessary but inferior. The context for creativity that it has provided, so necessary for human survival and well-being, has not been considered a creative act at all. Mom cleaning up after us "just happens," like childbirth "just happens," with the woman simply having to be there, passively, for it to occur. In the dominator system, women are considered on a par with nature in this respect. They are irrational natural phenomena to be molded and shaped according to the wishes of their masters. Women's creativity is supposed to be unconscious, without the interference of thought, will, or purpose.

For too long we have thought about creativity as a predominantly male phenomenon that occurs in lone individuals and is only hampered by society, never supported by it. A new view of creativity derived from systems theory sees creativity as occurring in a much broader context. This view restores value to the practices and creative contributions women have made to society for thousands of years.

A systems, partnership view of creativity holds out great promises and explores, as Frank Barron indicates, the ecology of creativity: All creation is collaboration. It is also, therefore, not just a more ecological form of creativity but a more creative way of being in our ecology.

There is a widely known four-stage model of the creative process—modeled on the birth process—that can help us better understand the problems inherent in the traditional view of creativity.

The four stages are preparation, incubation, illumination, and verification. First you realize what the problem is and get ready to deal with it; then you gather relevant information, after which you let it all stew for a while; suddenly, Aha!—the light bulb goes on over your head; and finally you see if you had the right idea and try to apply it.

The most famous of these four stages is illumination—the light bulb scene. It's the most dramatic moment, captured perfectly by Archimedes running naked through Syracuse shouting, "Eureka!" But then Archimedes ran home naked to try out the experiment he had thought of, and clearly he had a lot of work ahead. And he had been thinking about the problem long before the notorious streaking incident.

With our focus just on the dramatic moment of illumination/insemination, and then the appearance of an invention/baby seemingly fully formed out of a lab or a womb, we've not paid any attention to all the other steps. All the attention is on the flower, and no attention is paid to the roots and the soil and the air and the sun—the whole system, in other words.

The partnership, systemic model of creativity draws our attention to aspects of our world that have not been widely recognized as worthy.

From cooperation in biology to love in psychology to gestation and education in childbirth and child rearing, to a large extent it's women who are directing our gaze to this whole new universe. But then, it's not exactly new, is it? The dominator paradigm has relegated these aspects of life to a lower status, and kept them in their place, in the home. They are women's issues, and as such, their concerns do not surface in the public space of policy and law making or, much worse, in the way we as citizens think about these issues. Women may hold up half the sky, as the Chinese saying goes, but their concerns and perspectives, the areas they value and pay attention to, have yet to penetrate the public sphere where decisions are made and public consciousness is shaped. Who does this women's work in government?

As Riane Eisler has written, "Without a higher social valuing of the 'women's work' of cleaning, it is not realistic to expect adequate funding for the environmental housekeeping necessary to deal with our ecological problems. Nor, as long as men continue to be socialized to obsess on 'war toys,' and to relegate the caretaking work to women, can we expect the funding to meet the basic needs of women and men worldwide—thus creating the economic and social

249

base for a peaceful and equitable society." She points out that research shows it would require only 25 percent of the awesome one-trillion-dollar global armaments budget "to massively reduce all the major global problems, from eliminating starvation and providing adequate health care to stabilizing the world's population and regenerating the environment."

This shift in priorities and budget allocations can come about only with an examination of, and a fundamental change in, our values—in other words, through an increased awareness of alternatives that necessitates paying attention to areas formerly ignored. Until recently we have taken women's work (work that in our system has been performed by women, not work that is somehow genetically determined to be performed by women) for granted; we have not explored either its significance or its real nature. Scott Coltrane, in his research on partnership parenting, points out that men and women see different worlds in the same house. We also see different worlds in the same planet. The dominator system has trained us in this way; women have certain patterns of attention and values that are crucial for system survival and maintenance but that go unrecognized and unrewarded. By doing some of each other's work, both in the public and the private spheres, we will be expanding our worlds in almost unimaginable ways.

Meanwhile, the enormous amount of hard work involved in maintaining and nurturing life has been largely unnoticed by economists and therefore does not appear in economic indicators. Technologies of conservation, Eisler has discovered, have been systematically downplayed. Statistics show that women do 66 percent of the work in our world and get 10 percent of the rewards. The net effect is that in the way economists add things up—and governmental policies are shaped—the stereotypical contribution women make to the world economy is practically invisible. It is as though their work did not really exist. Public policy rolls along with almost no attention to the public dimension of those issues that in the private sphere have been attended to by women.

In fact in our gender-polarized society, these nurturing concerns have been conspicuous by their absence in the public sphere. With all creative energies fueled by a decontextualized creativity, we have produced great instruments of pollution such as cars, factories, and chemical compounds, with little or no thought (until now) for the environment, human or otherwise. Mom does not suddenly appear to clean up our toxic waste dumps, and Mother Nature is not up for it either.

For Isabel Allende "environmentalism is a nurturing approach to the world, to society, and to reality. We have been pushed and forced to take that nurturing approach because we have trespassed all limits. In a way that is what's happening with society and with the world: the world is talking back to us and saying, 'Hey, this is your last chance. You'd better watch it!' There is a point where you don't make a choice; the choice is made even if you don't want to, because the circumstances push you to a point where you have to make the changes."

Viewing our creative efforts as separate from the environment means engaging in a fundamentally antagonistic relationship with it. It is because of this relationship that we have trespassed all limits, as Isabel Allende said. We have depleted the very context from which our creativity emerges. We have not dealt with the "women's issues," with cleaning up after our creative acts and products, assessing their impact on the system as a whole. Cleaning up is not glamorous, not creative somehow. Because of our reductionistic focus on the ability of genius to transcend environment, we have neglected to create an environment that nurtures our growth and development.

From Peripheral Invader to Resident Mind-set

Once upon a time, ecology and the environment were the concern of a few romantics who cared deeply about the little and not-so-little animals and the lovely plants that live in this world with us. The environment was something outside us, something that would take a few bruises in the inevitable march of progress. In fact, being outside us, being the other, nature was made a party to the dance of domination and submission.

First we thought nature dominated humans. Then, with technological progress, human beings began to learn how to control and dominate nature. Any attempt to stand in the way of progress was thought of as foolish and reactionary, since there was a certain linear inevitability about human development. But as our scientific understanding changed, and our view of the world changed along with the world itself, the dichotomies and the domination began to make less and less sense.

Scientists have recently realized that they know absolutely nothing about 90 or so percent of the matter in the universe, so-called dark matter. We also don't know what our genetic potential is, Sheldon Margen reminded us. We don't know where we come from, and we don't know where we're going. We thought we pretty much

251

had power over our environment, until we realized that power over was perhaps the wrong thing to want. And this shows us that perhaps we do not even know the kinds of questions we should be asking ourselves and the kind of hopes we should entertain.

Our predominant worldview has seen us as separate from nature, everything an isolated atom, unable or unwilling to influence anything else. It has pitted us against nature, both within us and without; and it has stressed only one side of our creativity, without concern for the nurture of the environment from which creativity emerges, whether psychological, social, political, or ecological.

Now all that is changing, and we are beginning to see the world as a large ecosystem of interrelated elements constantly shaping, and being shaped by, one another. In such a web, it is important to be careful, as Isabel Allende suggests. It is important to be aware of the fact that we do not really know what we are doing. But we do seem to be doing it together, and we need to respect one another's ignorance and our search for greater understanding—not necessarily arriving at any ultimate principles, but at least attempting to coexist more peacefully and to develop together.

The linking of systems, nature, and cooperation is at the core of the Gaia hypothesis. The Gaia hypothesis came about through the exploration of space. It was developed by scientist Jim Lovelock when NASA asked him to study the possibility of life on Mars. This made Lovelock ask larger questions such as, What is life? The only place he could find out was on Earth. Somewhat symbolically, perhaps, as we move away from the planet we begin to see it as a whole and therefore develop a new understanding.

Eventually he came to see the Earth as a whole system, a single, tightly coupled process that allows the Earth to self-regulate through a series of feedback loops. Very simply put, the Gaia hypothesis sees all life on Earth as engaged in an ongoing process that creates a viable life-support system for itself. Within a mechanism similar to the one used in a thermostat, the balance of the planet is maintained as the whole system works to keep the equilibrium it needs in areas as diverse as the oxygen content of the air and the symbiosis of the forest floor.

Biologist Lynn Margulis is usually linked with Lovelock in the development of the Gaia hypothesis. Margulis is distressed by the religious overtones some people have been reading into Gaia. She's wary of those who equate Gaia with Mother Earth and ignore the science in favor of feel-good spirituality. She prefers to spend her time studying the population in the hindgut of a particularly voracious kind of termite. There she can observe the one and the many, the relationships of the parts to the whole and the whole to the parts. A large microbe is one whole cell, but the cell is made up of other living creatures, like bacteria, all working cooperatively to keep things going. Margulis is one of the major proponents of symbiosis, believing that evolution occurs through cooperation rather than Darwinian competition, as we saw, and this work was essential in making sense of the self-regulating, self-organizing abilities of Gaia.

With Lovelock and Margulis we go from the macrocosm of the planet to the microcosm of bacteria. And it seems that the old dictum applies: As above, so below. What they both see are systems, systems that self-regulate to keep themselves in decent shape. A cooperative effort keeps the systems viable and livable, from the planet as a whole to the individual cell and the bacteria that live in it.

The greater the autonomy of any system, the greater the interdependence, research shows. We can translate that as "The greater the individual's freedom, the greater his or her embeddedness in a larger system." It's another way of saying that freedom brings with it responsibility, and that our freedom can be increased by our interaction with others rather than reduced. The old dichotomy of individual versus society collapses.

But so does our view of animals and plants as fundamentally lower on the totem pole and expendable. As we become aware of the amazing self-regulating mechanism that is Gaia, we may begin to exercise some of the caution Isabel Allende says the pebble effect makes her feel. When we view ourselves as separate from the environment, we feel we can destroy it with impunity. When we view ourselves as environment, we become more respectful of our relationships to our world.

According to futurist Paul Saffo, "There's been steady environmental progress in a number of areas. We've solved the easy ones: we've gotten the easy recycling and wilderness protection done. From here out, the environmental problems are just going to get more complicated, with more trade-offs and more headaches. I think that leads to what Mark Twain says: 'I'm all for progress; it's change I don't like.' I think we're going to see a strong antienvironmental movement in the United States in the next two to three years. That means change is clustering at the extremes, that we will have more militant environmentalists, the Green Movement, and more equally militant organizations opposed to the environmentalists. In my business, when change clusters in extremes like that, it's a sure sign that more fundamental change lies ahead and that eventually a consensus will emerge.

"The wild card is the environment itself. There is evidence that southern Chile is on the cusp of the ozone hole. There are rumors of blinded sheep and fish and fears over harm to humans. Because Chile is so remote, these events may never affect public opinion. But imagine if the same thing happened in a U.S. urban area, or if we had another Chernobyl, and this time it was a true meltdown. That would change attitudes about the environment very quickly. I think we're going to go through short-term opposition to environmental change. We'll probably lose some advances. But over the long term, we're headed ever more aggressively on the path of solving the problem as it becomes clear that this is a business issue, a national security issue, and that everything depends on the environment. So in the short term, I'm a pessimist; in medium term, I'm an optimist; and in the long term, I don't know yet because the question is, Can we respond quickly enough? Can we get one step ahead of the problem?

"The other factor is the tremendous void now left by the collapse of communism. National security against the Russian threat was the organizing principle of our society. Organizing principles are very powerful. We didn't protect ourselves from the Russians, we just built the best nukes in the world. Because we were so busy building nukes, we no longer built the best cars in the world. I would bet that the decline of Detroit started at the time of Sputnik, when we started throwing our resources away from commercial consumer goods to military goods. Well, now it's gone, and there is a vacuum in the American consciousness waiting to be filled by another organizing issue. Two candidates are now vying for attention—one is health care, and the other is environment. Personally I hope that the environment becomes the equivalent of national security, the equivalent of Sputnik, which mobilized us to improve our educational institutions, to do things in high-tech centers."

The implications of what Paul Saffo is saying are far-reaching. This could be a step toward partnership and away from domination at a very basic level, namely the organizing point of society. Perhaps we can draw some inspiration from the Tiruray of the Philippines who, as we saw, consider their role to be guardians of the rain forest.

Stuart Schlegel pointed out that "much of the Tiruray mode of social consciousness and interaction incorporates what in the West are considered female values: sharing, warmth, nonviolence. But to

Tiruray, these are neither masculine nor feminine qualities; they are simply human. Or since these values characterize so many spirits as well, perhaps we should say they are simply personal or natural. Tiruray culture stresses sharing, not taking away; caring for, not oppressing; mutual responsibility, not domination.

"Tiruray see themselves as at one with nature, and this unity lies at the heart of everything that is, seen and unseen. This unity is a kind of unbroken cloth; it's a fabric that binds everyone and everything together. So all of reality is a single, complex, interrelated life system: a system that embraces all living beings and all the natural world and that was created and exists to express cooperative interdependence. And thus both people and things are to be cared for and nurtured, not exploited or shaped to one's private will. In such a universal system, the basic idea of radical human egalitarianism is not just possible, it's fundamental. Absolutely fundamental. They couldn't live their system of life with any other understanding." The Tiruray seem to experience this human interconnectedness to a far greater extent than we do, even though we're becoming more and more aware of the need to act upon it, rather than merely understand it intellectually.

"I know I've said this before," Stuart Schlegel stressed, "their society is not utopian, in the sense that there is not an absence of all violence by any means. They don't always live up to their ideas. Sometimes they do give each other a 'bad gallbladder.' But they have certain ideals, and these ideals give rise to a social life that largely institutionalizes the ideals even though they break them from time to time."

Understanding ecology and our relationship to the environment is not a peripheral issue anymore. It is not a cute romantic concern for the survival of little critters or a concern for natural beauty—a luxury we believe we can ultimately do without. Many of the explorers on the frontiers of a new paradigm that we have met here are thinking about ecology as an organizing social principle, an inspiration, and a fertile metaphor for reimagining the world. Frank Barron is studying the ecology of creativity; Hazel Henderson, the interface of economics and ecology; and Riane Eisler is writing a new book exploring the relationship between economics, ecology, and gender.

For some years, William Irwin Thompson has seen biology as having the same relationship to the coming paradigm that physics had to the previous one, in terms of its influence on our thinking.

255

Physics gave us its machine metaphor; biology may provide us with an ecological metaphor, one of living creatures and partnership with nature, of connectedness rather than separation.

In the final analysis, the new way of seeing the world will depend on what each of us comes to believe, both as separate individuals and as living cells in the body of Earth.

Conclusion

In the year 999 a lot of people sat around waiting for something incredible to happen. Nothing cosmic happened, beyond the crazy things they did themselves. At the end of the twentieth century, some of us likewise seem to be waiting for something to occur, something remarkable, like a nuclear apocalypse or a fundamentalist rapture, when the chosen will be lifted to the heavens while driving our cars or shopping at Kmart. Or a new age might dawn, and the dolphins will ask the extraterrestrials to come down and visit as we wave our crystals at them.

According to Paul Saffo, "The millennium is really a huge social Rorschach blot of unprecedented dimension. We're warming up to it; you can see the first signs: our President is using the word *millennium* in his speeches, the number of religious tracts about biblical prophecies and the like is growing. Someone told me the Grateful Dead have reserved space in the Great Pyramid in Egypt for a New Year's Eve concert in 1999. Travel agents are taking reservations for trips to new age power spots like Sedona and Ayer's Rock, Australia. We are entering a 'silly season' leading up to the millennium.

"Anyone who doubts that this sort of thing has an effect needs to be reminded of how Cortés conquered the Aztecs: This ragtag band of adventurers from Cuba managed to subdue the entire Aztec empire. They had the good fortune of arriving at the end of the fifty-two-year calendar cycle, and in the Aztec calendar system that was the time when the end of the world was supposed to come. They arrived from the east and matched the prophecy, so for the Aztecs there was no point in fighting.

"The same thing, I think, happened during the Iraq-Kuwait war. Billy Graham made a public statement to the effect that this was Armageddon. And it came at a convenient time, because all the people who had wanted the Soviet premier to be the Antichrist found that the Soviets stubbornly refused to go along with prophecy. Gorbachev made a lousy Antichrist because he was so charming. Saddam, on the other hand, is a perfect Antichrist, since he's not a nice fellow. Baghdad is only a couple miles down the road from the Babylon of Isaiah. My suspicion is that a significant minority in this country never questioned the Gulf War because they thought it was biblical prophecy fulfilled."

The end of the world is probably not everybody's idea of a good time, and people who like to have a good time are probably not going to be the ones lifted up to the heavens in rapture anyway. Rest assured, Paul Saffo told us, things are going to get weird around the millennium. And as the saying goes, When the going gets weird, the weird get going.

In the meantime, some others, like mystic David Spangler, are proposing that the new age is already here, and we're just not looking hard enough. This is an interesting idea, and something to keep us busy while we wait for the cosmic fireworks. What if this is really the end of the dominator world, not the whole world? What if a real positive change involved, among other things, a different way of seeing and being in the world? A way of seeing the world that made us behave differently? And what if we could begin acting on it right now? A change of mind and a change of heart?

Riane Eisler's cultural transformation theory, with its templates of the dominator and partnership systems, articulates the two fundamental alternatives facing us in the new millennium. As Eisler states, partnership proposes not revolution but transformation.

"Its ultimate faith is in life, not death," she writes in *The Partnership Way.* "Inspired not by the Blade, but by the Chalice—the ancient symbol of life-enhancing and transformative power—it is a statement of faith in the creative power of our higher aspirations: our age-old striving for truth, beauty, and justice. Above all, it is a statement of faith and hope in us, in our technological power as humans to deconstruct the myths of dominator reality and reconstruct ourselves and this planet into the new synergisms suitable for a world of partnership and peace."

The choice is clear, and the responsibility is ours. Partnership is not something we "buy into" but something we create together. The dominator and partnership templates provide us with the framework for beginning to make sense of the seemingly overwhelming complexity of our age. But the realization of partnership in our lives depends on our actions.

What if we could create pockets of partnership wherever we go? Roddy Frame had an interesting little anecdote in this regard. "The last record we made was really popular in Spain. We had a little moral dilemma because we were attracting so many people that they ended up putting the concert in a bullring. Now, I think bullfighting is pretty ugly, and quite cruel. But then I came to the conclusion that we could take our own vibes in there and for a while create a good vibe where there used to be an ugly, killing vibe. We brought some good vibes to an arena that's regularly used for a fairly cruel, prolonged, ritual slaughter." Sometimes, Roddy shows us, it might be more effective simply to go ahead and do something positive—leading by example—and act rather than protest.

We rarely find a total dominator system, with no partnership hope anywhere. Right now, as the whole world is in turmoil at all levels—social, political, economic—a rigid system has been shaken and is therefore more fluid, more chaotic. Established ways of doing things are breaking down, and people are trying to find new ways of thinking, being, and organizing their relationships. New political affiliations, new economic systems, new relationships, new family structures are being created by people in all walks of life who have found the old ways wanting—they just don't work for them anymore.

The shift from a dominator to a partnership society is a much greater change than the one that occurred with the Industrial Revolution because it implies a momentous transformation in the basic way that human beings relate to the world. Following the three main threads running through this book, the shift would be toward a holistic, systemic conception of human beings, which embraces both genders equally rather than focusing on just one. It would focus on relationships of partnership rather than domination or submission. And it would see the difference between men and women as a source of creativity—as symbolized by childbirth and child rearing—rather than an indication of superior or inferior ranking.

259

We're moving into uncharted territory, learning how to create new worlds as we go. Perhaps it's not such a utopian dream to suggest that we could become a learning society, devoted to exploring ways to live together more creatively, systematically ridding ourselves of old prejudices and preconceptions. What used to be a utopian dream is increasingly becoming a pragmatic necessity.

One of the main features of the movement to partnership is the role of an expanded attention. Partnership gently directs our attention to an entirely different world, a universe next door. Many of the researchers and scholars we spoke to studied subjects that no one had paid much attention to but that had been there right under our noses: cooperation and symbiosis in nature, the relationship between mind and body in healing, love and happiness in psychology, the nature of peace and conflict resolution in politics, the potential in working with nature rather than trying to control her.

In academic disciplines and public life, we find aspects of existence that have been totally ignored or dismissed in a cavalier fashion. This is the result of Western society's habitual public-private, male-female, important-trivial dichotomies. The time has come to heal these splits, which have engendered some of the more bizarre and often destructive expressions of the dominator system. In this drastically polarizing system, we find the greatest potential for healing in those very oppositions we have generated. We can begin to see, for instance, the role of gender in the creation of our world— both literally and figuratively. The royal road to wholeness seems to lie in the relationship to the "opposite" sex in both the private, intimate world of our personal lives and the public world of policy and business. By paying attention to our differences and similarities, women and men can begin to learn from each other what it means to be whole persons.

Much has been made recently of the so-called overview effect, seeing a photo of planet Earth from space. For some it's a significant experience that brings home the fact that we are all indeed on one big, beautiful planet. Others are less impressed. So what if you can't see borders and nation-states and different cultures, they say. They're still there; and after all, you can't see people or birds either. We thought we'd ask someone who'd not just seen the photo but could actually have taken it from his privileged position on the moon: astronaut Edgar Mitchell.

"We're talking about awareness and a shift in perspective, of perceiving information from a different viewpoint. Our sensory mechanisms—when I say sensory, I extend it to include intuition as well—really screen out most of the information that's available to us from our environment. We're only receiving a tiny fraction, something like one billionth, of the information presented to our sensory mechanisms. All we're really doing when we have one of these experiences, an overview experience, if you like, or a peak experience, is simply opening our awareness to perceive information that's already there and organizing that information in a different way. It results in a very high experience, because you say, 'I never saw that before.' That's right, you never saw that before, but that's only because you screened it out. So it really doesn't take going into space to do it, it merely takes the willingness, the ability, and the mechanisms whereby you're willing to perceive and consider and organize information somewhat differently.

"I'm reminded of the story of the mule. The first thing you have to do is get his attention, and, as the old saying goes, often that requires hitting him right between the ears with a baseball bat. Well, I describe this basic experience as my baseball bat. It caused me to see things and to perceive them in a totally different manner, but the information was there all along. People like to say it was a mystical experience or a divine experience. I don't believe that. I don't like to call things supernatural or unnatural or mystical or whatever. It's just perception. You suddenly are able to perceive new information or organize it differently."

The fact that in the past we focused so much of our attention on some phenomena rather than others—often denying that issues like happiness and love were worthy of serious study or effort (relegated to women's magazines or literature) or that cooperation was a significant phenomenon or that "women's issues" were crucial to human survival and were in fact human issues—meant, among other things, that we restricted our search for alternatives, solutions, and answers to a limited scope. This scope was fundamentally a pessimistic one. In psychology and politics, for instance, the fundamental assumption was that human beings were barely in control of a seething cauldron of emotions and violence that could erupt anytime. It was also a male framework, but a schizoid, grotesque distortion of "maleness," with terribly exaggerated features.

In that framework you could get away with saying things like, "Girls don't want sex, they want love. And boys don't want love, they want sex." Here we have the either/or kind of mentality that splits off male and female into two different camps and ensures the twain shall never meet—God forbid you should be some kind of weird mutant hybrid. Fortunately we're beginning to see beyond this kind of nonsense.

261

We all know how it's possible to be both sad and happy at the same time. Aristotelian either/or logic does not work in the realm of feelings. In fact the events that affect us the most are often the ones where there is precisely such a mixture of feelings, of the bittersweet, of sweet memories and distant longings, of paradoxes that don't resolve themselves but just linger, and we somehow manage to live with them.

Our knowledge about the world turns out to have been very one-sided, focusing our attention on dominator dynamics. We thought dominator dynamics were all that we could expect, but it seems that we found only what we were looking for. It was either domination or submission, and we were just waiting our turn. Many of the partnership elements in our lives were either ignored, suppressed, or trivialized.

This shift in attention is pretty dramatic. Taking some of the factors into consideration, looking at them as a whole, in other words, from a partnership perspective rather than as isolated omissions or oversights, we realize that it's impossible to go back and live in the old world. You can never see the world the same way again.

The difference is akin to a sexual awakening. One day the little boy is saying girls are yucky and don't know diddley about baseball scores, and the next day he blushes and stutters as he tries to figure out what to say to the cute redheaded girl who has moved in next door. And it's never the same again.

With a partnership perspective we begin paying attention to different things, seeing TV shows differently, exploring political issues from a renewed perspective, looking at our relationships from a different angle. What was once funny or profound may now seem dull and even brutish. What once we didn't even know existed may suddenly open up a rich vein of ideas, information, and inspiration. With this new perspective, we don't bring in answers so much as ask new questions, challenging why things have to be the way they are.

For many of the people we spoke to, the idea of partnership, and the idea of challenging the existing system, was an enormous motivating force. Like Isabella's experience at the end of law school, we've realized that the world does not have to be bound by a particular set of (dominator) rules, and it's now up to us to reimagine the world together. We are also realizing that our attention must shift to a world we had not seen but perhaps knew in our hearts was there. An essentially new world is waiting to be shaped by our thoughts and actions. This world is not determined by the stars or by genes, cosmic cycles, or limited resources. The responsibility rests with each one of us to contribute something to the future, to the world our children will be living in.

Bela Banathy believes that "many people feel that they can't make any difference. So why care? Why do anything? they say, because the big guys are doing it for me, are telling me what life is going to be like. But in critical times in a society's development, chaos theory and evolutionary theory show us that we don't have to have massive reactions. A few people who care deeply and respond to a situation can give direction to the evolution of a society. It's up to us. It has to be done in our lives, in our communities and families, and in the groups of which we are a part.

"The most important aspect is to be committed as an individual to developing yourself toward the ideal you feel you ought to become. You should utilize all the numerous resources this society has available for you to learn how to do so. You must be able to nurture yourself and develop into that desired state, that ideal state.

"We cannot change society without changing ourselves. And when you have entered the path, you have to become a missionary for it, learning how to realize this ideal for every individual you meet. That also means that each learner—and we are all learners—will have his or her own program of life learning, and not a prescribed curriculum dictated from higher up. It should empower the person, promote the idea of learning how to learn, so as to enable self-directed learning.

"As a member of the community, speak up whenever you can and wherever you can. Go to those public forums, go to those meetings of the supervisors, go to the school board meetings and speak up for the need to create a good climate and resources for learning. Eventually you should learn how to design systems as part of your own learning program. Again, in your own life, experience the possibility of learning and transformation so you can truly believe in it. Then voice that belief in whatever context you are able to. Definitely make it work in the life of your family, and make it work in all your relationships."

Bela Banathy points to the fact that when we feel helpless, when we wonder what we can do to change our situation, we are confronted with the possibility of learning about how to help ourselves rather than looking for ready-made answers. We need to seize this opportunity to learn how to learn, how to become informed, and how to shape our ideals and shape our own future. Sometimes we feel stuck, wishing we could do something but not knowing what to do. In these cases, rather than focusing on the content of what we

263

need to learn, we might nurture our capacity to learn, so that we can respond to many different situations—learning how to fish rather than going out to buy a fish.

Whenever we wonder about what we can do as individuals in the face of seemingly overwhelming problems of global proportions, we may also want to remember the pebble effect, and the way our actions can ripple outward to inspire, motivate, and inform others.

"The struggle we are engaging in is not a battle between the good guys and the bad guys," the well-known Buddhist scholar and systems scientist Joanna Macy asks us to remember. "That means we can be relieved of self-righteousness, and this is an enormous gift, because we can shed the feeling that we need to have all the answers. That need to possess an absolute truth is the legacy of the old paradigm. Instead what you get with the systems view of the radical interrelatedness of all phenomena is a line between good and evil that runs through the landscape of every human heart. Then you know that each act of pure intention to participate in the self-healing of our world has repercussions throughout the web of life that we cannot discern or measure.

"A dominant form of disconnectedness today," Joanna Macy points out, "is the notion that the awareness we have of the fate of our planet, of our collective dilemma, is a private and individual perspective. That gives people the sense that the pain they feel for our world is essentially reducible to a personal pathology. The sense of distress for what is happening to our world, whether you look at it in economic, political, military, or, above all, environmental terms, is an apprehension that goes beyond one's personal ego and one's individual needs and wants. This is not a private concern so much as an expression of our interconnectedness.

"I've been doing quite a bit of work with psychologists and psychotherapists. They're also finding that the model of the self that they have been trained in, that all the literature and the tradition has told them is what they are supposed to heal, is a false model. The systems view lets us see that real healing of the individual is that which allows us to participate in the healing of the larger whole. This is not wishful thinking. I'm not preaching some new spiritual glue. These are elegant concepts based on data showing the self-organization of open systems. I cannot begin to express my debt to systems theory for two things: for helping people find sanity in this time, and for helping them find momentum to engage their gears to participate in the self-healing of this world. Systems theory does not have a shallow fix-it mentality. It shows us that we're not outside the global, political, economic, or ecological systems. We cannot, the new worldview shows us, stand outside it. Power is not sitting isolated behind the controls and pushing this button or pulling that lever, standing outside life and manipulating the environment. It's engaging in a much more profound participation in life."

Dominique DiPrima feels that people want action rather than preaching, role models and examples rather than Sunday-go-to-meeting-preachers. Isabel Allende also values this kind of consistency. "I want my writing and my life to be as honest as possible," she said. "I try to live the way I talk and the way I write, and vice versa. You will seldom find in my books something that I do not practice in my real life. This horrifies my mother, especially in the sex scenes! When I talk about food in my books, it's because that's the way I am with food. Same with other ideas. You will always find in my books certain things that are issues in my life: feminism has always been present; social issues, inequalities, dictatorship, repression, violence. There is an obsession with poverty and with marginals: people who are not sheltered by the big umbrella of the system, who stand on the borderline. Those people are always the protagonists of my books. What you find in my books, in my writing, I also do in my private life."

Bela Banathy sees us engaged in a journey where we learn together how to live together. Learning together requires great attention. One fundamental dimension of attention is the ability to listen. It was surprising to us how many of the people we spoke to brought this up. In the process of conflict resolution, for instance, simply listening to each other is perhaps the most important step. It is essential in relationships between the sexes and between parents and their children. John Todd reminded us of how he listened to nature, showing that in order to begin to understand the world around us and live in some kind of harmony and partnership, looking and listening attentively is of paramount importance.

How remarkable, then, that we should not be listening to each other, because it seems like such an easy thing to do. But listening involves much more than just shutting up for a while, nodding, and saying, "Yeah, yeah," when the other person is speaking, while we wait to get into the act again. Not listening is a cornerstone of the dominator system.

When I don't listen to you, I don't care about you and what you have to say. I may claim that I do; in fact I may even say that the reason why you should shut up and listen to me, goddammit, is precisely because I do care, and I know what's best for you. But how

265

much can I really care if I don't even pay attention to what you're saying? Am I then not just interested in getting things done my way, to prove that I am right?

When two people who are supposedly engaged in discussion don't listen to each other, or listen just to see what they can pick apart in the other's argument, you have two people trying to figure out who can come out on top, who can win the argument, right or wrong. This is the dominator dynamic.

Partnership is created in dialogue, and dialogue is created in partnership. This does not mean that in a partnership dialogue we just nod and smile a friendly smile and agree with each other at all costs. A partnership dialogue involves both parties listening, questioning, probing, exploring, but also trying to build something together. This does not necessarily have to be a consensus. The two of us can remain in disagreement about an issue while at the same time honestly exploring the implications of each other's criticism and questioning our own assumptions.

For most people real dialogue occurs most often with friends, the people we can share our feelings and ideas and wild dreams with. What does it mean to be friends, to have a friend, a best friend or a group of friends? How are our relationships with our friends different from those we have with strangers? What makes a real friendship special for us?

Ashley Montagu told us we should teach our kids that the world is filled with friends we do not yet know, and Hazel Henderson reminded us of the importance of trust, a basic trust in life and in human decency. One of Joanna Macy's books is entitled *World as Lover, World as Self*. If we were to think of another metaphor for the world, what might it be? Would it be world as enemy, world as vale of tears, world as nuisance? Or world as playground, world as laboratory, as experiment, as banana peel, as journey? Or all of the above? Certainly world as friend does not strike us as a bad one.

But in view of some of the things that go on in the world, does that not seem unrealistic, or even a bit foolish? Isn't it a way to set ourselves up for disappointment, particularly when we're confronted with people who are not quite as benevolent as we think we are?

"When I was five or six," David Loye told us, "and went off to school for the first time, I was looking forward to this wonderful experience of getting out, being a grown-up child and entering the world of school. And as I approached the schoolhouse full of anticipation, enthusiasm, and hope, a little kid half my size came rushing toward me and I thought to myself, 'Ah, here comes my first friend.' And he rushed up and hit me as hard as he could in the stomach. I was absolutely devastated. He didn't know me. I didn't know him. There was no conceivable reason for him to do this. Afterward I tugged at the teacher to try to get some explanation for this shattering experience, for which I'd been wholly unprepared. But she brushed me off, too busy on the first day of school to bother with me. When time came for me to go to school for days afterward, I would just hide in the closet because I couldn't stand it. My mother would drag me out and push me out the door.

"What held me together in those years was the advantage of two models of rock-firm love and unshakable moral strength. One grandmother, one grandfather. They gave me my only rudders during a time when I was overwhelmed at the hostility and indifference in this otherwise potentially wonderful world."

Despite it all, David Loye has followed the moral example, the partnership alternative, rather than the game of domination and submission he could so easily have fallen into. But his experience is one that is all too often encountered in dominator systems: the removal of trust. No trust in ourselves, in others, or in the world we live in.

The partnership world is based on trust. What if we were actively to create an environment in which the trust of friendship could blossom? What if we were to attempt to create in our every encounter the kind of atmosphere psychologist Erik Erikson called basic trust? We might do this in an environment that relishes difference and accepts conflict as precursors not of war but of creativity, inquiry, and new understanding.

Children will explore if they have this basic trust in themselves and in the world, if they know there is a home base for them to return to. David Loye has called this matrix of trust the nurturing, feminine matrix of creativity, the environment that allows us to be creative. Trust, therefore, increases our willingness to be creative and to take risks. When we live in fear, some of us may still explore, but the majority will not. The dominator world is ultimately stultifyingly boring and lacking in imagination.

The new vision of a society based on partnership points our attention to the boundaries of our imagination. Where are we stuck, left without a vision, incapable of going further? Where have given up on ourselves and those around us, and declared that we cannot go any further? We said we could not run a four-minute mile or stop the fighting in Western Europe or curb our aggression or educate the masses or free the slaves or give women the vote. And every time it seemed obvious that it was possible after it occurred—and not just obvious but necessary.

How much are we still not seeing? Two hundred years ago slavery and the subordination of people to those more powerful or more privileged seemed perfectly normal. Today they are aberrations. How many things like this, things that we take for granted, appear as normalcies we cannot conceive of questioning?

Along with a deconstruction, a profound questioning, of our deepest assumptions must come a parallel reconstruction, a revisioning and reimagining of the world. We must not aggravate errors of commission with errors of omission. We must not fail the ethical imperative to imagine the world otherwise, in the words of philosopher Richard Kearney.

In a noisy Berkeley café, Art Aron looked up from his cappuccino and reminded us to stress that partnership is also fun. "It should not degenerate into some painfully earnest, humorless attempt to 'do good,'" he said.

"It's a release, a relief," Joanna Macy pointed out, "it's not hard work at all." Why is hell often portrayed as the center of fun and paradise as a dull affair with angels strumming harps on clouds in what must be a truly soporific vision of the beyond?

Dominator polarizations make domination and the "illicit" seem dangerous and pleasurable; so sex gets lumped in there too because it's just too much fun, and holiness really means sexlessness and ultimately bodylessness. Partnership means going beyond the illegal-fattening-or-immoral dilemma set up by the dominator system. It's not true that all the fun things conform to one of those three descriptions. Our system simply labels them as such.

So what is morality, after all? As David Loye has shown so convincingly, societies tend to have an ostensible and an operational code of ethics. The ostensible code says we should be good, loyal, dedicated, caring, decent people. The operational code says that if we want to get ahead, we have to lie, cheat, steal, and be pretty vicious. Sometimes we assume that this is just the way things are. This implies that anyone who pays too much attention to the way things should be is a dreamer, a wimp who can't take the real world, or just a damned fool.

Public figures illustrate this dynamic very clearly. Many religious leaders have succumbed to improper financial dealings or engaged in what for them should be inappropriate sexual conduct.

They've shown us the seedy side of fundamentalist Christianity, Buddhism, and various cults. Politicians often spout pieties of all sorts, and then wheel and deal behind everybody's back.

A continuous tension is created between what we should do to be good and what we should do to survive or have fun. Jesus may have said that the meek shall inherit the earth, but sometimes it seems like the meek will end up on the streets if they're not careful.

Using the results of brain research as well as evolutionary studies, David Loye builds the case for the idea that we not only have an organic moral sensitivity but that true morality is also innately pleasurable. Morality is not, in other words, something tagged on by society like an old-fashioned, sober-sided hat to top off the brute beast of humanity. It is something that is a natural part of us. If we consider the role of feelings and empathy, we realize that human beings can indeed have an almost instinctive Golden-Rule mentality, and using it can make us feel good. It's only natural for us to feel like not doing unto others what we would not want done unto ourselves.

Slowly we are learning how to let go of old habits of mind, heart, and body, and re-create ourselves in a variety of new images. We are beginning to pay attention to many aspects of our lives that we have largely ignored, taken for granted, or trivialized. We have before us a momentous task, but one that challenges our creative and critical faculties as they have never been challenged before. We are up to the task, and we can begin to make a difference, by paying attention, listening, learning, and taking risks, and maintaining our independence of judgment.

Speaking to the people in this book was for us a rewarding and inspiring process. The ideas, projects, actions, and people we came across showed us the force of the movement toward change, toward partnership. And yet the movement to partnership is sometimes found in the most ordinary places, with the people we meet every day, famous or not. A smile in a grocery store, a helping hand when we have car trouble, or a kindly spirit, like the old Chinese lady in Beijing who rushed Alfonso into her home because it was seven o'clock and he had not had dinner yet—these acts of connection and attention are in many ways what keep our public world intimate and human, no matter how high the skyscrapers.

A world of partnership, in which human beings do not persecute and kill one another, in which women and men treat one another decently and have equal rights and opportunities, in which we do not leave our brothers and sisters to die in poverty on our streets, a world in which we can afford to dream our dreams with some hope of achieving them and where our playfulness and inquisitiveness are not chased out of us like the threats to authority that they are—is this too much to ask? We think not. We believe it is possible to create a world in which women and men will be equally responsible for their fate—not a world where there is never any pain or suffering, where tears are never shed and harsh words are never spoken—but a world in which human beings act responsibly toward one another and toward the planet. It is a world that we can create together.

Introduction

The theoretical background for the organizing framework of this book (systems, partnership, and creativity, which, filtered through the mind of Isabella Conti, became ways of being, relating, and thinking) is explored in great detail in Montuori, A. 1989. *Evolutionary competence: Creating the future.* Amsterdam: J. C. Gieben; which in turn was influenced by Banathy, B. 1987. The characteristics and acquisition of evolutionary competence. *World Futures* 23:123–44. The reader interested in exhaustive references is referred to *Evolutionary competence.* The classic work on paradigms is Kuhn, T. 1970. *The structure of scientific revolutions.* Chicago: Univ. of Chicago Press. The Zen story by Janwillem van de Wetering is in his *Empty mirror: Experiences in a Japanese Zen monastery.* New York: Ballantine, 118–19. Paul Watzlawick's classic work is Watzlawick, P., J. H. Beavin, and D. D. Jackson. *Pragmatics of human communication: A study of interactional patterns, pathologies, and paradoxes.* New York: W. W. Norton. Also of great interest are Watzlawick, P. 1976. *How real is real?* New York: Vantage; and the amusing and easy to read—a cross between a Jewish-mother joke and a Zen story—Watzlawick, P. 1988. *Ultra-solutions.* New York: W. W. Norton. Riane Eisler's work is of course the reference for her cultural transformation theory and the partnership-dominator template that prompted this book: *The chalice and the blade: Our history, our future.* San Francisco: Harper San Francisco, 1987; and with David Loye, the 1991 workbook *The partnership way.* San Francisco: Harper San Francisco. Of considerable interest is the 1983 precursor, Eisler, R., and D. Loye. 1983. The "failure" of liberalism: A reassessment of ideology from a new feminine-masculine perspective. *Political Psychology* 4:375–91. For a good introduction to the applications of chaos theory to the social sciences, see Loye, D., and R. Eisler. 1987. Chaos and transformation: Implications of nonequilibrium theory for social science and society. *Behavioral Science* 32: 53–65. For perspectives on social transformation, see Capra, Fritjof. 1980. *The turning point.* New York: Bantam (recently made into a movie titled *Mindwalk*). Vitally important is the brilliant book by William Irwin Thompson, now sadly out of print but worth digging out in secondhand bookstores or hassling the Sierra Club for: Thompson, W. I. 1986. *Pacific shift.* San Francisco: Sierra Club. The work of Ervin Laszlo probably serves as the most extensive introduction available to systems thinking, by one of the leading philosopher-scientists of our time: Laszlo, E. 1987. *Evolution: The grand synthesis.* Boston: New Science Library. Laszlo, E. 1972. *The systems view of the world: The natural philosophy of the new developments in the sciences.* New York: George Braziller. Laszlo, E. 1972. *Introduction to systems philosophy: Toward a new paradigm of contemporary thought.* San Francisco: Harper & Row. Also Churchman, C. W. 1968. *The systems approach.* New York: Laurel. The reference to Einstein (p. 22) is from Overbye, Dennis. Einstein in Love. *Time,* April 30, 1990. The Luria research is cited in Restak, R. 1979. *The brain.* New York: Warner, 266–70. Our perspective on creativity is profoundly influenced by the work of Frank Barron. See Barron, F. 1990. *Creativity and psychological health.* Buffalo: Creative Education Foundation (original work published in 1963). Barron, F. 1988. Putting creativity to work. In *The nature of creativity,* ed. R. Sternberg, 76–98. Cambridge: Cambridge Univ. Press. Forthcoming is Barron's *No rootless flower: Towards an ecology of creativity.* Also of considerable interest from a partnership perspective is Loye, D. 1988. Hemisphericity and creativity. Group process in the dream factory. *Psychiatric Clinics of North America* 11:415–26. On beginner's mind, see Suzuki, S. 1970. *Zen mind, beginner's mind.* New York: Weatherhill, with an introduction by Richard Baker-Roshi.

271

Preview of Coming Attractions

Tom Stone learned the seven principles of Kwanzaa from a book by Eric V. Copage, *Kwanzaa: An African American Celebration of Culture and Cooking*, published by William Morrow in 1992. We have reproduced them here by kind permission of the publisher.

The Self

Two crucial articles by Susan Hales on self-esteem, moral behavior, and the social construction of the self are Valuing the self: Understanding the nature of self-esteem. *Saybrook Perspective*, Winter 1990, 3–17; Rethinking the business of psychology. *Journal for the Theory of Social Behaviour* 16 (1986): 57–76. Dean Ornish's work is summarized in his 1991 best-seller *Dr. Dean Ornish's program for reversing heart disease*. New York: Ballantine. Art and Elaine Aron's research on happiness is summarized in Aron, A. and E. N. 1987. The influence of inner state on self-reported long-term happiness. *Journal of Humanistic Psychology* 27, 2 (Spring). For psychological change from a "mythical" perspective, see Feinstein, D., and S. Krippner. 1988. *Personal mythology: The psychology of your evolving self*. Los Angeles: J. P. Tarcher. Anyone even remotely interested in the advances in mind-body healing, paranormal phenomena, and the human capacity for change should get Murphy, M. 1992. *The future of the body*. Los Angeles: J. P. Tarcher, an encyclopedic yet remarkably well-written tome exploring all these issues and more. Charles Hampden-Turner's (1981) *Maps of the mind* (New York: Macmillan) is a wonderful book to browse through while learning all about different psychological theories.

Relationships

The differences between men and women have generally been synthesized from Gilligan, C. 1982. *In a different voice*. Cambridge: Harvard Univ. Press. The Arons' work on love is found in Aron, A. and E. N. 1986. *Love and the expansion of self: Understanding attraction and satisfaction*. Washington, D.C.: Hemisphere. The polls on expectations and love are from a Yankelovich poll reported in *New Woman*, October 1990. Myriam Miedzian's comments are from an interview in *Time*, September 6, 1991. For Don Dutton's work on marital violence and intervention, see Dutton, D. G., and C. E. Strachan. 1987. Motivational needs for power and spouse-specific assertiveness in assaultive and nonassaultive men. *Violence and Victims* 2, 3 (1987). Dutton, D. G. Interventions into the problem of wife assault: Therapeutic, policy and research implications. *Canad. J. Behav. Sci./Rev. Canad. Sci. Comp.* 16, 4 (1984).

Working

Henderson, H. 1992. *Paradigms in progress*. Indianapolis: Knowledge Systems. Henderson, H. 1981. *The politics of the solar age*. Garden City, NY: Doubleday Anchor. Henderson, H. 1978. *Creating alternative futures*. New York: Putnam. For the systems approach in business, see Senge, P. 1991. *The fifth discipline*. New York: Doubleday. Also Harman, Willis. 1991. *Creative work*. Indianapolis: Knowledge Systems, which explores work within the larger context of the social change Harman himself has so well articulated in his writings and particularly in his (1988) *Global mind change*. Indianapolis: Knowledge Systems. Charles Hampden-Turner's (1990) *Charting the corporate mind* (New York: Free Press) is very interesting specifically for its discussion of dilemmas, dichotomies, and thinking styles.

Community

Philip Slater has two excellent books, his classic from 1970 on individualism, and his critique of American democracy from 1991. Slater, P. 1991. *A dream deferred: America's discontent and the search for a new democratic ideal*. Boston: Beacon Press. Slater, P. 1970. *The pursuit of loneliness*. Boston: Beacon. Robert Bellah and associates have followed up their excellent *Habits of the heart* with *The good society*, exploring the problems of individualism and democracy in transition. Bellah, R. N., R. Madsen, W. M. Sullivan, A. Swidler, S. M. Tipton. 1985. *Habits of the heart*. Berkeley and Los Angeles: Univ. of California Press. Isabel Allende refers to the PBS series and accompanying book by Keen, S. 1986. *The faces of the enemy*. San Francisco: Harper & Row. On the responsibility that comes with freedom, see Fromm, E. 1965. *Escape from freedom*. New York: Avon. For more on norm changers and maintainers, see Loye, D. 1977. *The leadership passion*. San Francisco: Jossey Bass. Also Loye, D. 1971. *The healing of a nation*. New York: W. W. Norton. This award-winning book deals with the problem of race and prejudice. See also Loye, D. 1990. Moral sensitivity and the evolution of higher mind. *World Futures* 30:41–52. This is a preview of his forthcoming magnum opus on moral sensitivity. Robert Anton Wilson's funny and often frightening satire of our irrational rationalism when we cling desperately to beliefs and opinions is in Wilson, R. A. 1987. *The new inquisition: Irrational rationalism in the citadel of science*. Phoenix: Falcon Press. This deals mainly with denial and repression of the odd or paranormal. Also Wilson, R. A. 1990. *Quantum psychology*. Phoenix: New Falcon Press (a guide to unprejudiced thinking). His 1983 *Prometheus rising* (Phoenix: New Falcon Press) is an often hilarious but penetrating view of the human condition. On education and systems design, see Banathy, B. 1991. *Systems design of education: A journey to create the future*. Englewood Cliffs, NJ: Educational Technology Publications. Thompson's already mentioned *Pacific shift* is a must, as is his wide-ranging speculation with David Spangler in *The reimagination of the world* (Santa Fe, NM: Bear & Co.), and his *American replacement of nature* (New York: Doubleday), both 1991.

The Environment
The quote is from Ehrlich, P. R. 1986. *The machinery of nature*. New York: Touchstone, 13. An excellent introduction to the implications of ecological thinking and biological metaphors is Thompson, W. I., ed. 1991. *Gaia: Emergence*. Great Barrington, MA: Lindisfarne Press. See also Thompson, W. I. 1991. *Imaginary landscape: Making worlds of myth and science*. New York: St. Martin's Press. The quote from Lynn Margulis is from her (1987) Early Life: The microbes have priority. In *Gaia: A way of knowing*, ed W. I. Thompson. Great Barrington, MA.: Lindisfarne Press. This is the first volume in the Gaia series. Eugene Linden. Lost tribes, lost knowledge. *Time*, September 23, 1991 (on the loss to humanity of ancient medicinal wisdom—not to mention the loss of humanity and the inhumanity of humanity to the nonhuman). The quote from James Burke is from Burke, J. 1978. *Connections*. Boston: Little, Brown & Co., 155. The PBS series is extremely interesting and highly recommended, full of examples of social and technological interconnectedness.

273

277

Index

For information regarding seminars, lectures, and consulting services based on the material in this book, please contact:

Barnes and Conti Associates, Inc.
940 Dwight Way, Suite 15
Berkeley, CA 94710

Phone: (510) 644–0911
Fax: (510) 644–2102